T0320117

Systemic Vulnerability and Sustainable Economic Growth

Skills and Upgrading in Southeast Asia

Bryan K. Ritchie

Professor of International Relations, James Madison College, Michigan State University, USA

Edward Elgar

Cheltenham, UK • Northampton, MA, USA

Published by
Edward Elgar Publishing Limited
The Lypiatts
15 Lansdown Road
Cheltenham
Glos GL50 2JA
UK

Edward Elgar Publishing, Inc.
William Pratt House
9 Dewey Court
Northampton
Massachusetts 01060
USA

A catalogue record for this book
is available from the British Library

Library of Congress Control Number: 2009940744

Mixed Sources
Product group from well-managed forests and other controlled sources
www.fsc.org Cert no. SA-COC-1565
© 1996 Forest Stewardship Council

ISBN 978 1 84844 822 3

Printed and bound by MPG Books Group, UK

Contents

Figures

Tables

Abbreviations

2SLS, 3SLS	two and three stage least squares
ADB	Asian Development Bank
AFTA	Asian Free Trade Association
APITD	Action Plan for Industrial Technology Development
ASEAN	Association of Southeast Asian Nations
BIOTEC	National Center for Genetic Engineering and Biotechnology
BOI	Board of Investments
BS	Barisan Socialis
BUILD	BOI Unit for Industrial Linkages
CITREP	Critical IT Resource Program
CPTE	Council on Professional and Technical Education
DSD	Department of Skills Development
DSI	Disk Storage Institute
EDB	Economic Development Board
EPU	Economic Planning Unit
FDI	foreign direct investment
GDP	gross domestic product
GERD	gross expenditures on R&D
GNP	gross national product
HRDC	Human Resource Development Corporation
HRDF	Human Resource Development Fund
IDA	Infocomm Development Authority
IDEMA	International Disk Drive Equipment and Materials Association
IKMAS	Institute of Malaysian and International Studies
IKTBN	National Youth and Sports Higher Skills Training Institute
ILP	Industry Linkages Program
IMF	International Monetary Fund
IRP	Industrial Restructuring Program
IRPA	Intensification of Research in Priority Areas
IT POWER	IT Program for Office Workers
ITAF	Industrial Technical Assistance Fund
ITE	Institute of Technical Education
LIUP	Local Industry Upgrading Program

MARA	Majlis Amanah Rakyat
MASTIC	Malaysian Science and Technology Information Center
MBC	Malaysian Business Council
MDC	Multi-Media Development Corporation
MIDA	Malaysian Industrial Development Authority
MIGHT	Malaysian Industry–Government Group for High Technology
MIMOS	Malaysian Institute for Microelectronic Systems
MLSW	Ministry of Labor and Social Welfare
MMU	Multi-Media University
MNC:	Multi-national Corporations
MoE	Ministry of Education
MoF	Ministry of Finance
MoHR	Ministry of Human Resources
MoI	Ministry of Industry
MoM	Ministry of Manpower
MOSTE	Ministry of Science, Technology, and the Environment
MSC	Multi-Media Super Corridor
MTDC	Malaysian Technology Development Corporation
MTEC	National Metals and Materials Technology Center
MTI	Ministry of Trade and Industry
NAFTA	North American Free Trade Association
NCB	National Computer Board
NDP	New Development Plan
NECTEC	National Electronics and Computer Technology Center
NEP	New Economic Plan
NICs	newly industrializing countries
NITC	National Information Technology Council
NPB	National Productivity Board
NSTB	National Science and Technology Board
NSTDA	National Science and Technology Development Agency
NSTP	National Science and Technology Plan
NTUC	National Trade Union Congress
NUS	National University of Singapore
OECD	Organisation for Economic Co-operation and Development
OLS	ordinary least squares
ONEC	Office of the National Education Commission
PAP	People's Action Party
PDC:	Penang Development Corporation
PORIM	Palm Oil Research Institute Malaysia
PSB	Productivity and Standards Board

PSDC	Penang Skills Development Center
R&D	research and development
SDF	Skills Development Fund
SDL	Skills Development Levy
SHRDC	Selangor Human Resources Development Center
SIRIM	Standards and Industrial Research Institute of Malaysia
SME	small- and medium-sized companies
SNEF	Singapore National Employers Federation
TDRI	Thai Development Research Institute
TIC	technical intellectual capital
TISTR	Thailand Institute of Scientific and Technical Research
TSDF	Thai Skills Development Fund
UMNO	United Malays National Organization
VC	venture capitalist
VITB	Vocational and Industrial Training Board
WTO	World Trade Organization

Preface

The thinking behind this book started long before there was any notion it might turn into a book, and long before my time at Emory University or James Madison College at Michigan State University. Over 15 years ago, as a young executive in the computer industry, I found myself traveling around the world to market and sell software. No PhD was needed to quickly see that some countries were far out in front technologically, and that the number of such countries was comparatively small. Countries such as Korea and Taiwan were making tremendous gains on countries such as France and England. Singapore, Australia and Ireland began to emerge as technological leaders. Even traditionally poor countries like Thailand, the Philippines and Malaysia in Southeast Asia, Mexico in North America and Brazil and Argentina in South America began to transition from agriculture to manufacturing and exporting, generating huge gains in wealth and poverty reduction as a result. So astounding was this rapid transformation among the countries of Southeast Asia that the World Bank declared the region an 'economic miracle,' and new hope emerged that all countries might be able to 'upgrade' their economies and compete in a global market.

Yet as promising as the thesis was that countries were like geese and the leaders would pave the way for the followers, it soon became apparent that not all countries shared the same capacities for upgrading. While foreign direct investment and export industrialization might cause economic growth to surge for a period, sustainable development depended on key capacities for innovation and technology creation, assimilation and dissemination. Without such capacities, the churning global economy's peaks and troughs exposed weaknesses in many growing economies that led to economic meltdown. Mexico, Argentina, Thailand, Russia, South Korea all felt the brunt of heavy market pressures in response to weak economic and political institutions that threatened the very foundation of national structure.

The gap in capacity for sustainable upgrading can be characterized as a difference in the ability to innovate. Upgrading begins with diversification from agriculture to low-wage manufacturing in areas such as toys, textiles, and basic food processing of agricultural products. Further upgrading moves from low-wage manufacturing to more sophisticated and advanced manufacturing in electronics, automobiles and parts, machinery, and other more exacting and demanding products and processes. The next critical step is to move from building someone else's designs to creating your own. Each of these steps requires tremendous amounts of information and knowledge, much of it tacit or 'learned through experience.' Nor is the necessary accumulation of knowledge between each stage linear. Rather, the required information and knowledge grow exponentially. Thus, to successfully move into the frontier of economic development, into the realm of indigenous innovation and technology creation and promotion, countries must be capable of developing the political and economic institutions that facilitate the creation, acquisition, transmission and application of an exponentially growing amount of knowledge.

Whether societies learn how to create and manage knowledge and information depends on their institutions. Institutions, or the rules of the game, determine who benefits from the interactions of society and who does not. The big question, then, is why some countries have created institutions that result in the benefits of economic gains accruing to a broad, cross-class group of people while other countries have institutions that ensure gains will only accrue to a narrow group of elites. While the former countries have been able to use their institutions to manage flows of information and knowledge in ways that enable upgrading, the latter group has not, miring them at various stages of development that lags behind innovation and technology creation and thus ensuring that the wealth gap between them and the economic leaders will widen over time.

Because knowledge and innovation are so critical to long-term economic upgrading, this book focuses its analysis on the education and training systems in developing countries. These institutional systems are often microcosms of the state's entire institutional system, mirroring and highlighting the strengths and weaknesses of national bureaucratic policy processes, political parties, interest groups and firms and industry. Because education and training is so critical to so many social aspects of a country, it is typically an endeavor that demands attention and resources, thus making it both a tool to help understand where countries have come from as well as a vehicle to change the future direction of where they are headed.

The most compelling finding of this book is that the way we organize our social interaction as evidenced in our political coalitions shapes powerfully the ways we create our economic and political institutions to manage and reward the creation and flow of information and knowledge. This finding is important for the prospects of economic upgrading, but also might help us understand what, when and how different kinds of political organization, including democracy, influence economic outcomes.

To generate these findings has taken significant resources. Books that rely on serious research do not emerge without financial and institutional help. Research for this study has been generously provided by the Andrew W Mellon Foundation through grants from the Social Science Research Council, the Department of Education's Fulbright–Hays Fellowship and grants from Emory and Michigan State universities. I am indebted to each of these groups for providing their resources to a project I have felt so deeply about.

Successful research also requires emotional and intellectual support. As with any project such as this one, the end result includes very little original thought. I am indebted to numerous individuals, many of whom have shaped my life in fundamental ways through relationships that have become sweet and very meaningful over time. None of this project would have happened without the support of my eternal companion, Susan. She has supported the elevation of my dreams while providing gravity and traction to my effort. Few have her ability to see the really important things in life for what they are. As Susan is to my emotional growth and stability, Rick Doner has been to me intellectually. I have been blessed to have mentors who become friends and colleagues. Rick's support has gone far beyond simply challenging the way I think; it has extended to inviting me to learn how to ask the right questions, and then being willing to go on the journey with me to find the answers.

Others have also played an important role. While it will be impossible to name everyone, Allen Hicken, Greg Felker, Rajah Rasiah and Patarapong Interakumnerd have all had a special impact on the project through relationships as friends and colleagues that now spans more than a decade. To them and everyone else who has contributed, I say thank you, without laying to anyone's charge but my own the mistakes and weaknesses that remain.

B.K.R
22 November 2009
East Lansing, Michigan

To Susan and Rick

1. Introduction

Recognize that the only resource you have is your people, their brains, and their skills.
E.J. Mayer, former director of the Industrial Planning Department of Israel's Ministry of Commerce and Industry

The quality of a people determines the outcome of a nation.
Lee Kuan Yew, Senior Minister of Singapore

According to one prominent development economist, economic development has been an 'elusive quest' (Easterly, 2001). But while this is true in many regions of the world, there is one region where at least five countries – Indonesia, Malaysia, the Philippines, Singapore and Thailand – have *averaged* over 6 percent growth since 1970 (World Bank, 2005) and one country, Singapore, is achieving levels of technological capacity found in developed countries. In all five countries the manufacturing sector has expanded, a broadening and diversified range of goods is produced and exported, and a growing emphasis has been placed on technology products. Such diversification or 'structural change' is a significant achievement. In fact, the World Bank (1993) was so impressed by this diversification that it suggested that Southeast Asia was an example other developing countries should emulate.

But diversification may no longer be enough for sustainable development. This is not to argue that diversification or even large infrastructure and other heavy industrial developments are not evidence of economic progress. But although second-generation development projects typically have high capital and management requirements, their technology requirements are well known and can often be acquired and used 'off the shelf' even if only contracting outside consultants. By comparison, 'new economy' initiatives to move into higher-value-added products at high levels of efficiency with local inputs requires far more tacit, sophisticated and often unknown skills, knowledge and technologies than before.[1]

Why is sustainable upgrading necessary for economic prosperity? Firms are producing products or providing services in ever-more sophisticated ways and more quickly and efficiently than ever before. Product cycles that used to be measured in years, sometimes decades, are now measured in months despite an exponential rise in product and process complexity. Global supply, product, value and, increasingly, innovation chains are expanding rapidly. These observations apply across industries such as microelectronics, software, chemicals, life sciences, bio products (including energy), logistics and telecommunications. One software industry executive observed, 'Competition in this industry is with yourself. If you are not the source of your own product's obsolescence, you are behind the curve.'[2] IDEMA, the hard disk drive industry association, likens the task of positioning read/write heads accurately over magnetic disks spinning at thousands of RPMs to maintaining the flight of a Boeing 747 17 cm off the ground while staying perfectly centered over the dividing stripe of a road.[3] While these are clearly extreme examples, there are few industries free of these pressures, even if comparatively less severe.

Industry pressures spawn new incentives at the national level to develop technical capacity. Prior economic transitions from agriculture to first-stage, labor-intensive manufacturing require policy capacity to create a stable macroeconomic policy environment that encourages investment. By comparison, later shifts from first-stage manufacturing to second-stage industrialization require that local firms be able to adopt and integrate existing technologies and then, ultimately, innovate and create new technologies. Transitioning to a third-stage innovation-intensive economy puts the emphasis squarely on new knowledge creation, especially tacit knowledge. Sustainability comes from mastering new tasks associated with knowledge creation, dissemination and assimilation. As David Landes put it, 'It is not want of money that holds back development. The biggest impediment is social, cultural, and technological unreadiness – want of knowledge and knowhow' (1999: 269).

The problem is that the closer an economy gets to the technological frontier, the less knowledge is available from other sources about how to move forward. To the extent that industries experience rising wages without concomitant rises in quality and productivity, or in other words, innovation, they must retreat from the technological frontier and increasingly compete on price, which forces a 'hollowing out' as industries move to chase the lowest wage costs. This leaves a large pool of under-educated people unemployed. If new, more technologically advanced firms begin to form or set up operations, they often cannot find sufficient qualified workers. Mismatches between labor capacity and business needs results in a labor shortage amidst high unemployment.[4]

Thus, upgrading by maintaining robust innovation trajectories at the technological frontier requires increasing the technical brainpower, or what I call technical intellectual capital (TIC),[5] of the population.[6] Hence, educating and training the labor force *in technical skills* becomes a critical component for economic upgrading (Felker, 1999; Mowery and Oxley, 1995; Nelson, 1993; Booth and Snower, 1999).

Yet although developing countries are realizing that the primary developmental task has shifted from diversification to upgrading, only a few have been successful. To be fair, many have not yet even made the transition to economic diversification, let alone upgrading. On the other hand, very large economies, like China and India, have already moved significantly toward upgrading, driven in large part by huge markets and vast human capital, much of it educated abroad. There are in the middle, however, a fair number of 'intermediate' states that have made the initial transition to a diversified economy, but are now feeling increasing pressure to upgrade. These states find themselves in an ever-tightening economic vice, neither wage cost competitive with China or India, nor technologically competitive with Japan, Europe and the USA.

Nowhere are these pressures more evident than in Southeast Asia. Yet despite similar pressures for change, close examination reveals large differences among the various countries of this region in their levels of technological upgrading in general and skills development in particular. At the high end, Singapore has been able to create technological capacity that approaches that of the developed countries. Malaysia and Thailand exhibit vexingly mixed results, with some industries making more progress than others, but where in the aggregate technological capacity lags based on what other indicators of development would predict (see Table 1.1). What accounts for these differences?

Groundbreaking research by Peter Evans (1995) and Richard Doner (1992) explained that different kinds of growth depended on different kinds of interaction between the government and the private sector. Countries with tight linkages between government and businesses characterized by 'embedded autonomy' were more likely to succeed in the long term than places that lacked such relationships. While necessary as a first step in understanding what separated the successful from the unsuccessful, identifying the institutional capacity behind embedded autonomy pushed the question further back, prompting one to ask: where do these relationships come from? In earlier work I have argued with Richard Doner and Dan Slater that institutions that promote economic upgrading are the product of 'systemic vulnerability,' which is made up of three variables: resource scarcity, external security vulnerability and domestic coalitional breadth (Doner et al., 2005).

In this earlier argument, resource endowments interacted with security threats and coalitional structures to create incentives for institutional design. This book extends that early argument by unraveling the relationship between structural conditions, coalitional politics and microeconomic

Table 1.1 Comparative technology indicators for Asia

	Indonesia	Japan	Korea	Malaysia	Philippines	Singapore	Taiwan	Thailand
IMD world competitiveness ranking (2008)	51	22	31	19	40	2	13	27
R&D exp. (% of GDP, 2000–2005)	0.0533	3.145	2.643	0.6915	0.1117	2.25	N/A	0.2614
S&T human resources (per million capita)	215 (2000)	5719 (2005)	2770 (2005)	319 (2005)	N/A	4479 (2000)	2980 (1995)	159 (1995)
High-tech exports % of man nf. exports (2005)	16	22	32	55	71	57	N/A	27
Internet hosts per million capita (2005)	0.001212	258	20	15	3	271	N/A	5
Internet users per 1000 capita (2005)	73	668	684	435	20 (2000)	324 (2000)	N/A	110

Sources: World Bank, *World Development Indicators*, various years. Business International Indices of Corruption and Institutional Efficiency and are measured from 1980 to 1983. Transparency International Corruption Perception Index. Malaysian Science and Technology Information Centre, *National Science and Technology Databook*, 1998; Singapore National Science and Technology Board, *National Survey of R&D*.

outcomes. The important change in the argument is to move coalitional politics into an intervening position between structural conditions and microeconomic outcomes.

Treating coalitional structure as an intervening variable suggests tantalizing possibilities about how structural, exogenous conditions, such as the resource curse, might operate through political preferences and incentives to shape economic institutions. It also shows that selecting and implementing appropriate economic policy is not simply a matter of determining what to do, but instead is the product of complicated and heavily vested interactions among political entities who just as often have as a goal the acquisition of political power as a means to generate economic returns. Finally, a coalitional approach might provide leverage on the question of democracy and upgrading. To the extent that productive linkages between government and industry are best maintained through broad and participative linkages, then politics that encourage broad participation will be most effective at producing economic upgrading, whether or not they use democratic means to do so.

COOPERATION AND SKILLS DEVELOPMENT

Creating technical intellectual capital is more complex than simply organizing and applying existing resources. Although large stores of knowledge are explicit and available 'off the shelf,'[7] there is an equal amount of knowledge that is internal, individual, and must be learned 'on the job,' or through direct experience.[8] This implicit or tacit knowledge is critical for innovation and must be endogenously created.[9] But as Merilee Grindle (2004) notes, tasks associated with educating and training demand greater information flows, monitoring and enforcement, as well as the ability to reconcile distributional allocations and manage complex outcomes with long time-to-payoffs. Each gives rise to new and complex collective dilemmas that resist easy resolution.

Three tasks with respect to education and training are particularly bedeviled by these collective dilemmas. First, creating an education and training infrastructure to provide *general* skills and talents must overcome large investment costs and slow time-to-payoff hurdles. These challenges are usually met through government financing of general, public education and training.[10]

Second, *specialized* skills are created by firms as they educate and train scientists, engineers and technicians in firm- and industry-specific processes and products. Yet in an environment of high labor mobility, trained labor is easily 'poached' by competing firms (Pigou, 1912). This, in the parlance of the economist, is a classic problem of positive externalities. If all firms were to train without regard to investment appropriation, a substantial pool of skilled labor would exist from which all firms could draw. But precisely because positive externalities mean that someone is paying for something they are not getting (or getting what they are not paying for), firms are dissuaded from training and are instead motivated to 'free-ride' on the training efforts of others, leading to a socially suboptimal, low-skill equilibrium (Soskice, 1991).

In his seminal work on human capital development, Becker (1962) argued that in fact there was no skills-development externality. If training could be disaggregated into general and specific components, then in a competitive labor market the individual would find it in her best interest to invest in acquiring general skills, and both the firm and the individual would find it in their interest to share the cost of acquiring specific skills. All that would remain is for the individual and the firm to negotiate over the portion each would provide.

Recent work, however, argues that Becker's theory is based on a set of untenable assumptions. First, as Stevens (1999) points out, differentiating between general and specific skills may be virtually impossible.[11] But second, Streeck (1989: 97) argues that even if skills can be disaggregated, a technologically demanding international economy may actually require firms to provide fewer specific skills and more 'generally polyvalent skills that can be put to a variety of as *yet unknown* future uses' in order to maintain or enhance competitive advantage (italics in original). Streeck also points out that beyond the vagaries of skill specificity is the problem of uncertainty. Becker's model, like all neoclassical economic models, assumes perfect information. Since individuals cannot know perfectly what skills will be in demand and since firms cannot know perfectly what skills will maximize their return, both face powerful disincentives to invest in training. As rates of technological change accelerate, or as the time to acquire education or training lengthens, uncertainty increases and education and training decreases. Third, it is essential that economic actors, especially firms, demand high-level technical talent. Institutions, policies, or private information designed to facilitate cooperation for education and training will have little impact if there is no demand for the skills once they are created. Demand is best fostered when firms conduct innovation (Booth and Snower, 1999; World Bank, 1997; Zeufack, 1999). Firms are more likely to invest in innovation when full investment appropriation is assured and monopolies are controlled (Metcalfe, 1995).

What all of this means is that creating new skills and knowledge is not easy. To sum it up, the appropriate supply and demand of technical intellectual capital is contingent upon society's ability to provide necessary public goods, promote positive externalities and stimulate demand without fostering uncompetitive behavior. How do we get all three conditions?

Although the market knows what training it needs, it does not always provide appropriate incentives that result in an optimal supply of skills. Some scholars argue that strong states capable of functioning autonomously from the demands of special interest groups can overcome the market's failures.[12] But government solutions to these market failures are usually not very effective. Governments often fail for reasons of moral hazard, distance from and unfamiliarity with market signals, and the tendency to subordinate economic necessities to political maneuverings. One certainly doesn't need to look far to find examples of government policies making a mess of the economy, including the current financial crisis in the USA.

But even if governments have the capacity and focus to create and implement the right policies, experience teaches us that few if any governments have the knowledge to address increasingly complex development problems without the input of the private sector.[13] Furthermore, there is no good explanation why some states might be capable of finding and implementing the precise mechanisms through which government capacity is translated into specific outcomes or encouraging and applying private sector preferences and capacity to support major policy initiatives while others are not (Wade, 1990).

That markets and governments by themselves are not sufficient to foster the required amount of education and training suggests that institutions capable of facilitating the cooperation necessary for education and training might reside between the two, or be a combination of both. Different combinations of market and government institutions have generated similar capacities for skills upgrading. *Handwerk* apprenticeship guilds in Germany and institutions restricting labor mobility in Japan have been able to resolve collective dilemmas hindering firm-level training (Thelen and Kume, 1999).[14] In France and Eastern Germany, similar apprenticeship institutions have emerged through the information activities of private business associations. Private information, usually supplied by business associations, can provide the impetus for firms to expect that other firms will also train, thus overcoming the lack of trust that can restrict cooperation (Culpepper, 2003). In Europe the widespread practice of financing business through non-equity sources of capitalization can extend a firm's decision-making horizon, allowing it to adopt a long-term perspective toward investments made in skills development (Finegold, 1991). Strong labor unions in Germany regulate firms to fulfill their social obligation as a 'place of learning' as much as a 'place of production' (Streek, 1989). And finally, government research funding coupled with student loan programs in the USA has encouraged widespread access to higher education.

Clearly a wide variety of institutional structures might provide the capacity needed to overcome market and government failures that can block upgrading,[15] and, moreover, these institutional structures are changing over place and time. For example, developmental state theorists have argued that a strong, autonomous and embedded state was able to create patterns of reciprocity between government and business that fostered key institutions for upgrading.[16] This policy strategy, however, might only have been possible due to prevailing geopolitical conditions. In an attempt to corral the expansion of communism, the USA and other Western powers were willing to maintain a global economy that tolerated domestic trade restrictions on imports into the Northeast Asian countries while welcoming their exports (Cumings, 1984). Using this 'technonationalist' approach, Korea and Taiwan were able to implement Listian 'greenhouse' modes of technological development based closely on Japan's example (Keller and Samuels, 2003).

This explanation, however, cannot account for Singapore's success. In contrast to the Northeast Asian countries, the countries of Southeast Asia pursued a very different developmental track.[17] With growth occurring toward the end of the cold war, the global economy was much less tolerant of 'technonationalist' development strategies. Instead, these countries pursued more globalist development strategies, in which foreign direct investment (FDI) played a primary role, albeit to differing levels (Doner and Ritchie, 2003).

We can see, then, that it is not the particular institutions that matter, but rather their functionality and capacity as demanded by the requirements of a particular time. If countries are to upgrade their skills in the current global economic environment, they must create the capacity to overcome the investment appropriation dilemmas associated with education and training, and encourage foreign-owned firms to transfer core technologies to local firms. Because both challenges are hindered by market failures, countries must figure out how to simultaneously coordinate the development efforts of key actors in firms, business associations, unions and universities without providing incentives for government policy failure. Taken together, these tasks require the capacity of society to create institutions that reduce barriers to information flow and collection, improve transparency within corporations and government, encourage more and broader participation from economic actors, resolve sticky distributional conflicts, create short-term incentives to compensate for long-term payoffs, monitor performance including resource allocation and usage, and impartially enforce sanctions for infractions of development policy, regardless of how politically connected the offending group might be. Anything less will constrain the creation, acquisition, assimilation and dissemination of ever-more sophisticated knowledge and skills necessary for upgrading.

This book argues that the cooperation needed to accomplish these tasks is shaped significantly by coalitional politics. The nature of the interaction between political elites and mass actors shapes incentives for policy choices, which over time are regularized into institutional forms, which have long-lasting impacts on performance outcomes.

COALITIONS AND COOPERATION

The structure of coalitions influences the ability of social groups to cooperate to overcome collective dilemmas. A growing consensus among scholars is that broad coalitions facilitate the provision of public goods.[18] Active participation in the policy process by a broad cross-section of coalition members improves policy credibility by 'tying the hands' of the ruling elite. Broad participation, the active involvement of economic actors in policy design and implementation, holds all actors accountable for outcomes, which allows ruling elites to maintain sufficient autonomy from any one interest group, making cooperation possible to resolve completely the collective dilemmas that bedevil third-stage upgrading initiatives.

Broad and participative coalitions shape political interactions for the acquisition and distribution of resources. If we accept, as Knight (1992) argues, that those in power will create institutions that maintain their power,[19] then the breadth of the support base upon which rulers depend for power will shape institutional formation and change. When political elites depend on a broad coalition of support to stay in power, they must provide side payments to a wide cross-section of society (Doner et al., 2005). This is done most efficiently through the provision of public goods (Bueno de Mesquita et al., 2003). Public goods such as education and training infrastructure, public housing and welfare redistribute and reallocate resources in ways that improve equality and access to power.

Even so, it is not enough simply to provide public goods. In order to ensure that public goods lead to technology-enhancing institutions, coalition members must also be involved in the policy-making process. Involvement ensures access to policy and institutional creation, which enhances distributional equality.[20] Once governments are committed to supplying public goods, they apply the full complement of brainpower in a society to the problems of innovation and upgrading. Broad participation is the only way the necessarily massive bi-directional information flows can be created to ensure the accumulation and dissemination of technical information *and* the necessary input to resolve the distributional and coordination conflicts that arise as a result, especially with respect to monitoring and enforcing compliance. To coordinate participation of a broad coalition while simultaneously checking rent-seeking, governments must create and maintain cooperative public–private linkages among government, business, labor, academia and other relevant social actors that hold actors accountable to one another. In other words, broad and participative coalitions are the force behind the institutions that encourage embedded and autonomous relationships between government and the private sector.

Explaining the origins of developmentally friendly coalitional structures is tricky. Much of the political-economy literature points to domestic conflict, either among elites or between elites and the masses, as the primary factor behind coalitional formation (Waldner, 1999). Excellent studies also exist that connect resource endowments and domestic divisions, primarily ethnic fragmentation, to the probability of growth and the provision of public goods (Sachs and Warner, 1997; Easterly and Levine, 1997), but there is little if any explanation of the causal mechanisms between structural conditions and economic outcomes.[21] This book focuses on the influence of coalitional politics as the mechanism through which structural conditions influence microeconomic outcomes.

'Systemic vulnerability' shapes preferences of ruling elites for particular coalitional structures.[22] Scarce resources expand coalitional breadth by forcing governments to generate revenues from a broad cross-section of groups and people in society, usually through taxation.[23] As mentioned above, in return for taxes paid, government must supply goods, which for efficiency purposes are usually public in nature, which also encourages an expansion of the coalition in a virtuous cycle. Plentiful resources, on the other hand, provide options to generate income from a narrow cross-section of society. Side payments given in return can be private in nature and targeted to these few individuals or groups. Military vulnerability increases pressures on limited resources. Domestic fragmentation, especially when it manifests itself through conflict, makes cross-class coalitions more difficult by encouraging confrontation rather than cooperation in the use of available resources.

Coalitional structure in turn shapes social bargaining around key decisions, which over time result in institutions, both formal and informal. At key junctures in time, society is faced with critical choices over which they must bargain and that have long-lasting effects. Decisions made or not made at these junctures are shaped by preferences of political and economic elites. Such choices are especially evident either during periods of state-building or at critical junctures when crises, conflicts or other events 'open' the institutional structure for change. During transitions to independence in Malaysia and Singapore, and to a constitutional monarchy in Thailand, key decisions were made or not made that shaped, in a path-dependent way, important outcomes in the education and training institutional infrastructure in each country. As I detail in Chapter 5, decisions surrounding language of instruction, the degree of bureaucratic fragmentation allowed, the extent to which labor is involved, and the level of focus on technology and science influenced the focus and performance of education and training systems for sustainable economic upgrading by facilitating or hindering close interconnections between business, government and academia. These interconnections are the necessary 'touch points' that foster cooperation to resolve the collective dilemmas surrounding education and training.

This book focuses on the origins of institutions that facilitate the capacities needed for improving technical intellectual capital. It argues that these institutions are significantly shaped by coalitional politics – the aggregations of raw political preferences, whether formally incorporated into the political structure or not,[24] behind policy choices.[25] Preferences for both upgrading and the nature of coalitional politics are influenced heavily by levels of systemic vulnerability, the influence of which is highest at points of new institutional creation, such as state formation.

The entire argument is graphically depicted in Figure 1.1: systemic vulnerability (the independent variable) is a sufficient cause of coalitional structure (the first intervening variable), which in turn is at least a necessary input, and perhaps also sufficient, for institutionalized public–private linkages (second intervening variable), which then determines the level of technical intellectual capital creation that is possible (the dependent variable).

Chapter 2 explains the theory in more detail. Chapter 3 then tests these ideas to establish plausibility and generalizability. As in all quantitative analyses, there is little ability to do more than guess at causal mechanisms. Nevertheless, the findings reveal a strong correlative relationship between systemic vulnerability, coalitions and skills upgrading, as well as interactive relationships between resource endowments and ethnic fragmentation and conflict.

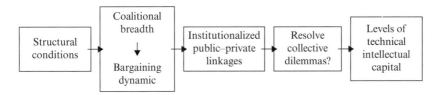

Figure 1.1   Argument outline

The book seeks to establish causality by examining three cases – Malaysia, Singapore and Thailand. These three cases provide strong quasi-experimental control on a number of variables, including, among others, religion, development strategy, regional considerations, culture and processes of industrialization. In addition, the comparative control extends to both cross-sectional and longitudinal analysis, allowing the analysis to move beyond assuming predictive outcomes to entertaining the possibility of conjunctural causation.[26]

Chapter 4 begins the process-tracing analysis by examining the historical processes through which systemic vulnerability has influenced and continues to influence coalitional form and function in the three Southeast Asian cases. The second part of this analysis identifies how these structural conditions influence preferences coalitional actors have for (1) prioritizing economic redistribution relative to overall economic expansion and (2) fostering innovation and technological development.[27]

Chapter 5 shows how coalitional preferences influenced the four key policy and institutional choices made during the process of forming an education and training system as part of larger state-building processes. This is the key critical juncture when policy decisions among the cases diverge.[28] Chapter 6 examines the legacies of these initial choices on past and present policy decisions.

Chapter 7 then evaluates the mechanisms by which policy regimes result in institutional systems and the ways these institutional systems foster public–private linkages. In particular, the chapter examines the ways these linkages operate to facilitate the formation of technical intellectual capital in several technology-intensive industries. Since a significant advantage of process tracing is the ability to incorporate additional observations at different levels of analysis, the analysis refocuses the explanatory lens on government-led initiatives to create technological capacity in general and technical intellectual capital in particular *within* each of the three cases, thereby increasing the overall number of observations in the sample.[29] The initiatives include the creation and operation of a 'skills development fund,' incentives to promote higher-technology FDI, and incentives to connect public research institutions to private actors.

Finally, Chapter 8 explores the question of whether systemic vulnerability and coalitional politics influence policy change and implementation only during times of relative institutional vacuums, such as periods of state-building. In other words, is it possible that major crises or other causes of institutional upheaval alter decision calculi and create windows of time during which discontinuous change of significant policy and subsequent institutional formation can take place? To answer this question I evaluate the impact of the Asian financial crisis as a potential subsequent critical juncture.

Although the value of the analysis in this book is primarily focused on Southeast Asia, its findings on causal mechanisms may be applicable to countries and regions outside of Southeast Asia, industries beyond information technology, and more general relationships between politics and economics. One of the surprising implications of the findings from the application of this research to bigger questions of politics and economics concerns the connection between democracy and economic development. If broad and participative coalitions are in fact necessary for economic upgrading, the right question is not whether democracy is good for development, but whether democracy does enough to create broad and participative coalitions. Scholarly findings that democracy increases the provision of public goods (Baum and Lake, 2003) makes sense when looked at through a coalitional lens: democracy encourages a broader social coalition, which encourages the provision of public goods, as Riker (1980) and Bueno de Mesquita et al. (2003) would predict. But democracy tells us nothing about whether the coalition will be participative enough to encourage the right kinds of public goods, sufficient information creation, or needed oversight and sanctions. Democracy, therefore, is probably neither necessary nor sufficient for development. But it could be a precursor to coalitional structures amenable to development if it is constructed appropriately.

NOTES

1. On upgrading, see, e.g., Gereffi et al. (2005). On the distinction between structural change and upgrading, see Montobbio and Ramp (2005); and especially Waldner (1999).
2. Novell company board meeting, Provo, Utah, 1996.
3. IDEMA stands for the International Disk Drive Equipment and Materials Association (IDEMA). See also McKendrick et al. (2000).
4. Ironically, this condition arises just as easily in developed as developing countries, for example in Michigan where declining automotive manufacturers are laying off less-skilled workers while new IT firms cannot find enough higher-skilled workers.
5. Throughout the rest of the book I use the term 'technical intellectual capital' to include both scientific and technical knowledge. I realize, however, that the two are not interchangeable. As Parayil (1999) rightly points out, technology is not simply applied science. Rather technology is, as the word suggests, techniques. Thus, technology can be used without the scientific understanding of the theories behind them. But more important, science and technology develop differently. As Kuhn (1962) observes, scientific progress is often conflictual and discontinuous. On the other hand, technology is best understood as an evolutionary and cumulative process. I do my best to distinguish between scientific progress and technological development. But if I have to privilege one over the other, appropriate techniques can be effectively applied, indeed even improved

upon, without a complete understanding of the scientific and theoretical principles behind them.

6. Dunning argues that intellectual capital has emerged as the key wealth-creating asset in most industrial economies (1998: 47). Similarly, measuring the contribution of human capital by deducting both natural capital and produced capital from the total stock of wealth, the World Bank (1997) finds that human capital makes up more than two-thirds of per capita wealth in Organisation for Economic Co-operation and Development (OECD) countries and just under two-thirds of total wealth in most developing countries (cited in Auty, 1998).

7. Explicit technology is embodied in equipment, blueprints, schematics etc.

8. As early as 1957, Solow calculated that technological change accounted for over 87 percent of total economic growth, leaving less than 12 percent to be accounted for by the traditional factors of capital and labor. 'But for all practical purposes, Solow and other neoclassical economists conceptualize technology as an exogenous factor that is outside the production process (function)' (Parayil, 1999: 71). But knowledge also has a large tacit component. That is, insofar as equipment, blueprints, white papers and multimedia presentation can be transferred around the world, knowledge is explicit. But where equipment must be used and maintained, not to mention improved upon, and where blueprints, papers and presentations must be read (heard) and understood, and where processes must be learned by doing, knowledge is tacit.

9. See Romer (1986); Lucas (1988); and Grossman and Helpman (1991).

10. Baum and Lake (2003) argue that countries with higher levels of participation in the policy process (particularly democracies) are more likely to provide these public goods.

11. In all fairness to Becker, the ability to differentiate between general and specific skills is almost certainly much harder today than in the late 1950s when he was writing. In the twenty-first century the pace of technological change means that firms often cannot tell what skills they will need tomorrow. New, industry-specific skills rapidly become general skills in a very short period of time. In this environment negotiating over what portion of investment will be borne by the individual as opposed to the company is difficult at best, but perhaps impossible. Such would not have been the case in a more Fordist production operation of the mid-twentieth century.

12. See Ashton et al. (1999). Gerschenkron (1962) suggested that for 'late' developing countries, a strong state was necessary to overcome collective dilemmas of capital accumulation and risk aversion. Statist theory finds its strongest support in the literature on how the developmental states of Japan, Korea and Taiwan were able to steer private industries through the gauntlet of technological upgrading by implementing far-sighted industrial policy (Johnson, 1982; Amsden, 1989; Wade, 1990).

13. For more on this point, see Culpepper (2003).

14. In Germany, the *Handwerk* sector was given monopoly training rights whereas in Japan institutions restricting labor mobility allowed firms to fully recognize the return on their investment made in skills development. The USA and the UK, on the other hand, lack institutions that lead to this outcome.

15. This insight fits with recent research that shows that countries have unique systems of institutions that interact in complex ways to influence processes of innovation (Nelson, 1993; Dosi et al., 1988; Freeman and Soete, 1997; Rasiah, 1999b). Searching for a single configuration of policies and institutions, 'institutional monocropping' is probably not very useful (Rauch and Evans, 2000).

16. See Amsden (1989), Wade (1990), Johnson (1982), Woo (1991) for more on the developmental state.

17. See Booth (1999), Bernard and Ravenhill (1995), Dittmer (1992), and Cai (1999) for various perspectives on this debate.

18. On this point, see Doner et al. (2005); Root (1996); and Bueno de Mesquita et al. (2003). For a contrasting view, see Waldner (1999).

19. Knight argues that while the incentives behind institutional formation and evolution

may be economically driven, the process is primarily political. That is, no institution is created or altered in a vacuum, but within an existing institutional system. This existing system confers asymmetric power on the actors involved. Thus institutions are formed or altered through a complex bargaining process that reflects current power relationships.

20. Baum and Lake (2003) argue that democracies are better at producing public goods because of the participation of their citizens.

21. Of the few examples where authors link structural factors to policy outcomes, the best include Engerman and Sokoloff (2002) and Easterly and Levine (1997). Sokolof and Engerman argue that natural resource scarcity created economic and political equality that enhances entrepreneurship and political participation. Easterly and Levine argue that ethnic divisions account for much of the poor growth record in newly developing countries.

22. In earlier writings I have thought of systemic vulnerability as including coalitional structure (see Doner et al., 2005). In this book I focus on the core elements of systemic vulnerability, to which I add ethnic structure and then examine the effects on coalitional structure, which now gets treated as an intervening variable.

23. See Shafer (1994) for a version of this argument.

24. For my purposes, coalition does not imply political incorporation. Coalitions of social interests can provide benefits and resources to, as well as receive benefits from, political elites whether or not they are incorporated into the formal political system. This observation leads to important insights when considering whether democracy is the ideal form of political structure to encourage coalitional structures beneficial to skills formation.

25. Analysis of coalitional politics has been largely ignored by political scientists. A key exception is the work of David Waldner (1999). Perhaps the reason, as Waldner notes, is that arguments invoking coalition-driven mechanisms often devolve into little more than descriptions of interplay between powerful actors while ignoring the independent role of the state (1999: 4). But if 'calculations of rulers and would-be rulers' motivate the formation of coalitions to pursue particular objectives, coalitional analysis becomes the heart of any politics of economic development (Wade, 1990: 309).

26. See Ragin (1987) for an interesting alternative to comparative methodologies based on Mill's methods as well as a discussion of conjunctural causation.

27. The data I use in this section are archival data and other secondary historical sources, combined with over 120 interviews I conducted in all three countries between 1998 and 2005.

28. See Collier and Collier (1991) for a further description of the usefulness of critical junctures in qualitative analysis.

29. See King et al. (1994) for a discussion on the appropriateness of expanding sample size in this manner.

2. The political economy of technical intellectual capital formation

By the beginning of 2000, the hard disk drive industry in Thailand and Malaysia was changing. Efforts to upgrade operations in both countries ran into a long-standing problem of a lack of qualified, skilled workers. Components that could be created more cheaply were moved to lower-cost countries, such as China. Those that required higher-technology processes were moved back to Singapore or even to the USA and Japan.[1] Thailand and Malaysia were caught in a vice, neither price competitive with China nor technologically competitive with Singapore. In the space of less than a decade, over 30 000 jobs moved from Thailand and Malaysia to China. All the evidence suggests that for many years both the Thai and Malaysian governments were aware of severe deficiencies in skilled labor. Why did both countries inadequately address the shortfall?

This book argues that coalitional pressures on the ruling elites during earlier institutional formation created a system unable to respond to these emerging needs. These institutions, supported by similar coalitional configurations, also crippled policy responses designed to overhaul the system.

Where did these coalitions come from and how did they influence policy decisions? Systemic vulnerability creates preferences for coalitional size and levels of participation. Broad and participative coalitions increase incentives to create institutional structures that facilitate collaborative and productive public–private linkages that drive innovation and upgrading. When coalitions are narrow and disconnected from policy making, incentives exist to create institutions that encourage redistributing resources from the general population to a select few, which hinders processes of skills upgrading.

The remainder of this chapter explains a new theory of coalitional origins, shows how coalitions shape the institutional structures behind productive public–private linkages, and then applies the new theory to explain outcomes in education and training in Southeast Asia.

A THEORY OF COALITIONAL ORIGINS

Riker (1980) observed that rational actors form coalitions only as broad as necessary to achieve their ends because payoffs must be shared among the members of the winning coalition. Again, as mentioned in Chapter 1, these coalitions are made up of actors who vote for, or otherwise provide support to, the ruling elite. They may or may not be formally incorporated into the political system as parties or other political units. Fewer members of a winning coalition mean more rewards per actor. When the number of coalition members is broad enough, the best strategy for repaying political support is the provision of public goods. But what things motivate elites to first expand their coalition and then to provide increasing opportunities for coalition members to participate in the public policy process?

Inter-elite conflict for political power is one reason elites might expand their ruling coalition (Waldner, 1999). This theory suggests that conflicting elites reach out to popular sectors for support against other elite groups. The more conflictual the political process, the more likely additional support will be sought, thus widening the winning coalition.

Another important impetus for coalitional breadth is the means by which governments generate the wealth necessary to buy political support. Every government must generate revenues to stay in power. When revenues can be generated easily through relationships with a small number of industries or sectors, then Riker's logic prevails and coalitions are kept narrow and small. On the other hand, when revenues can be generated only by extracting small amounts from numerous people, such as by extensive and comprehensive tax systems, pressure mounts on the government to expand the coalitional size.[2] In return for taxation, the government must reward those that supported them.

Both of the first two theories can explain why coalitions are broader or narrower, but they say little if anything about pressures to allow coalitional actors to participate in policy processes. If wealth generation is seen simply as a function of number of contributors, we can only predict changes in coalitional breadth. If, however, we examine the technological complexity of the process of generating wealth, we can also say something about participation. Upgrading an economy requires massive amounts of technology and information, which must be derived from and shared with as many of the intellectual resources and capital in a society as possible. The more difficult and complex the technological demands of the industries that create a nation's wealth, the broader and more participative the coalition must be to support the country's political economy. In contrast, when societies depend on less technologically demanding industries, such as selling raw materials and natural resources to generate wealth, the processes usually require less participation from a narrower coalition.

Once created, coalitional structure has feedback effects. Narrow coalitions create incentives for elites to implement rents that encourage fragmentation, resulting in further coalitional narrowing. Without broad input, those in power create institutions and policies that benefit themselves and in the process marginalize the rest of society politically, economically and socially. Broader coalitions allow more participation. Participants, in turn, push for institutions that benefit themselves. The more people who participate in policy processes, the more likely the outcome will be compensation in the form of public goods (Bueno de Mesquita et al., 2003). The result is reduced income inequality, which facilitates consolidation, rationalization and cooperation, which also leads to further coalitional expansion.

Elite conflict, wealth extraction, wealth creation and resource distribution, the variables known to influence coalitional structure, are shaped by systemic vulnerability – the combined influence of levels of resource endowments, external military security and domestic fragmentation and conflict. So far there has been little exploration of the impacts of systemic vulnerability on coalitional structure. In the following sections I explain how the component parts of systemic vulnerability shape coalitional breadth and participation. I also show that these variables are not just additive, acting in isolation, but interact to create unobvious outcomes.

THE RESOURCE CURSE

Early economists held that rich resource endowments had a positive impact on growth (Viner, 1952; Lewis, 1955). Natural resources provided or facilitated a ready source of foreign exchange, capital for fledgling manufacturing sectors, export taxes and state-owned monopoly extraction (growing), processing and transportation companies.

An increasing weight of evidence, however, points to a resource curse (Nankani, 1980; Auty, 1994). Contrary to expectations, developing countries with poor natural resource endowments outperformed their resource-rich counterparts.[3] A growing literature suggests several potential explanations as to how the resource curse operates (Ross, 1999). But while this literature is most often interested in explaining 'why these hardships lead to persistently slow growth – the resource curse' and then also explaining 'why governments fail to take corrective action' (ibid.: 307), this book is more interested in the impact the resource curse has on coalitional makeup and function.

Revenue Generation

Every government must generate revenues from its citizens to fund its operations and provide public goods, such as defense, health and education. International political-economy theory has long understood that industrial makeup influences political outcomes, which influence coalitional breadth.

Resource-intensive industries tend to have large returns to scale (Engerman and Sokoloff, 1994). As a result, the productive capacity in associated industries is often owned and controlled by a small group of powerful business elites. The wealth generated by resource sectors also often accrues to such groups (Auty, 1994; Mahon, 1992). Not only does this wealth take the form of income (wages), but also assets. Because of their small size, as Olson (1971) would predict, these small groups are able to act collectively and exert tremendous influence on the state, especially to maintain protection or other favorable policies. When economic wealth is concentrated in the hands of a few, inequality of income and asset distribution rises (Deininger and Squire, 1996). Income inequality encourages feedback effects as fewer wealthy people create policies and institutions that provide more private returns.

Rarely does the state remain outside the power coalition built on resource abundance. Large returns to scale in resource-intensive industries, which often leads to high asset specificity, increases exposure to exogenous events in the global economy (Shafer, 1994). A common strategy to protect against such risks is to create a narrow coalition of state and industry elites to act collectively to press for their interests in government. The primary interest shared by both industry and government officials is to preserve the large revenue flows generated by the industry, which then contribute to a large proportion of state revenue. Over time the state adopts the industry's interests as its own. At its extreme, when commodities provide the bulk of state revenues and where state spending provides the majority of private income, there is little if any need to generate income through general taxes (Luciani, 1995). As the state becomes increasingly dependent on resource-generated dollars, its institutional capability to generate revenue declines and public spending is increasingly accepted as a substitute for state capacity (Karl, 1997).

Conversely, when asset flexibility and low barriers to entry and exit characterize the dominant industrial sector, it is likely to be made up of and controlled by a large number of small and medium-sized firms. The large number of these firms makes it much harder to organize and act collectively to demand industry-specific rents from the government. The government, for its part, cannot extract revenues from a single or small number of large firms or industries, but instead must extract revenues from the taxes on numerous economic actors, which requires formal institutions that have high attachment value and penetrate deeply into society (Robinson and Ritchie, 2010).[4]

In return for taxation, states must be accountable to those from whom resources have been extracted. Narrow political distribution of rents is less tolerable in such societies. In addition, those who have been taxed demand participation rights and inclusion in the ruling coalition. Once incorporated, both formally into the political structure or informally through other mechanisms, actors have access to the policy-making apparatus and can influence policies and institutions for their good, resulting over time in a more equitable distribution of assets. This allows the middle and poorer classes to borrow to acquire skills through education and to set up new businesses as a way of becoming 'yeomen' participants in the economy (Auty, 1998).

Inter-Elite Conflict

Less clear is the impact of resource endowments on inter-elite conflict. On the one hand, resource endowments create sources of wealth, the acquisition of which might justify conflict. Fighting elites might also rely on resource endowments to fund the conflict, by-passing the need to reach out to popular sectors.

Poor resource endowments may reduce incentives for inter-elite conflict, but might also intensify competition over what does exist. But again, it's not clear whether in the process elites reach out to popular sectors or not, although it's clearly much more likely in the second scenario. The impact of resource endowments on inter-elite conflict can be clarified by theorizing (which I do below) and testing (which I do in Chapter 3) the interplay of ethnic fragmentation with resource endowments.

Technology and Revenue Generation

Another perspective is that resource endowments may not cause cognitive failure as much as alter priorities and preferences for innovation and technological development, which then influences growth in the long term. Building on the idea that resource endowments influence industrial economies of scale, Engerman and Sokoloff (1994) suggest that the nature of the industrial sector influences economic preferences and motivation. Resource-intensive industries that are more scale sensitive and benefit from mass labor and fewer elites, characteristic of the antebellum Southern United States, encouraged stagnation of innovation and upgrading. In the North, farming was less sensitive to scale economies, which encouraged broad participation in the economy from 'yeoman' farmers. Broad participation encouraged expansive social coalitions that created institutional incentives for innovation and entrepreneurialism.

A rich natural resource endowment provides an exploitable source for generating foreign exchange with minimal amounts of science and technology.[5] Any advanced technology necessary to exploit resource industries is usually available 'off the shelf,' minimizing the need for tacit technologies necessary for innovation. After periods of set-up and familiarization, specialized resource-extracting assets are easily nationalized.[6] Since little or no local technology is needed to capture the rents generated from primary commodity industries, the demand for developing local technical intellectual capital is also low (Mahon, 1992; Wood and Berge, 1997).

On the other hand, poor resource endowments require that countries rely on technological upgrading, the key to which is innovation, to generate foreign exchange.[7] Governments therefore feel tremendous pressure to upgrade technologically, which in turns creates pressures for education and training. Without a large resource endowment, elites generate revenues through expansive economic growth. The industrial pattern in resource-poor countries does not facilitate income and asset redistribution. Rather, the pattern is one of lifting the low and middle segments of the population while limiting the income growth of the upper class (Auty, 1998). Thus social groups are more equal and, without dramatic power asymmetries, broader and more participative coalitions are likely.

DOMESTIC FRAGMENTATION AND CONFLICT

It is well known that domestic cleavages and conflict influence coalitional structure. Polarized societies are more prone to competitive rent seeking (Easterly and Levine, 1997), which creates strong incentives against cooperation, and hence more narrow coalitions. Rodrik (1999: 79) confirms that the sharp drop in growth throughout the developing world after 1975 can be partly explained by divided societies[8] that encouraged distributional conflict and weak institutions[9] that were unable to manage that conflict. In many societies, ethno-linguistic fragmentation is the most difficult of domestic cleavages to overcome. Ethno-linguistic groups tend to cleave together and form ethnically centered political parties, which have ethnically centered political agendas, often narrow in scope (Horowitz, 1985). The result is that ethnic polarization facilitates the formation of narrow ideological camps that conflict on virtually every point (Easterly and Levine, 1997: 1206).

Domestic fragmentation also motivates political elites to form coalitional relationships with economic actors on a communal basis.

Homogeneous societies, on the other hand, are less likely to see politics in communal terms. While society might still divide around class or special interests, these divisions are likely to be less numerous without the compounding influence of ethnicity.

Social divisions, especially those based on ethnic differences, create strong preferences for prisoner dilemma games that are detrimental to political and economic development (Easterly and Levine, 1997; Weingast, 1997; Mahon, 1992; Doner and Hawes, 1995).[10] They facilitate corruption (Mauro, 1995) and postpone macroeconomic stabilization (Easterly and Levine, 1997). Ake (1996) argues that the struggle for power among competing groups marginalizes every other enterprise.

Finally, highly fragmented societies also do not create institutions to facilitate participation from coalitional actors that is critical for technological development. The result is fewer public goods. Moreover, for the public goods that are provided, Alesina and Spolaore (1997) show that they are less satisfactory to the population. Take education as an example: fragmented groups in society have different preferences for everything from language of instruction to curriculum.[11]

EXTERNAL THREATS[12]

War has a powerful influence on coalitional breadth and participation. But whether war broadens or narrows the coalition, and provides incentives for economic actors to participate in economic policy making, 'ultimately depends on how war makes states generate revenue' (Doner et al., 2005). Many have argued for a tight correlation between war, state-building and economic prosperity. Charles Tilly famously declared that 'War made the state, and the state made war' (Tilly, 1975: 42). Others point to Asia's dominant economic success as inextricably connected to military security and survival (Woo-Cummings, 1999: 322).

The mechanisms for how external threats increase coalitional breadth are similar to those operating under internal unrest. External threats create an atmosphere of 'political contestability,' which compels leaders to create economic institutions that promote growth and facilitate wealth-sharing for popular sectors (Campos and Root, 1996).

But these findings seem to work best for Asia. In the Middle East and Latin America, state formation is impacted by external threats differently. In these areas, even when mass coalitional pressures are evident, external threat is not always associated with growing institutional capacity and economic growth.[13] This apparent conflict of outcomes is evident even within regions, reflected in Campos and Root's inability to provide a systematic explanation for the much weaker commitments to education and training and more sporadic and superficial consultative mechanisms in the Association of Southeast Asian Nations (ASEAN-4) than in the NICs.[14] The critical factor explaining this variation is whether threatened states will be 'forced to turn inward to meet the financial challenges of war' (Centeno, 1997: 1579).

INTERACTIONS

In addition to the additive influence of the component variables of systemic vulnerability, it is clear from the foregoing discussion that there are numerous potential interactions among them. First, ethno-linguistic fragmentation and domestic conflict are often wound very tightly around specific industrial sectors, usually involved in primary commodity production from natural resource sectors. If we put resource endowments on the 'y' axis and ethnic fragmentation and external conflict/threat on the other, the resulting matrix provides a framework in which to understand coalitional outcomes at different levels of systemic vulnerability (see Table 2.1).

Comparing outcomes across the cells in the table exposes interesting insights. First, no one variable of systemic vulnerability is associated with a particular outcome. Fragmented societies have both broad and narrow, more and less participative coalitions. The same is true for high external threats and levels of resource endowments. Second, only in two cases does there emerge broad and participative coalitions simultaneously. One is in cell 4, indicative of Singapore, Israel, South Korea and Taiwan. The other is in cell 2, which is indicative of Japan and Germany. But although the current state of external threat is very low for these countries now, it wasn't always that way. Both countries experienced high levels of external threat during the first half of the twentieth century, which was during their periods of state-building.

Third, countries in cells 1 through 4 have no easy sources of foreign exchange. Financial resources must therefore be based on innovation and technological upgrading, which are difficult without the broad participation and cooperation of a large and cross-cutting coalition (Ritchie, 2005a). Countries with wider ethnic variability, such as South Africa (cell 1) and Pakistan (cell 3), tend to have internal conflict and competition among these groups that hinders cooperation to produce joint goods. Conversely, when countries lack ethnic competition, as in Japan (cell 2) and Singapore (cell 4), they experience fewer obstacles in generating cooperation. Since the population is more equally situated (Auty, 1998), institutional systems are designed more for jointly beneficial outcomes. Broad and participative

Table 2.1   Coalitional structure and systemic vulnerability

	Low external threats		High external threats	
	More fragmented	More homogeneous	More fragmented	More homogeneous
Fewer resource endowments	(1) Broad with participation in ruling party and competition among elite groups (Nepal, South Africa, India)	(2) Broad, but with participation limited to members of ruling party/ group (Japan, Germany)	(3) Narrow with participation within parties/ groups (Pakistan)	(4) Broad with wide participation across groups and classes (Singapore, Israel, South Korea, Taiwan)
More resource endowments	(5) Narrow with high participation within competing political and economic parties/groups (Indonesia, Zambia, Angola, Kenya)	(6) Narrow with low participation primarily from ruling elites (Saudi Arabia, Thailand)	(7) Broader but participation is limited to consultation and then only within ruling groups/party (Malaysia, Tanzania, Uganda, Philippines)	(8) Narrow with little participation outside of ruling group/ party (Vietnam, Syria, Somalia, Egypt)

coalitions emerge that change the payoff structure of societal bargaining to approximate a game of harmony focused on development. The dominant strategy is to cooperate to control monopoly rents and expand the size of the overall economy.[15] When levels of external threat are high (as in cell 4), the pressures to win at this game are even more pronounced. This game is win–win and expansive. As external threat diminishes (cell 2), however, it is possible that, although participation remains high, it becomes more competitive, resulting in a game that looks more like battle of the sexes than harmony.

Fourth, countries in cells 5–8, starting with the left and moving along the bottom, can rely on resource endowments to generate foreign exchange. As with the top row, coalitional breadth and participation varies based on the interaction of the three variables. When resource wealth is coupled with low external threats, coalitions are narrower. Within fragmented societies, such as Angola or Kenya (cell 5), participation coalesces around ethnic divisions. Although participation can be high within different parties and/ or groups, only the group in power effectively influences policy outcomes. In more homogeneous countries, such as Saudi Arabia and Thailand (cell 6), there is little reason to extend participative rights to actors outside the ruling elite. If resource endowments are especially high, as in the oil-producing states, citizens are often paid for their political acquiescence.

When external threats are higher, more fragmented societies tend to create broad coalitions, but which have little cross-cutting participation, as in Malaysia and Uganda (cell 7). Interestingly, it may be the existence of resource endowments that make it possible for broader coalitions to create more consociational political structures by buying cooperation.[16] Malaysia appears to have done this by giving different groups control of different portfolios within the bureaucracy as a means to control the flow of goods, revenues and services to targeted populations. But despite the broadening of the coalition, the top of the elite structure is still very narrow and participation extends primarily to consultation rather than participation and accountability. Nor is this always the outcome. One ethnic group might control the resource endowment and use it to subdue other groups. In this case the coalition will remain narrow. Civil conflict can occur if too many of the benefits of the resource wealth are withheld from most of the population. Countries similarly situated but without a rich resource endowment might lack the resources to co-opt different ethnic groups in a consociational manner. Narrow, ethnically concentrated groups often quarrel over the few resources that do exist that might propel them to political power. The powerful exclude the weak from the few resources that do exist. The dominant incentive is to pursue prisoner's dilemma bargaining tactics, which ultimately increases pressures for violent internal conflict, civil war and/or national disintegration.

In both cases of high fragmentation, coalitions prioritize redistribution (rarely equal) over development, or expansionary economic policies. The set of payoffs from this bargaining dynamic resembles a zero-sum, highly redistributive prisoner's dilemma game in which coalitional politics centers on the ability to appropriate monopoly rents and, most often, to provide private goods to a select and privileged few.

HOW BROAD AND PARTICIPATIVE COALITIONS LEAD TO GOOD POLICY

Broad, cross-cutting coalitions, which encourage all actors to be actively engaged in policy-making processes, facilitate the intensive cooperation, information sharing, careful monitoring and appropriate enforcement necessary to overcome collective dilemmas that hinder the formation of institutions necessary for skills development. The important causal mechanism between coalitional breadth and participation on the one hand and institutional linkages within society on the other is side payments. Side payments are those remunerations given by the elite to social actors in return for political support. The type, timing and duration of side payments create preferences for institutions that will maximize the payoffs to individuals in the coalition. As the size of the coalition increases, *ceteris paribus*, coalition members' share of supplied private goods decreases, making the utility calculus for cooperation more favorable by lessening the difference between belonging and not belonging to the winning coalition (Bueno de Mesquita et al., 1999). When leaders must rely on a broad range of social actors for political support, they tend to provide public goods as the most efficient form of side payments in return for political support.[17] Furthermore, as resource endowments decrease, the likelihood rises that ruling elites will provide public goods as side payments to coalition members (Doner et al., 2005; Root, 1996).[18]

But public goods are more difficult to design and implement, and require more cooperation and interaction among the coalitional actors than is necessary to provide private goods. The provision of more advanced public goods requires more intensive cooperation to design, implement, monitor and maintain (enforce). Narrow coalitions have less need for connective public–private linkages and therefore do not create the institutions necessary to facilitate these linkages, or, if they already exist, allow them to weaken and decay.[19]

The provision of public goods is important for several reasons. First, public goods increase equality. Political processes underlying institutional formation and maintenance reflect power asymmetries among the various parties involved (Knight, 1992).[20] Game-theoretic, rational-choice frameworks assume intentional actors, strategic options and payoffs associated with certain choices (Scharpf, 1997). Strategies and choices, however, do not exist in a vacuum. The reality is that actors, whether individual or aggregated, must operate within a certain institutional structure, which shapes and constrains their behavior through both positive and negative social incentives. Providing public goods creates an environment where all members of society can gain in influence and power, in turn influencing the institutional structure in ways that pay off for them personally. Since by definition all have access to these goods, income equality is enhanced.

Income equality is important because lower inequality increases the purchasing power of low-income families for superior goods, such as education and training (Birdsall et al., 1997). Education and training, in turn, advance an individual's earning potential, further reducing income inequalities and providing further resources with which to participate in the institutional system. In short, equality puts more people in a position to be linked to the policy process if the political institutional structure allows it. Clearly democracy offers the best possibilities here. But other options certainly exist, as I show later in the analysis on Singapore.

Furthermore, as equality among actors increases, power asymmetries diminish, further reducing barriers to participation and cooperation. Since each actor in the coalition desires to create institutions that best serve his or her purposes, institutions are created to facilitate dense information exchanges and to create checks and balances that ensure public–private relationships do not devolve into rent-seeking or collusion. Broad coalitions may lead to some public goods, but broad *and* participative coalitions lead to institutions that increase trust, accountability, credibility and transparency while providing public goods since actors are 'vested' in the projects over which they have an active participating role.

As income equality increases and group participation rises, linkages between organizations, both public and private, move from uni-directional information providers, to bi-directional consultative, to bi-directional participative. What do these ideal connective linkages, necessary to accomplish upgrading tasks, look like? Importantly, they must extend beyond government and big business. New skills required for a changing global economy means that labor must be included. Costs and complexities associated with R&D make the inclusion of academia, especially universities (Yusuf and Nabeshima, 2007), vital. Also, the fact that R&D is increasingly being carried out by small and medium-sized entrepreneurial firms is a strong argument for extending connections to firms of all sizes.

The linkages I speak of are less like the ones theorized by developmental state scholars[21] and more like the 'embedded autonomy' envisioned by Peter Evans (1995). Whereas the developmental scholars suggested that the state could control all state–society relationships, scholars such as Richard Doner (1992) and Weiss (1995) recognized that all the players in government–private sector relationships were critical to the interaction. It is true that productive public–private relationships are not possible in an environment of minimalist states or acquiescent societies. Capacity for statecraft remains a necessary ingredient, but in conjunction with an assertive and involved private sector (Doner and Hawes, 1995).

This book pushes these ideas further and suggests that the relationship between the state and private sector needs to increasingly function in an integrated, more balanced and interdependent way. More balanced public–private linkages facilitate good economic policy in at least three ways. First, they better balance multiple preferences of both the state and society for resource allocation, including economic growth, domestic stability and external security. Second, they facilitate balanced negotiation and complex bargaining with a broader range of actors in a more demanding environment. Third, they create autonomy for the state from any single, dominating interest. The state is therefore able to formulate neutral, technocratic policy and to demand help from the private sector to monitor and assist in compliance and enforcement. At the same time, such state–society relationships demand transparency and accountability from the government on policy direction and decisions. Trust and legitimacy come from repeated cooperative interactions, which the state cannot break if it desires continued future cooperation from a naturally skeptical and profit-oriented private sector (Hicken and Ritchie, 2002).

PUTTING IT ALL TOGETHER

To summarize the entire argument, systemic vulnerability influences the breadth and participation of political coalitions through the nature, type and timing of side payments. Coalitional breadth and participation shape the linkages among economic actors in society. These linkages, or the lack thereof, what Evans called 'embedded autonomy,' facilitate policy processes and institutional creation in an endogenous fashion that in turn influences skills development and upgrading. The entire argument is laid out in detail in Figure 2.1.

Systemic vulnerability creates incentives (as described above) for particular coalitional structures that include the state and extend to economic actors, whether or not formally incorporated into the political structure. Coalitions that are broadly cross-cutting and also provide extensive opportunities for coalition members to be actively engaged in making and implementing economic policies are able to foster institutional structures that tightly integrate the interaction of actors across economic activities. Such tightly networked groups have the capacity to overcome collective dilemmas and meet the high demand for innovation and technological upgrading generated by the systemic vulnerability. Applying this framework can help us understand the processes of skills upgrading in Southeast Asia.

In Malaysia, a rich natural resource endowment, fluctuating levels of military vulnerability and primarily ethnic but also rural–urban domestic unrest interacted to created preferences for a coalitional structure that, while broad at the bottom, was a narrow alliance of interests at the top with little active participation beyond periodic consultation. Rich resources made revenue generation easy for the political elite. At the same

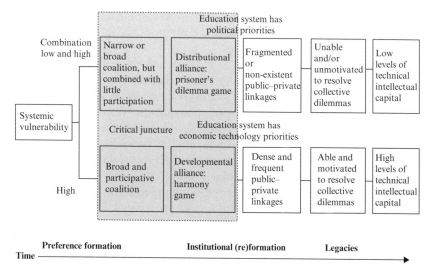

Figure 2.1   Detailed argument outline

time, competing ethnic factions were constantly vying for government-generated rents. Finally, external security conditions in Malaysia never rose to a level that would force the ruling elite to expand membership or participation within the ruling coalition.[22]

Preferences for coalitional structure generated by conditions of systemic vulnerability are evident through early decisions by the British to 'assign' ethnicities to industries, which economically segregated the races. Chinese predominately worked in the tin mines, Indians on the rubber plantations, and Malays on the rice farms. The Malay privileged government used resources extracted from primary commodity sectors to pay for majority, Malay-friendly, affirmative action policies. To make subsidies for the majority palatable to the minority ethnic groups, Malaysia relied on rapid economic growth through first-stage structural reform. The result was a coalition of interests, primarily ethnic, that appeared broad at the base, but was actually a narrow, corporatist alliance made up of each of the elites of the various ethnic groups.

Although Malaysia's coalition was 'a cohesive state elite centralized authority and policy initiative . . . from the top down, and drew business into policy networks under its firm control,' these corporatist links were superficial and 'relied heavily on less formal personal or clientelist ties to individual corporate groups' (Felker, 1998: 11). The result was a less participative coalition. Actors were consulted to some degree (Biddle and Milor, 1999), but the consultation never extended to responsibility and accountability for actual policy formation and implementation. As a result, policies had low credibility and lacked the effective implementation to transform institutional capacities.

In Thailand rich natural resource endowments and a relatively homogeneous population influenced coalitional structure in at least two ways. First, taxes generated from rice agriculture provided a steady source of revenue to fund narrow coalitional relationships between the Thai political elite and the Bangkok-based Chinese–Thai economic elite (Crone, 1988). Second, abundant resource-generated revenues also provided sufficient means and objectives to encourage inter-bureaucratic rivalry and fragmentation over redistributive objectives.

Although Thailand was more ethnically homogeneous than Malaysia, resource-generated income from rice agriculture created divisions between rural and urban communities. The processing, finance, supply chain and exporting of rice grown in rural communities was controlled by the Chinese–Thai elite in Bangkok. These elites formed clientelistic relationships with the government elite, also in Bangkok. The farmers often found themselves on the outside of this coalition.

As with many other countries in Southeast Asia, Thailand's early state-building began with high levels of military vulnerability to outside powers, particularly Great Britain and Europe. High levels of external threats encouraged restructuring of the Kingdom's political institutions away from narrow relationships between the royal family and nobles to include a broader coalition of economic elites. Later stages of external vulnerability, such as the Vietnam conflict, also correlate with coalitional broadening and institutional change (Doner et al., 2009). Nevertheless, external threats were either not intense enough or not of sufficient duration to change coalitional trajectories shaped by resources and social cleavages. The majority of conflicts were of the small border dispute variety. More serious conflicts, such as the Vietnam War, were mitigated by protection and resources provide by the US military presence.

The result has been an odd ebbing and flowing of coalitional patterns of breadth, at times appearing narrow and at times broad. But the power behind the military regimes as well as the fragmented parliamentary democracies has always been a fairly narrow political elite supported by rice agriculture and a large land frontier. In the words of one scholar, changes in the political structure, including the supporting coalitional structure, have been more 'rearranging the deckchairs' than substantive change.[23]

Finally, in Singapore, a scarce natural resource endowment coupled with relative ethnic homogeneity and heightened levels of external military threats both forced and facilitated the development of a broad social coalition between the state and private economic actors. Without an economic safety net woven from the income of primary commodity exports, Singapore had to depend on expansive rather than redistributive economic growth to survive. Initial fragmentation and political competition between labor, the civil service and foreign business was quickly seen as economically and politically unsustainable, especially in the face of hostile neighbors. To respond to external threats with few natural resources, Singapore, like Israel (and Thailand), mobilized every Singaporean between 19 and 25 to serve in the country's security forces. The same mentality extends to the economy. Participation from a broad cross-class developmental coalition is necessary to compensate for the systemic vulnerability felt by the island nation. Although the country is ruled by a single party, the People's Action Party (PAP), the political elite have created a corporatist structure in which numerous social groups, including labor, participate in the policy-making and implementing process.

Each country's coalitional structure fostered specific forms of strategic interaction and bargaining among economic actors. These strategic interactions led to policy choices, made in equilibrium, that were regularized into institutional configurations.[24] These choices were especially important during 'critical junctures'[25] in time.

In Malaysia and Singapore the initial juncture was political independence. In Thailand, it was a major political transition from dynastic monarchical rule to parliamentary democracy. Subsequent critical junctures included periods of full employment and, potentially, the Asian financial crisis. Critical junctures open windows of opportunity where institutional systems might be overhauled, abandoned, and/or created (Gourevitch, 1986).[26]

Early survival for Singapore at the point of independence required the newly dominant Lee faction to quickly broaden the political coalition. Moreover, the rapid redeployment of British forces, the failed union with Malaysia, and a long history of labor unrest forced the government to focus intently on economic expansion as opposed to redistribution. Whereas the economic game in Malaysia and Thailand was zero-sum, in Singapore it had to be multiplicative for survival's sake. In other words, since there were few if any resources to distribute, personal gain was the byproduct of collective gain. Broad coalitions became more participative over time, leading to significant political cooperation, coordination and integration.

In addition to pressure for broader coalitions, independence created intense pressure for technological upgrading. Broad developmental coalitions were able to agree on how to reform the education and training system by (1) quickly adopting English as the language of instruction and (2) connecting training programs to multinational corporations (MNCs). As pressures to upgrade mounted during the late 1970s and early 1980s, and again in the late 1990s, Singapore responded by creating and expanding institutions to foster technical training, facilitate technology dissemination from foreign MNCs to locally owned firms, and coordinate development efforts among labor, academia and business (Schein, 1996; Wong, 2001; Doner and Ritchie, 2003; Ritchie, 2005a). These efforts were facilitated by institutions that increasingly and more effectively linked public and private actors together in bi-directionally participative policy initiatives.

Like Singapore, Malaysia has experienced critical junctures at independence and as the economy neared full employment. But levels of systemic vulnerability shaped different coalitional responses. Malaysia's superficially broad coalition ostensibly sought to transfer wealth from the minority Chinese population to the majority Malay population. In practice, however, wealth was transferred from the broader Chinese population to the narrow coalition of Chinese business and Malay political elites (Jomo, 1993). Even so, as important as redistribution was, it had to be balanced with some level of overall economic growth if the government was to also maintain the support of the Chinese masses.

The institutional system reflected the priorities of the coalition. Priorities for educational reform were initially centered on political unification in a federal system as a way to balance various ethnic groups. Malay was chosen as the language of instruction, and political and social sciences were emphasized over science and technology. As in Thailand, labor was largely excluded from the economic coalition. The result has been sufficient capacity to create institutions that look similar to those in Singapore, but which function primarily to maintain social balance through a complex mix of income growth and redistribution. Institutionally these objectives continue to be facilitated through consultative mechanisms that foster one-way information flows from the private to the public sphere. Yet at the same time, pressures to increase skills to address labor shortages continue to push the ruling elite to address technological development. But existing patterns of top-down consultation frustrate most of these efforts. The result is development processes that remain mired at the high end of first-stage manufacturing.

In Thailand political transformation was not accompanied by serious economic threat and so educational reform focused on political objectives rather than technological upgrading. But here, unlike in Malaysia, a lack of intense ethnic conflict ironically allayed incentives to generate rapid economic growth, so much so that policy makers initially chose a path of socialist economic development that emphasized equality. The coalitions that emerged were focused on transferring wealth primarily from the extensive farm-based rural population to the narrow coalition of Thai politicians and urban-based Chinese businessmen (Christiansen, 1993). The incentive for these narrow coalitions was to view economics as redistributive and zero-sum. Policies were thus designed to extract and redistribute, not to expand. As fragmentation within both the state and the private economy increased, pressures to acquire one's 'fair share' also increased.

Narrow coalitions created few incentives for cooperative linkages, consultative or otherwise, between the narrow coalition of ruling elites and the private sector. When future critical junctures during times of crisis did increase pressures for upgrading, Thailand's institutional structure impeded change. In particular, a fragmented bureaucratic structure created numerous 'veto points' that made change in response to outside pressures either efficient or long-lasting (Doner et al., 2009).

The legacies of these early policy and institutional decisions continue to make it difficult in both Malaysia and Thailand to form institutions facilitating close linkages between public and private actors. As a result, it is harder to complete tasks necessary to encourage the formation of technical skills. Lacking cooperation and trust,[27] distributional coalitions unify and consolidate education and training systems in vague and unfocused ways to further politically or socially expedient ends. More than simply lacking institutional capacity, both countries de-emphasize technical and scientific capacity, despite loud rhetoric about the need for technological progress, which makes it difficult to create, replicate and expand technical skills and knowledge. Ultimately, society sees education and training as secondary and non-'mission-critical.'

NOTES

1. Interview with Seagate official, 2005.
2. This is an extension of the argument made in Shafer (1994).
3. As Sachs and Warner (1997) show, between 1971 and 1989, states that relied on high levels of primary resource exports as a percentage of GDP grew more slowly than resource-poor states. Auty (1998) explains that rapidly diminishing transportation costs immediately after World War II may have been the difference between the initial salutary effects of large resource endowments and their subsequent detrimental effects. This suggests that when resource endowments figure prominently in competitive specialization, asset specification and the international division of labor, their effects are especially pernicious. On the other hand, if high transportation costs rendered primary commodities less tradable on the international market, the domestic market was more likely to exploit the resource to develop capacity and specialization in other areas. This in turn suggests that the nature of the resource endowment may also be important. A balanced endowment of industrial metals, timber, agriculture and foodstuffs, petroleum

and so forth would be much more beneficial than a single, large concentration of any one resource.

4. This argument is a natural extension of Shafer (1994).
5. Nation states develop preferences from their position in the international system (Krasner, 1984). Foremost among these preferences is to maintain sovereignty. To do so, a country must have the capacity to defend itself as well as provide economically for its people. Foreign exchange is important for both tasks.
6. Ross (1999) reports that whereas in the late 1950s almost all extractive enterprises in the developing world were foreign owned, but the late 1970s virtually all had been nationalized. But even where nationalization has not been complete, the flow of revenue to the state has not suffered. For example, in Malaysia, Exxon and Shell have been given contracts to extract crude oil and natural gas from peninsular Malaysia, East Malaysia (Borneo) and Malaysian territorial waters. Both companies, however, pay almost 90 percent of their gross revenue directly to the state in extraction fees. An executive at Exxon remarked that while such fees are usually high in every developing country, Malaysia extracted by far the greatest amount of any country in which Exxon did business.
7. While it is true that resource-poor countries with significant human resources might succeed in establishing low-technology, labor-intensive industries to generate foreign exchange, this solution is only temporary. At some point rising wages will force the country to upgrade technologically or suppress real income growth. The latter strategy is almost certain to end in the removal of the ruling elite. I assume rulers are rational and wish to maintain their incumbency and will therefore pursue the former.
8. Proxied by inequality and ethnic fragmentation.
9. Proxied by the quality of governmental institutions, rule of law, democratic rights and social safety nets.
10. Fearon and Laitin (1996) argue that all ethnic relationships are not conflictual. Instead, institutions can help contain disputes between individual members of various groups. This leads to a variety of conflict-free equilibria.
11. See Easterly and Levine (1997).
12. This section draws heavily on Doner et al. (2005).
13. On Latin America, see Centeno (1997: 1569). On the Middle East, see Barnett (1992).
14. Campos and Root (1996: 58–9).
15. Harmony games are characterized by a payoff structure in which all parties derive the greatest benefit from cooperation and the least benefit from defection. If one party cooperates and the other defects, there is a disproportionately greater benefit to the defecting party. Nevertheless, the total of the sucker's payoff is less than the cooperative payoff, making cooperation more likely. See Snidal (1991) for a complete analysis of various games and their attendant payoff structures.
16. See Lijphart (1975).
17. See Root (1996); Doner et al. (2005); Baum and Lake (2003); Bueno de Mesquita et al. (2003).
18. Waldner (1999) argues persuasively that narrow, cohesive political coalitions are not beholden to popular segments of society, which allows them to focus on resolving both 'Gerschenkronian' dilemmas of capital accumulation and risk tolerance, as well as 'Kaldorian' dilemmas of increasing returns and technological upgrading. Broad coalitions, he argues, must use state resources to compete for popular support among mass-based groups. When the time comes to 'discipline capital' and promote industrial upgrading, the resources are not available to do so. As convincing as this story is, it glosses over the motivations for technological upgrading. Why do narrow coalitions prefer technological upgrading? In other words, narrow coalitions might be a necessary but not sufficient condition for upgrading.
19. Ross (2001) argues that resource wealth caused political institutions in Indonesia to wither over time.
20. Cf. Christiensen (1993), who applies this dynamic to the rice industry in Thailand.

21. See Johnson (1982); Woo Cumings (1999).
22. Malaysia's main military disputes have been with its border neighbors, including Malaysia's *Konfrontasi* border dispute with Indonesia, and disputes over water with Singapore and border definitions with Thailand. Although fairly constant, these conflicts, with the short exception of *Konfrontasi*, have not risen to the level of severity to change the coalitional structure.
23. Personal conversation with Richard Doner.
24. Bates et al. (1999: 8) argue that institutions 'induce choices that are regularized because they are made in equilibrium.'
25. See Collier and Collier (1991) for a discussion of the appropriate use of critical junctures in comparative politics.
26. Influential research in comparative politics points to the importance of decisions, some seemingly very small, at 'critical junctures' in time (Collier and Collier, 1991). More on critical junctures in Chapters 4 and 5.
27. Credibility can also be thought of as trust, which Schoppa (1999) argues is necessary for cooperation within a bargaining framework.

3.   Some preliminary evidence

This book claims that systemic vulnerability shapes the breadth of coalitions and the level of participation of its members. As breadth and participation rise, the ability to create productive public–private interactions also rises, increasing society's ability to develop institutions that lead to higher levels of intellectual capital, a core ingredient of long-term, sustainable economic upgrading. Alternatively, less vulnerable conditions create incentives for more narrow, less participative coalitions. The results are fewer productive linkages, fewer institutions capable of handling the tasks of upgrading and, hence, less technical intellectual capital.

What is the evidence behind these arguments? This chapter conducts preliminary tests on these hypotheses by evaluating correlative evidence, both qualitative and quantitative. The point is that before explaining *how* things happen, it would be nice to know how confident we are *whether* they happened. After evaluating the strength of correlative relationships in this chapter, I then explore in subsequent chapters the causal relationships behind the correlations through comparative process tracing – the work of examining causal explanations both over time and across cases.

Three steps are useful in determining the extent and strength of hypothesized relationships. The first, qualitative matching within the countries of Southeast Asia, provides control for regional variation and considers the counterfactuals on several key variables. This effort is designed to eliminate potential alternative correlative relationships, thereby relieving any worries of omitted-variable bias. The second is a regional comparison between Northeast and Southeast Asia using both qualitative and quantitative data. Whereas the first effort is designed to eliminate variables, this second strategy is designed to discover variables that might correlate. The final approach is to employ three-stage, least-squares analysis on quantitative, worldwide data to explore the potential generalizability of any discovered correlations.

VARIATION WITHIN SOUTHEAST ASIA

Malaysia, Thailand and Singapore can provide significant insight into the processes behind economic growth and development. All three have been among the top performers in the developing world since the mid-1980s. Using these three cases from the same region provides a high degree of comparative control by eliminating many potentially confounding interregional variables such as timing, development strategy, investment sources and so forth (Diesing, 1971). Yet these cases also co-vary on other important variables (see Table 3.1). For example, Malaysia and Singapore approximate a natural experiment, having shared a similar political and economic history with final separation coming only in 1965. Thus these historical similarities cannot be the cause of differing levels of technical

Table 3.1　Case similarities and differences

Variables	Malaysia	Singapore	Thailand
Resource endowments	High	Low	High
Ethnic composition	Fragmented	Homogeneous	Homogeneous
Coalitional structure	Broad, but with little participation	Broad and highly participative	Narrow with little participation
Colonialization	British	British	None
State strength	Mid to high	High	Low
Elite conflict	Low to mid	High	Low
Institutional structure	Macro growth with micro distribution	Developmental	Macro growth with micro distribution
Economic strategy	Import substitution and export processing zones.	Integration into the global economy	Import substitution and export processing zones
Foreign investment	High	High	Mid to high
Tariffs structure	High (except for EPZs)	Virtually none	Mid to high (but falling in most areas and none in EPZs)
Language of education	Malay	English/Chinese	Thai
Bureaucratic fragmentation	High (especially at the line ministry level)	Low	High
Extent to which labor is included in education and training	Low to non-existent	High	Low to non-existent
Early technical focus	Primary commodities	Industrial technologies	Primary commodities

intellectual capital. On the other hand, Thailand is relatively dissimilar from the first two countries in terms of religion, language, culture, economics and political and economic history. In this case these variables cannot account for the similar levels of technical intellectual capital found in Thailand and Malaysia. Finally, with respect to the hypothesized causal variables, Thailand falls between the other two cases. Like Singapore, Thailand is relatively ethnically homogeneous. But like Malaysia, Thailand has a rich natural resource endowment.

Each country's unique combination of structural conditions and resulting coalitional structure correlates highly with significant variation on a number of indicators of developmental outcomes (see Table 3.2).

COMPARING NORTHEAST ASIA TO SOUTHEAST ASIA

Although recent transitions from diversification to upgrading have been rare, a large majority of the successful cases are located in Northeast Asia. As a result, one interesting analytical and theoretical division commonly found in the political-economy literature is between the 'developmental states' of East Asia and the more 'neo-liberal,' corporatist, or authoritarian developing states of Southeast Asia, Latin America and Africa (Booth, 1999; Doner and Ritchie, 2003; Pempel, 2004, Doner et al., 2005). Booth (1995) accurately argued that despite similar growth trajectories, the ASEAN-4 were in fact very different from the East Asian NICs in a variety of areas. Important differences exist in education, financial structures, business organization, labor, land holdings, military vulnerability, resource endowments and ethnic structure.

In East Asia, the correlation between resource endowments, ethnic composition and developmental states is high. Because these countries lacked a rich natural resource sector to underwrite rent-seeking activities, the focus was on expanding the overall economic pie. To do so required elites to increasingly draw a widening number of active participants into its coalition over time, including peasants and labor. Broader, more participative coalitions created critical institutional capacity that provided key public goods, which in turn facilitated technological upgrading (Root, 1996; Doner et al., 2005).[1] These public goods included land reform, public education, public housing and open markets (but with close oversight), to name a few (Doner et al., 2005). Managing the provision and maintenance of these public goods required institutions that facilitated close public–private linkages, which could be drawn upon to further technological upgrading and development when the incentives were right to do so.

Table 3.2   Comparative structural conditions and technology indicators for Southeast Asia

		Thailand	Singapore	Malaysia
1975 ethnic composition (Herfindahl concentration index)[a]		0.5942	0.6083	0.5071
2007 ethnic composition (Herfindahl concentration index)		0.5942	0.6156	0.3273
1975 commodity exports (% of GNP)		20.33	0.01[b]	58.87
Income equality (0 = complete equality)	1975	41.74	(1973) 41	(1976) 53
	1989	(1990) 48.80	39	48.35
Scientists, engineers, and technicians (per 1 million capita)	1995	159	3081	175
	2000	(2001) 400	4478	319
	2002	(2003) 494	4733	356
	2004	(2003) 494	4997	503
R&D expenditure (% of GDP)	2000	0.252	1.91	0.49
	2002	0.244	2.16	0.69
	2004	0.255	2.25	0.60
Tertiary enrolment (% of gross)	1970	13.0	7.8	4.0
	1980	12.7	18.6	4.1
	1990	19.0	. . .	7.2
	2000	35.0	. . .	23.0
	2004	44.0		31.0
Secondary enrolment (% of gross)	1975	26	52.0	42
	1992	37	78.9	60
	2001	67	. . .	65
	2004	72	. . .	72
Public education expenditures (as % of GNP)	1975	3.6	2.9	6.00
	2000	5.41	. . .	6.20
	2004	4.23	. . .	6.25
Number of political parties	1998	11	5	15
Winning coalition size	1970	0.50	0.75	0.75
	1990	0.75	0.75	0.75

Table 3.2   (continued)

		Thailand	Singapore	Malaysia
Ministries responsible for technical education and training	2001	7	3	4

Notes:

[a]   The Herfindahl concentration index, which is defined as Ethnic fragmentation = $\Sigma(f\_i^2)$, i = 1,. . ., I I, where Σ means 'the sum of the following, for all i,' where 'i' is the designator for the ith ethnic group, and where 'f_i' is the fraction of the total population of the country accounted for by the ith ethnic group. Essentially, it is the sum of the squares of the top 'i' ethnic groups. The index returns a measure between 0 and 1, with 1 equal to complete homogeneity and 0 equal to complete fragmentation.

[b]   Primary commodity production as a percentage of GDP.

Sources:
http://www.gov.sg/parliament/mp.htm
http://www.agora.stm.it/elections/election/malaysia.htm
Europa World Year Book in combination with *Fischer Weltalmanach* and www Malaysia on Line. *CIA World Fact Book*, 1999, 2007. World Bank *World Development Indicators* 2007. UNESCO *World Yearbook* 1999. Deininger and Squire (1996).

Without ethnic fragmentation or domestic unrest to sabotage cooperative linkages, development initiatives were able to accomplish complex developmental tasks.

Scarce resources also acted as a direct motivation for the East Asian NICs to develop. War provided a continuous source of income from the early 1940s through the late 1960s and early 1970s as the USA worked first to contain the Japanese and then the communists. But when funds from the USA dried up, these countries were forced to address the challenge of creating foreign exchange without a rich natural resource sector to fall back on.

Like the East Asian NICs, the ASEAN-4 also benefited from US involvement and resources during World War II, the Korean conflict and the Vietnam War. But unlike the NICs, when the USA began limiting its assistance, the ASEAN-4 turned largely to various resource sectors to grow. Foreign exchange generated from rice, sugar, oil, palm, rubber and other agricultural and commodity products reduced political pressures to expand technological capacity and to reach out to other sectors of society, especially labor.

The two regions also differ with respect to ethnic diversity. Whereas Japan, Korea and Taiwan are relatively homogeneous societies, most of the ASEAN-4 countries are highly diverse. Diversity has made it more difficult for the ASEAN-4 countries to form broader coalitions. Ethnic fragmentation in Malaysia limited incentives to empower Chinese and Indian elements of the ruling coalition. What at first glance appears to be a broad coalition is in fact a multiplicity of narrow coalitions presided over by the Malay political elite.

Different coalitional structures have created different preferences for the means of creating support to maintain power. In Northeast Asia, political support was generated through the provision of public goods that were broadly beneficial. By comparison, in the ASEAN-4, payoffs were more often private and targeted to maintain narrow power structures at the pinnacle of the state. When public goods were provided, they were often 'morsels' that, while public in form, most benefited a narrow few at the top.[2] Private-regarding side payments led to dualistic economies in which strong and protected local business sectors operated alongside a growing export sector that was largely foreign owned and operated. Narrow coalitions of political elites at the apex of political institutions privileged small groups over the rest of society either politically, economically, or both. Such institutions led to 'turf building' among the elite and further fragmentation not only between the public and private spheres, but also within government (Ritchie, 2005a). Such institutions were adept at creating and supplying private goods, but constrained the formation of public goods. The result was little pressure to create the institutions that would foster deep and overlapping public–private linkages.

Using a bivariate analysis of resource endowments and ethnic fragmentation, we can see how the so-called 'developmental states' cluster together while those that have been less successful in upgrading their economies cluster in different regions. Correcting for Singapore's misleading statistic that reflects the fact that Singapore is a large *re*-exporter of commodity products from the region, but has virtually no natural resources of its own, one can see a tight cluster of the developmental states. Interestingly, those emerging economies in Southeast Asia that have been most successful in diversifying their economies, namely Thailand and Malaysia, but also the Philippines and Indonesia, also cluster together. The laggards occupy the extremes of either or both axes (see Figure 3.1).

WORLDWIDE ANALYSIS

Can we find the same correlations in other regions of the world as seem to exist in Asia? Ideally we would be able to estimate the entire theoretical argument simultaneously. In the model we want to estimate two primary questions: (1) what is the impact of structural conditions on coalitional structure; and (2) what is the impact of coalitional structure

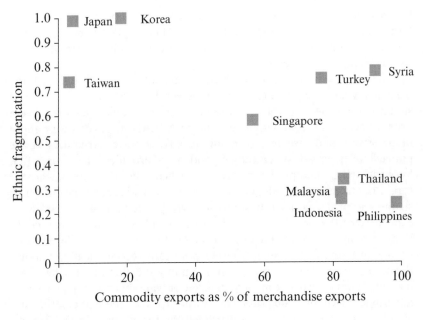

Source: *World Bank Development Indicators* 2007, CIA.

Figure 3.1   Clusters of developmental states

on skills upgrading? One option is to estimate each equation separately using standard ordinary least squares (OLS) analysis. However, although OLS will work, the best solution may be to use instrumental variable estimation.

Instrumental variable estimation has several advantages. In addition to allowing us to estimate the entire model simultaneously, this approach provides mechanisms to deal with measurement error problems. For example, we have hypothesized that coalitional breadth and participation is a key variable leading to levels of technical intellectual capital in each country. However, we cannot measure coalitional structure directly. This analysis uses two proxies, an index of winning coalitions developed by Bueno de Mesquita et al. (2003) and the Gini coefficient measuring income equality developed by Deininger and Squire (1996). Both measures probably do not correctly reflect real coalitional breadth or participation, at least not efficiently, which leads to measurement error. This error might correlate with the error term in either the structural equation or the equation of the dependent variable. If measurement error correlates with the error in the structural equation, using OLS estimators will be inconsistent, causing the inferences to be invalid. The problem can be fixed using two- or three-stage least squares (2SLS or 3SLS). Theoretically, although 2SLS will be more robust than 3SLS, 3SLS will be more efficient if the system of equations used in the estimation is correctly specified.[3] Assuming correct specification, the analysis uses only three-stage models.

Nonetheless, finding acceptable measures for the variables is tricky. The analysis reduces systemic vulnerability into measures for resource endowments, external conflict and internal unrest. First, resource endowments (*COMMEX*) are measured, as in Sachs and Warner (1997), by a measure of the amount of primary commodity exports as a percentage of GDP. While this measure can be criticized as not inclusive of those resources consumed internally, it does capture the realized foreign exchange benefit, which is the hypothesized causal motivator for incentives to which the ruling elite respond.

External conflict is measured by two variables, *WAR* and *MILITARY*. *WAR* is a measure of conflicts contained in the correlates of war data. *MILITARY* is a measure of expenditures on military as a percentage of GDP.

Domestic unrest is captured by a number of measures, including *CONFLICTINDEX, RIOTS, ELF60*. *CONFLICTINDEX* is an aggregate measure of upheaval and unrest and includes phenomena such as strikes, assassinations, demonstrations, civil conflicts etc. *RIOTS* measures the number of organized confrontations with government. *ELF60* are ethnic data from the KGB (see Mauro, 1995) that reflect ethno-linguistic fragmentation. Because the theory hypothesizes an interactive relationship between resource endowments, ethnic fragmentation and security exposure, the model includes two multiplicative terms, one for resources and ethnicity and the other for resources and external conflict.

The dependent variable of technical intellectual capital (Y) uses a measure of scientists, engineers and technicians per million capita. Although this measure suffers from several concerns, including different qualifications of 'scientists, engineers, and technicians,' it is probably the best we can do since other measures, such as expenditures on education, R&D expenditures, patents etc., say little about the technical capacity of the local institutional structure.

The most difficult variable to measure is the intervening variable of coalitional structure (*W22, EQUALITY*). Bueno de Mesquita, et al. (2003) use an index that is weighted heavily by voting considerations.[4] The problem with this measure is that many developing countries are only pseudo-democratic at best (Case, 2002). Coalitional breadth and participation must be measured in different ways. To compensate for these weaknesses, I also use the Deininger and Squire (1996) measure for income equality.

This variable captures the indirect impact of coalitional structure over time. The scale returns a number between 0 and 1, with 0 being complete equality and 1 being complete inequality.

While income equality is often used as a proxy for a multitude of concepts and variables, it captures an important dimension of coalitional structure. Insights gained from Knight (1992) and Olson (1982) suggest that coalitions between political and economic actors reflect relationships of power and influence. Second, these coalitions form only as broad as necessary to achieve desired ends (Riker, 1980; Bueno de Mesquita et al., 1999). Thus, where power asymmetries are high, coalitions will be narrower since a more even power distribution requires a broader coalition of actors to bargain over desired ends and means. Asymmetries of wealth are a good proxy for asymmetries of power. Thus, where inequality is high, so are asymmetries of power. In societies with a more equal distribution of income, power asymmetries are less pronounced. Inequality should therefore be associated with narrow coalitions and equality should reflect increased coalitional breadth.

Time is also clearly a factor. It is not clear, *ex ante*, how much time is needed for structural conditions to influence coalitional structure and coalitional structure to influence microeconomic outcomes. On the one hand, educating people could take as much as a generation. On the other, severe crises might provoke more immediate outcomes. To ensure that the analysis captures both long- and short-term change, we draw measures of the impact of variables over several decades by lagging the intervening and dependent variables from the independent variables by ten years. Measures for independent variables come from 1970–80. Coalitional measures come from 1980–90, and technical intellectual capital measures from 1995–2005. Finally, the analysis controls for GNP per capita (*GNP*), education expenditures as a percentage of GNP (*EDGNP*) and a measure for regime type (*POLITY*). Our expectations, then, for each variable in the model are depicted in Table 3.3. Following the theory, we utilize three-stage least squares to organize the variables into a structural equation:

$$(Y = \alpha + \beta_1(EDGNP) + \beta_2(GNP) + \beta_3(W22)$$
$$\text{or } \beta_3(GINI) + \beta_4(COMMEX));$$

and a reduced-form equation:

$$(W22 \text{ or } GINI = \alpha + \beta_1(ELF60) + \beta_2(GNP) + \beta_3(COMMEX)$$
$$+ \beta_4(CONFLICTINDEX) \text{ or } \beta_4 (RIOTS) + \beta_5(WAR)$$
$$+ \beta_6(POLITY) + \beta_7(ELF60*COMMEX)$$
$$+ \beta_8(ELF60*MILITARY) + \beta_9(MILITARY*COMMEX)$$

The results of the estimation can be seen in Table 3.4.

Table 3.3 Data description and expected relationships

Variable	Measure	Structure	Expected relationship with science and technology measure (Y)	Expected relationship with intervening variable coalitional breadth (W)
Y	Number of scientists and technicians *Source*: World Bank *Development Indicators*	0 – positive		
W22	Coalitional breadth *Source*: Bueno de Mesquita et al. (2003)	0–1 The higher this number implies broader winning coalition	+	
EDGNP	Ratio of government's education expenditure to GNP *Source*: World Bank *Development Indicators*	0–1 The higher this number implies higher spending in education	+	
GNP	Gross national product *Source*: World Bank *Development Indicators*	0 – positive	+	
GINI	Gini coefficients *Source*: Bueno de Mesquita et al. (2003)	0–1 The higher this number implies higher income inequality	–	–

Table 3.3 (continued)

Variable	Measure	Structure	Expected relationship with science and technology measure (Y)	Expected relationship with intervening variable coalitional breadth (W)
COMMEX	Share of agriculture, food, fuel, and ore exports values overt total export values. *Source*: World Bank *Development Indicators*	0–1 The higher this number implies that the country relies more on primary commodity as source of income	–	–
ELF60	Ethnic fragmentation *Source*: Bueno de Mesquita et al. (2003)	0–1 The higher this number implies the higher likelihood of the next different ethnic people within the country.	–	–
MILITARY	World Bank *Development Indicators*	% of GDP spent on military	+	+
CONFLICTINDEX	Internal conflict index *Source*: Bueno de Mesquita et al. (2003)	0 – positive The higher this number implies that the country has more internal conflict.	–	–
RIOTS	Numbers of violent demonstrations *Source*: Bueno de Mesquita et al. (2003)	0 – positive The higher this number implies that the country has more demonstration.	–	–

Variable	Description	Range/Coding		
WAR	Numbers of external wars. *Source*: Bueno de Mesquita et al. (2003)	0 – positive. The higher this number implies that the country has engaged in war	+	+
Polity	Polity IV (concomitant qualities of democratic and autocratic authority) *Source*: http://www.systemicpeace.org/polity/polity4.htm	–10–10. –10 (hereditary monarchy) to +10 (consolidated democracy) or The polity scores can also be converted to regime categories: we recommend a three-part categorization of 'autocracies' (–10 to -6), 'anocracies' (–5 to +5 and 'democracies' (+6 to +10)	+	+
ELF60*COMMEX	Interaction of ethnic fragmentation and primary commodity export. *Source*: Author's calculation	0–1		–
ELF60*MILITARY	Interaction of ethnic fragmentation and military. *Source*: Author's calculation			
MILITARY *COMMEX	Interaction of military and primary commodity export *Source*: Author's calculation			

Table 3.4 Three-stage least squares estimation for scientists, engineers and technicians per million capita

	Model 1	Model 2	Model 3	Model 4	Model 5	Model 6	Model 7	Model 8
Structural equation	3SLS	3SLS	3SLS	3SLS	3SLS	3SLS	3SLS	3SLS
EDGNP	468.053***	462.218***	466.182***	453.045***	309.907***	303.307***	310.880***	309.987***
	(46.68)	(46.472)	(46.531)	(46.750)	(70.483)	(70.543)	(71.073)	(71.129)
GNP	0.000	-0.000	-0.000	-0.000	-0.000**	-0.000**	-0.000**	-0.000***
	(0.000)	(0.000)	(0.000)	(0.000)	(0.000)	(0.000)	(0.000)	(0.000)
W22	1130.072***	1382.265***	1343.973***	1471.504***				
	(316.5)	(301.717)	(306.030)	(312.886)				
GINI					-128.679***	-131.134***	-129.734***	-130.303***
					(17.416)	(17.630)	(17.925)	(17.978)
COMMEX	-2385.175***	-2369.206***	-2380.926***	-2338.598***	58.967	121.508	82.900	96.575
	(330.29)	(330.533)	(331.551)	(332.688)	(562.740)	(567.553)	(573.415)	(574.684)
_cons	680.757*	658.492*	675.677*	614.657	6111.597***	6203.801***	6138.014***	6157.519***
	(399.14)	(391.413)	(393.434)	(396.133)	(738.731)	(744.336)	(754.425)	(756.021)
N	140	140	140	140	80	80	80	80
R-squared	0.780	0.771	0.780	0.781	0.782	0.780	0.781	0.781
Reduced-form equation								
Intervening variable	W22	W22	W22	W22	GINI	GINI	GINI	GINI
MILITARY	1.291	1.100	1.029	0.935	181.283***	171.167***	176.184***	173.049***
	(2.001)	(2.017)	(2.046)	(2.090)	(54.392)	(55.297)	(55.871)	(55.354)
ELF60	0.074	0.132	0.089	0.118	28.340***	24.347***	27.701***	27.952***
	(0.210)	(0.209)	(0.212)	(0.216)	(8.105)	(8.049)	(7.832)	(7.795)
COMMEX	-0.496***	-0.470***	-0.497***	-0.441***	39.999***	37.899***	39.151***	39.061***
	(0.102)	(0.100)	(0.101)	(0.100)	(2.878)	(2.729)	(2.623)	(2.615)

48

	(1)	(2)	(3)	(4)	(5)	(6)	(7)	(8)
CONFLICTINDEX	-0.000	0.000	-0.000**		-0.000	-0.000	0.000	
	(0.000)	(0.000)	(0.000)		(0.000)	(0.000)	(0.000)	
RIOTS	-0.040**	-0.041**			0.543	0.684		
	(0.019)	(0.019)			(0.462)	(0.466)		
WAR	-0.107				3.624*			
	(0.073)				(1.867)			
POLITY	0.029***	0.030***	0.028***	0.030***	-0.559***	-0.572***	-0.558***	-0.565***
	(0.002)	(0.002)	(0.002)	(0.002)	(0.058)	(0.059)	(0.058)	(0.055)
ELF60*COMMEX	0.118	0.025	0.077	0.047	-72.008***	-65.229***	-70.991***	-71.522***
	(0.288)	(0.283)	(0.287)	(0.293)	(14.412)	(14.310)	(13.953)	(13.874)
ELF60*MILITARY	-8.368***	-8.275***	-8.074***	-8.039***	-134.341	-121.012	-142.655	-142.420
	(1.909)	(1.922)	(1.951)	(1.994)	(100.089)	(102.071)	(102.310)	(102.322)
MILITARY* COMMEX	1.876	2.136	2.080	2.266	-180.694**	-173.096**	-169.956**	-165.911**
	(2.802)	(2.824)	(2.867)	(2.930)	(78.731)	(80.232)	(81.158)	(80.489)
_cons	0.936***	0.912***	0.938***	0.871***	21.468***	22.936***	22.213***	22.402***
	(0.069)	(0.067)	(0.067)	(0.062)	(1.664)	(1.526)	(1.461)	(1.383)
N	140	140	140	140	80	80	80	80
R-squared	0.651	0.691	0.680	0.668	0.874	0.867	0.864	0.864

Notes: *** $p<0.01$, ** $p<0.05$, * $p<0.1$. Standard errors in parentheses.
We can compare models 1 and 5, 2 and 6, 3 and 7, and 4 and 8.

Source: Author's calculation.

The results of the analysis suggest several conclusions. First, in the structural equation, resource endowments and coalitional structure influence the amount of technical intellectual capital as hypothesized. As resource endowments fall, the number of scientists, engineers and technicians rises. Likewise, as the coalition broadens and becomes more participative, levels of technical intellectual capital improve. The findings hold in Models 5 through 8 when the *GINI* coefficient, a better measure than *W22* for the participation of the coalition, is used.

The two control variables for the structural equation are *GNP* and expenditures on education as a percentage of GNP (*EDGNP*). The education expenditures variable is significant and its positive sign is as we would have expected: countries that spend more on education produce more technical intellectual capital (TIC) than countries that spend less. No big surprise.

On the other hand, GNP, contrary to what might be expected, was not significant. Several explanations might account for this. First, it is probable that levels of TIC are influencing levels of GNP rather than the other way around. Second, to the extent GNP is determining levels of TIC, it could be indirect. Finally, variables such as investment in education and levels of resource endowments might be explaining portions of the GNP variable.

In the reduced-form equation, resource endowments, ethnic fragmentation, and internal conflict and riots all influence coalitional structure as hypothesized. Fewer resource endowments lead to broader coalitions. Likewise, as societies become more ethnically fragmented or are involved in internal conflict, coalitions become narrower. What is less clear is the influence of the external conflict variable. *WAR* is statistically significant in Model 5, but not in the hypothesized direction. More war correlates with narrower coalitions. The same is true with the *MILITARY* variable. Although not statistically significant with the *W22* variable, it is highly significant with the *GINI* variable, but again in the direction that suggests that more military conflict results in narrower coalitions. Remember, however, that the theory argues an interactive relationship among the variables, which might change the coefficients at various levels of the other independent variables (more on this below).

Among the control variables, *POLITY*, a measure with autocracy at one end and democracy at the other, is highly significant. For the three equations with *W22* as the intervening variable, a positive sign indicates that as countries become more democratic, the winning coalition size increases. For Models 5 through 8, which use the *GINI* coefficient as a measure of coalitional breadth, a negative sign indicates that as the democracy score increases, the level of *inequality* falls, again suggesting that participation from a broad coalition increases. Finding the same result from both measures of coalitional breadth and participation increases our confidence that democracies encourage more participation from broader numbers of actors than less democratic countries. In other words, democracies are built on broader coalitions than non-democracies, again as we would have expected.

All of the equations have an interaction term for resource endowments, the most significant of the domestic conflict variables, *ELF60*, and *MILITARY*. Various of these variables are statistically significant in several of the equations, which means that there is a statistically significant change in one variable as the other interacting variable changes values. As theorized in Chapter 2, the three variables might have variable impacts on each other *depending on the value of the other variable*. For the interactive term, the significance of the impact one variable has on the other is measured *when the other variable equals zero*, and vice versa. When these variables take on other values, the substantive and statistical significance of the other variable changes. To figure out whether any changes in the values of one variable would have a significant impact on the other variable, it is necessary to evaluate the *conditional* influence of one variable *at various values of the other variable*. This can be done by computing the conditional standard errors.[5] For example, it may be possible that ethnicity's influence on the coalitional structure changes as the value of resource endowments changes. Whether the interactive term itself is significant indicates only whether there is a 'statistically significant amount of change in the relationship between each independent variable and the dependent variable with a one-unit change in the other independent variable' (Friedrich, 1982: 820).

The results in Models 1–3 and 5–7 in Table 3.4 suggest that *CONFLICTINDEX*, *RIOTS* and *WAR* are substantively insignificant or lack statistical significance. Although included for the readers use, the analysis considers only Models 4 and 8 for the conditional standard errors of the interactive terms.

For Model 4, which uses *W22* as the measure of coalitional breadth, the conditional variation for *MILITARY* and *COMMEX* can be seen in Table 3.5. A one-unit change in military expenditures when resource endowments are low *has no statistically significant impact on coalitional breadth*. But when resource endowments are more than 45 percent of total exports, military expenditures narrow the coalitional structure in significant ways. At the same time, a one-unit increase in resource endowments when military expenditures are low causes coalitional structure to narrow. But once military expenditures climb beyond 5 percent of GDP, resource endowments lose their influence. Both relationships are graphically represented in Figures 3.2 and 3.3.

Table 3.5 *Model 4 interaction computation with three-stage least squares (W22) (military expenditure and commodity exports)*

Value	Military expenditure at various values of commodity export			Commodity exports at various values of military expenditure		
	Marginal effect	Standard error	t-value	Marginal effect	Standard error	t-value
0	0.935287	2.090136	0.447477	−0.44052	0.099671	−4.41975
0.05	1.048583	1.951183	0.537409	−0.32723	0.145331	−2.25159
0.1	1.161878	1.813418	0.640712	−0.21393	0.274277	−0.77998
0.15	1.275173	1.677133	0.760329	−0.10063	0.415035	−0.24247
0.2	1.388469	1.542719	0.900014	0.012661	0.558749	0.022659
0.25	1.501764	1.410713	1.064543	0.125956	0.703609	0.179014
0.3	1.615059	1.281858	1.259936	0.239252	0.84903	0.281794
0.35	1.728355	1.157207	1.493557	0.352547	0.994764	0.354402
0.4	1.84165	1.038275	1.773759	0.465842	1.140693	0.408385
0.45	1.954946	0.927266	2.10829	0.579138	1.28675	0.450078
0.5	2.068241	0.827375	2.499762	0.692433	1.432896	0.48324

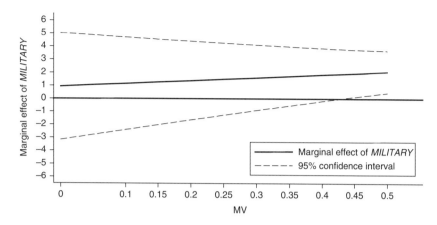

Figure 3.2 *Marginal effect of* MILITARY *on* W22 *as* COMMEX
changes (dependent variable: W22)

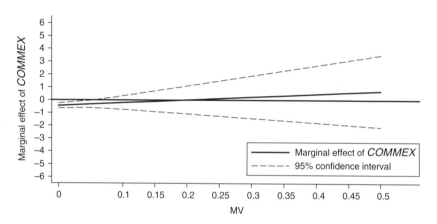

Figure 3.3 *Marginal effect of* COMMEX *on* W22 *as* MILITARY
changes (dependent variable: W22)

When *GINI* is substituted for *W22*, the results are even stronger. Military spending always narrows the coalition in that it increases income inequality. Commodity exports narrow the coalition when resource endowments are low, but again the effect cannot be distinguished from zero as resource endowments climb to more than 20 percent of GDP (see Table 3.6 and Figures 3.4 and 3.5).

When using the *W22* variable for coalitional breadth, the *ELF60* variable is not statistically significant at any value of *COMMEX*. But

Table 3.6 Model 8 interaction computation with three-stage least squares (GINI)

Value	Military expenditure at various values of commodity export			Commodity exports at various values of military expenditure		
	Marginal effect	Standard error	t-value	Marginal effect	Standard error	t-value
0	173.0485	55.35362	3.126236	39.06095	2.614771	14.93857
0.05	164.753	51.9502	3.171364	30.76542	4.495484	6.843628
0.1	156.4574	48.6417	3.216528	22.46989	8.122464	2.766388
0.15	148.1619	45.44886	3.25997	14.17435	12.00551	1.180654
0.2	139.8664	42.39783	3.298905	5.878821	15.95878	0.368375
0.25	131.5708	39.52147	3.329097	−2.41671	19.94056	−0.1212
0.3	123.2753	36.86067	3.344359	−10.7122	23.93662	−0.44753
0.35	114.9798	34.46541	3.336093	−19.0078	27.94083	−0.68029
0.4	106.6842	32.39463	3.293268	−27.3033	31.95014	−0.85456
0.45	98.38872	30.71405	3.203378	−35.5988	35.96283	−0.98988
0.5	90.09319	29.49045	3.054995	−43.8944	39.97789	−1.09797

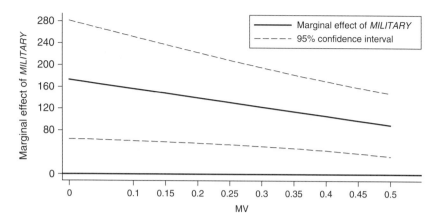

Figure 3.4   Marginal effect of MILITARY *on* GINI2 *as* COMMEX
changes (dependent variable: GINI2*)*

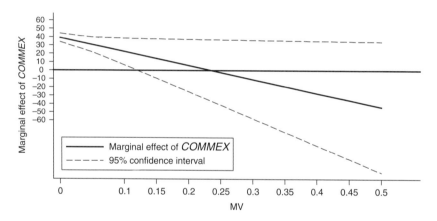

Figure 3.5   Marginal effect of COMMEX *on* GINI *as* MILITARY
changes (dependent variable: GINI*)*

as commodity exports rise coalitions become more narrow across every
meaningful value of ethnic fragmentation (see Table 3.7 and Figures 3.6
and 3.7).

The results change somewhat for the interaction when using *GINI* as
the intervening variable. When resource endowments are scarce, rising
fragmentation leads to rising inequality, or a narrowing of the coalitional
structure and a reduction in participation. But as commodity exports
exceed 20 percent of GDP, the influence reverses and more fragmentation

Table 3.7 *Model 4 interaction computation with three-stage least squares (W22) (ELF60 and commodity exports)*

Value	ELF60 at various values of commodity export			Commodity exports at various values of ELF60		
	Marginal effect	Standard error	t-value	Marginal effect	Standard error	t-value
0	0.11806	0.216349	0.545692	−0.44052	0.099671	−4.41975
0.1	0.122723	0.190244	0.645083	−0.43586	0.089844	−4.85126
0.2	0.127387	0.165225	0.770987	−0.43119	0.089051	−4.84209
0.3	0.13205	0.141868	0.930797	−0.42653	0.097513	−4.3741
0.4	0.136713	0.121136	1.128593	−0.42187	0.113172	−3.72767
0.5	0.141377	0.104604	1.351546	−0.4172	0.133519	−3.12467
0.6	0.14604	0.094501	1.545386	−0.41254	0.15674	−2.632
0.7	0.150704	0.092948	1.621375	−0.40788	0.181736	−2.24434
0.8	0.155367	0.100343	1.548358	−0.40321	0.207868	−1.93976
0.9	0.16003	0.114972	1.391905	−0.39855	0.234756	−1.69772
1.0	0.164694	0.134495	1.224533	−0.39389	0.262168	−1.50242

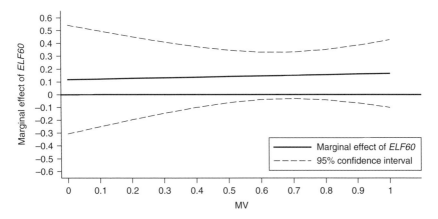

Figure 3.6 Marginal effect of ELF60 *on* W22 *as* COMMEX *changes
(dependent variable:* W22)

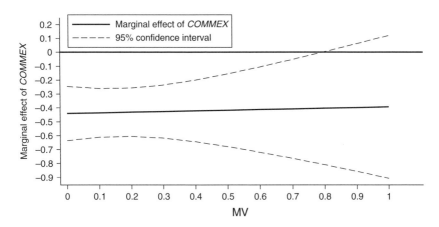

Figure 3.7 Marginal effect of COMMEX *on* W22 *as* ELF60 *changes
(dependent variable:* W22)

is associated with broader coalitions. This finding could perhaps shed some light on why some ethnically fragmented states can create conso-ciational bargains and others cannot (Lijphart, 1969). Sufficient resource endowments might be used to buy peace from contending ethnic groups. This might be why we see very few resource-poor, ethnically fragmented countries. Unable to compensate competing groups, they devolve into ethnically motivated civil conflict and eventual breakup.

The opposite relationship in the interaction is also interesting. When populations are highly homogeneous, commodity exports raise inequality. But again, the relationship reverses direction when ethnic fragmentation gets above 60 percent, about the level of Malaysia. At this point more resources reduce inequality and thereby broaden the coalition (see Table 3.8 and Figures 3.8 and 3.9).

The final interaction is between military expenditures and ethnic fragmentation. Military expenditures only influence $W22$ when ethnic fragmentation is very high, around 70 percent. In these cases military expenditures narrow the coalitions when fragmentation is high. When military expenditures are high, greater than 55 percent of GDP, rising fragmentation broadens the coalition. It's hard, however, to think of countries that would spend this much on the military (see Table 3.9 and Figures 3.10 and 3.11).

The relationship between *MILITARY* and *GINI* is almost opposite that of *W22*. In this case, rising military expenditures increase inequality when fragmentation is low. But after about 20 percent fragmentation, the relationship ceases to be significant. When military expenditures are low, ethnic fragmentation increases inequality. But by the time military expenditures reach 10 percent the relationship dissolves (see Table 3.10 and Figures 3.12 and 3.13).

CONCLUSION

The purpose of this chapter was to present some initial evidence to establish plausibility and generalizability. Structured comparisons within Southeast Asia, between Southeast and Northeast Asia, coupled with quantitative evidence on a worldwide data set reveal interesting correlations that support the hypotheses presented in Chapter 2. At the highest level, resource endowments, domestic fragmentation and external military conflict directly influence coalitional structure, which in turn influences levels of technical intellectual capital. Perhaps the most interesting discoveries, however, are in the interaction of these variables.

A combination of most similar and most different approaches to comparing the three countries of Southeast Asia provided control on many competing explanations. Colonization, investment strategy and industry orientation are all controlled through a comparison of the similar systems in Malaysia and Singapore. Comparing Malaysia and Thailand's different systems allows us to eliminate religion, development timing and political systems.

Moving up to a regional analysis comparing Korea, Taiwan and Japan and the ASEAN-4 countries allows us to see in some relief the operation

Table 3.8 Model 8 interaction computation with three-stage least squares (GINI)

Value	ELF60 at various values of commodity export			Commodity exports at various values of ELF60		
	Marginal effect	Standard error	t-value	Marginal effect	Standard error	t-value
0	27.95189	7.795272	3.585749	39.06095	2.614771	14.93857
0.1	20.79966	6.499302	3.200291	31.90872	2.001891	15.93929
0.2	13.64742	5.250295	2.599363	24.75648	2.242345	11.04044
0.3	6.495189	4.091487	1.587489	17.60424	3.146213	5.595375
0.4	−0.65705	3.12489	−0.21026	10.45201	4.314997	2.422252
0.5	−7.80928	2.576744	−3.03068	3.299776	5.584777	0.590852
0.6	−14.9615	2.713721	−5.51329	−3.85246	6.900021	−0.55833
0.7	−22.1138	3.455278	−6.39999	−11.0047	8.238982	−1.33569
0.8	−29.266	4.512607	−6.48538	−18.1569	9.591734	−1.89298
0.9	−36.4182	5.712993	−6.37463	−25.3092	10.95317	−2.31067
1.0	−43.5705	6.983048	−6.23946	−32.4614	12.32041	−2.63477

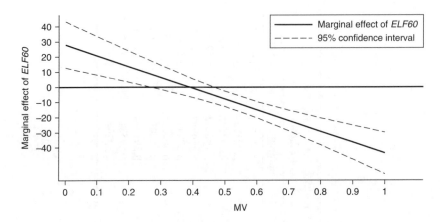

Figure 3.8   *Marginal effect of* ELF60 *on* GINI *as* COMMEX *changes*
(dependent variable: GINI*)*

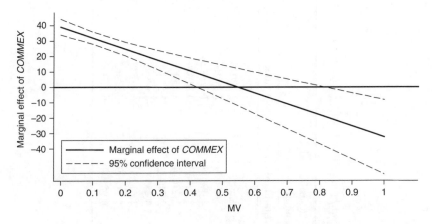

Figure 3.9   *Marginal effect of* COMMEX *on* GINI *as* ELF60 *changes*
(dependent variable: GINI*)*

of the hypothesized variables. Higher levels of vulnerability born of hard
budget constraints from resource scarcity in the face of conflict led ruling
elites to rely on upgrading as a strategy not just for economic prosperity,
but for social survival. When faced with similar challenges, the resource-
rich countries of Southeast Asia could rely on other mechanisms to generate foreign exchange and reserves. This safety net allowed education and
training infrastructure to be dedicated to political rather than economic
outcomes.

Table 3.9 Model 4 interaction computation with three-stage least squares (W22) (military expenditure and ELF60)

Value	Military expenditure at various values of ELF60			ELF60 at various values of military expenditure		
	Marginal effect	Standard error	t-value	Marginal effect	Standard error	t-value
0	0.935287	2.090136	0.447477	0.11806	0.216349	0.545692
0.1	0.131423	2.077585	0.063258	0.127387	0.165225	0.770987
0.2	−0.67244	2.084115	−0.32265	0.136713	0.121136	1.128593
0.3	−1.47631	2.109549	−0.69982	0.14604	0.094501	1.545386
0.4	−2.28017	2.153218	−1.05896	0.155367	0.100343	1.548358
0.5	−3.08403	2.214042	−1.39294	0.164694	0.134495	1.224533
0.6	−3.8879	2.290656	−1.69729	0.174021	0.068732	2.531869
0.7	−4.69176	2.381536	−1.97006	0.183347	0.050014	3.665897
0.8	−5.49563	2.485117	−2.21141	0.192674	0.031297	6.156393
0.9	−6.29949	2.599883	−2.42299	0.202001	0.012579	16.05875
1.0	−7.10335	2.724419	−2.60729	0.206664	0.00322	64.18121

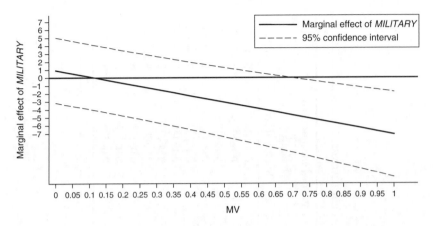

Figure 3.10   Marginal effect of MILITARY *on* W22 *as* ELF60 *changes (dependent variable:* W22)

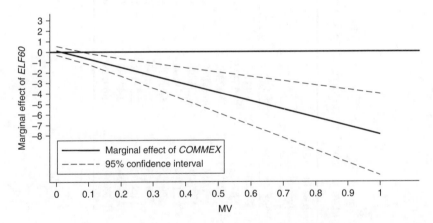

Figure 3.11   Marginal effect of ELF60 *on* W22 *as* MILITARY *changes (dependent variable:* W22)

Singapore is the exception in Southeast Asia that proves the rule. Although firmly part of Southeast Asia in terms of development strategies and trajectories, Singapore was able to leverage foreign direct investment into national technological capacity. Like the countries of Northeast Asia, Singapore shares a similar resource endowment footprint, external military condition, and its ethnic structure is more homogeneous than most Southeast Asian countries. Thus it was not that Singapore adopted 'developmental state'-like properties of its Northeast Asian neighbors,

Table 3.10 Model 8 interaction computation with three-stage least squares (GINI)

Value	Military expenditure at various values of ELF60			ELF60 at various values of military expenditure		
	Marginal effect	Standard error	t-value	Marginal effect	Standard error	t-value
0	173.0485	55.35362	3.126236	27.95189	7.795272	3.585749
0.05	165.9275	54.55308	3.041579	20.8309	8.040169	2.590854
0.1	158.8065	54.22547	2.928633	13.7099	10.99414	1.247019
0.15	151.6855	54.37935	2.789395	6.58891	15.14751	0.434983
0.2	144.5645	55.01068	2.627935	-0.53209	19.75782	-0.02693
0.3	130.3225	57.6311	2.261322	-14.7741	29.48334	-0.5011
0.4	116.0805	61.85392	1.876688	-29.0161	39.46591	-0.73522
0.5	101.8386	67.37853	1.51144	-43.2581	49.55042	-0.87301
0.6	87.59657	73.91361	1.185121	-57.5001	59.68523	-0.96339
0.7	73.35458	81.21558	0.903208	-71.742	69.84843	-1.02711
0.8	59.11259	89.09611	0.66347	-85.984	80.02922	-1.07441
0.9	44.8706	97.41487	0.460613	-100.226	90.22163	-1.11089
1.0	30.62861	106.0688	0.288762	-114.468	100.4221	-1.13987

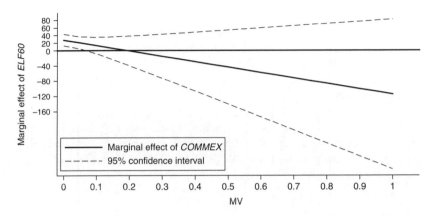

Figure 3.12   Marginal effect of ELF60 *on* GINI *as* MILITARY *changes (dependent variable:* GINI*)*

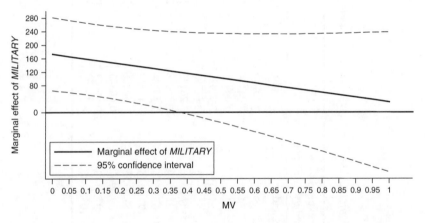

Figure 3.13   Marginal effect of MILITARY *on* GINI *as* ELF60 *changes (dependent variable:* GINI*)*

but rather that it was able to create similar institutional capacity through institutional structures more similar to its Southeast Asian neighbors, but whose capacity was far higher due to the exigencies of the external conditions facing the city state. In short, high levels of vulnerability like those in East Asia required Singapore to respond with mechanisms to increase wealth without the luxury of a rich resource endowment to rely on.

The quantitative analysis provides further corroborating evidence. Resource endowments, external security and ethnic fragmentation influence coalitional structure in a generalizable way. Coalitional structure, in turn, is a statistically significant predictor of levels of TIC. We also showed that levels of ethnic divisions interact with resource endowments in ways that might explain why some ethnically fragmented states can create consociational bargains and others cannot.

Having established a strong case for correlation among the hypothesized variables, it is now useful, in the chapters that follow, to go beyond cross-sectional analysis and examine the cases of Southeast Asia using methods of comparative process tracing. These methods illuminate the potentially complex interplay among different variables while maintaining an element of comparative control for idiosyncratic stimuli and variables impacting longitudinal processes.[6]

NOTES

1. Important parts of this argument are made in Doner et al. (2005). But I am modifying and extending this argument in several ways, most notably by arguing that coalitions are a function of vulnerability *and* ethnicity rather than an independent variable.
2. See Cox and McCubbins (2001) for a detailed analysis of different kinds of public goods.
3. Using three-stage least squares has several advantages and disadvantages compared to two-stage least squares. First, considering all the restrictions and knowledge in the entire system of equations makes it possible to specify coefficients and statistics for the variables in every equation. It also results in a smaller asymptotic variance–covariance matrix than the two-stage estimators. Thus the estimates are likely to vary from the two-stage estimates and be more efficient, although this added efficiency will come only as sample size increases (Kennedy, 1998). But herein lies the rub: if the system is misspecified, all of the parameters are affected rather than those of a single equation.
4. This measure uses items such as the electorate in political elections as an indicator of breadth.
5. See Friedrich (1982) for an excellent discussion of why and how to use interactive terms in multiple regression analysis.
6. In many ways this method parallels George and McKeown's method of structured, focused comparison (1978).

4. The origin of initial institutional decisions

In the mid-nineteenth century, military explorers were looking to expand the colonial empires of Europe and America. Admiral Perry sailed his iron-clad vessel into Edo (Tokyo) Bay, trained his guns on the emperor's palace and invited the Japanese to trade. Similarly, Sir Robert Bowring sailed up the Chao Praya River, trained his guns on the royal palace and Wat Phra Kaew temple, and offered the same invitation. As much as Japan and Thailand might not have wanted to trade under the unequal terms offered by these two powers, they were unable to withstand Perry's and Bowring's superior technology.

It is not as if Japan and Thailand were new to conflict. In fact, like most states, Asian nations were born and shaped amid conflict, both internal and external. Formal states in Korea and Taiwan began as Japanese colonies, while most of the capitalist countries in Southeast Asia were either British colonies, as Malaysia and Singapore, or heavily influenced by British power in the region, as was Thailand. Conflict, coupled with resource endowments and internal strife – systemic vulnerability – shaped the nature of the emerging states in Asia.

In this chapter I examine the impact of systemic vulnerability during times of state creation on the preferences of the ruling elite to create particular institutional systems for technological upgrading. In particular, the question is, how did vulnerability influence coalitional politics, which in turn generated preferences for particular institutions at a time when there were few institutions already in place to shape outcomes or when existing institutional systems were being destroyed or rearranged?

Institutional formation and change are easiest when few institutions exist and when pressures to change are high. Periods of state-building offer both a relative institutional *tabula rasa* as well as incentives for change. Waldner (1999) defines state-building as moving from a mediated to an unmediated state. In mediated states, political elites rule through intervening middle-level elites, for example barons, sultans, village headmen, warlords and so forth. Mediated states tend to be loosely formed with little formal extractive and oversight capacity. Thus the transition from a mediated to an unmediated state, then, entails two generic developments: the construction of institutional networks supplanting notables and linking the state to social classes and groups and the expansion of the state's provision of public goods, particularly as the state assumes responsibility for establishing infrastructure, regulating the economy, and managing ties to the global economy. (1999: 23)

Clearly this is not a process with sharply defined beginning and ending points. Nor does state-building occur simultaneously in every country or last for similar periods of time. But in each of the three cases at the core of this analysis, significant choices for institutional design and operation for education and training systems are made during periods of state-building, especially surrounding transitions to new political and economic institutional systems. Processes of state-building in Thailand begin in 1855 with the signing of the Bowring Treaty and continue until several decades after the establishment of a parliamentary democracy in 1932 (roughly 1950). For both Singapore and Malaysia, serious efforts at state-building are shaped during the latter years of colonial occupation by Great Britain, which sets in motion events leading to independence in the early 1950s. State-building efforts crescendo until the mid- to late 1970s.

Recall from previous chapters that coalitional structures influence political and economic priorities for redistributive or expansive political economies. Broader and more participative coalitions will favor the provision of public goods, which in turn leads to equality and expansive economic development. On the other hand, since people do not usually voluntarily give away their hard-earned assets to others, redistribution is easier when large power asymmetries exist, which is typical for narrow coalitions. Creating and maintaining power asymmetries is most easily and efficiently accomplished through political processes. Hence redistributive societies prioritize political over economic processes while expansive societies reverse the prioritization.

To the extent that ruling elites in each country responded to preferences generated by systemic vulnerability and its impact on coalitional politics, we should be able to see how strategic policy and institutional choices at the critical juncture in time shaped education and training systems to produce desired outcomes, either primarily political or economic. As I show in the next chapter, these choices have long legacies for the creation of technical intellectual capital (TIC). In other words, decisions for particular education and training policies and institutions made during the formative period of state-building dramatically shaped future levels of technical capacity and skills.

COALITIONAL FORMATION IN MALAYSIA, SINGAPORE AND THAILAND

Malaysia, Singapore and Thailand are three of the fastest-growing developing countries in the world. And yet prospects for sustainable future economic growth differ among the three cases. Having shown in the previous chapter that systemic vulnerability is correlated with levels of TIC, it's time now to understand *how* systemic vulnerability influenced coalitional structures in these countries and then how these structures influenced the 'embedded autonomy' that has driven institutional creation.

Malaysia

Malaysia is richly endowed with natural resources, including tin, petroleum, timber, copper, iron ore, natural gas, bauxite and palm oil. Of the three countries in this book's comparison, Malaysia is most ethnically diverse, fragmented into three main groups, with Malays and other indigenous people comprising roughly 65 percent of the population, Chinese comprising 20 percent, and Indians approximately 6–7 percent.[1] These high levels of ethnic fragmentation have led to almost continual internal conflict, although rarely bloody (the most visible case occurring in ethnic riots in 1969). In comparison, external military conflict has been more muted. Other than *Konfrontasi* with Indonesia, most external military conflicts have been of the border variety.

Before being granted independence in 1957, Malaysia, like Singapore, was a British colony. Originally Malaya (as it was called before independence) was valuable to the British for its strategic position on the main trading routes from India to China, particularly a series of ports through the Malacca Straits. During the first half of the twentieth century, however, world wars and intensive industrialization made tin and rubber valuable commodities for Britain. The lion's share of the local export economy was soon composed of large tin-mining operations and extensive rubber-harvesting plantations (Jomo, 1986; Bedlington, 1978). Both were highly sensitive to scale economies and created a division between British management and local labor. As is common in most colonial arrangements, the government largely ignored the development of indigenous firms and distributed income away from the local population and into its own coffers (Rasiah, 1996). Technology, to the extent demanded by the two resource industries, was largely supplied by British scientists and engineers. No incentives existed for the British to diffuse technology to the local economic sector; nor did local capacity exist had they wanted to.

The rise of resource-based industries created labor problems for the

British, as the vast majority of Malays were subsistence farmers. Like those in other cultures, Malays valued farming and viewed agriculture as an honorable profession while eschewing commercial and industrial labor. Cultural resistance to labor-intensive industries, however, made it difficult for the British to meet the labor needs of the rubber and tin industries. Therefore the British began encouraging substantial immigration from China and India to meet this demand. Between 1911 and 1957, 1 640 000 Chinese immigrants flooded into Malaya (Leete, 1996). Although partially in response to political turmoil in China, much of the immigration came from British efforts to recruit additional labor to exploit Malaysia's natural resources (Bedlington, 1978: 34). The British used Chinese laborers extensively in the tin mines and concentrated Indian labor in the rubber plantations. Over time these immigrants, especially the Chinese, expanded their economic activity and set up small trading, retail and merchant businesses. The British also began to use the Chinese to perform bureaucratic tasks, such as tax collection, that over time fostered feelings of animosity among the various ethnic groups (Jomo, 1986).

By the time of independence, Malaya was fragmented economically and politically. The Chinese soon emerged as the leading capitalist class behind the British. Indian immigrants comprised most of the organized labor class, and the Malays dominated the agriculturally based rural class (Jomo and Todd, 1994). The territory was further divided by location and class, with the Chinese being largely urban and the Malays largely rural, while the Indians divided themselves equally between the cities and the countryside.

After war in the Pacific ended, the British initiated steps toward Malayan independence. However, the British proposal for Malayan Union in 1945 sparked intense elite conflict between Malays and British. At the same time, the British were embroiled in an intense conflict to rid the area of a virulent communist insurgency. The Union proposed to unite both the Unfederated and Federated Malay States,[2] granting equal citizenship status to all the inhabitants of the territory in the process. English-educated Malays in the bureaucracy and civil service joined with aristocrats from royal families to oppose the action (Jomo, 1986). In 1946 the United Malays National Organization (UMNO) was created, bringing together in a political coalition both English- and Malay-educated Malays. The conflict continued until the proposal for Malayan Union was dropped, less than a year later. By 1948, negotiations over independence had resumed, but only between the British and the Malays, without the participation of any minority ethnic group. Although the Malaysian Chinese Association and the Malaysian Indian Congress political parties were later included with UMNO in a political coalition, both minority parties had little independent political power. Instead, this proto-consociationalist bargain served the interests of the Malay, Chinese and Indian elites while limiting the political participation of the greater Chinese and Indian communities.

The country of Malaysia was formed when Britain granted Malaya independence in 1957. Despite their dominant political position, however, the Malay population, including the political elite, controlled few of the productive assets in the country or, as in the resource sectors, the expertise to use them. To address this problem the political elite took several steps.

First, the government immediately established state-owned enterprises to assume the operations of the formerly British tin mines and rubber plantations (Jesudason, 1989). Nevertheless, once the British had abandoned these industries, only the Chinese and Indians had the knowledge and expertise to run them. Thus, ironically, the same Chinese and Indian foremen employed under the British system continued to run the newly nationalized operations.

Second, new public firms were established to exploit newly found resources such as petroleum, natural gas and palm oil. Again, management expertise was found mostly in the minority population. As a result, political elites developed narrow, patron–client relationships with business owners who were largely ethnic Chinese. By doing so, the former gained access to economic assets while the latter were able to insert themselves, at least indirectly, into the political system. Public firms, as in Thailand, became vehicles for these coalitions to pursue political power and economic return (Jomo and Gomez, 1997), creating incentives to further taper the membership of existing coalitions. Patronage-based coalitions 'were free to pursue personal and group interests without giving much consideration to anyone else' (Crouch, 1996: 197). This coalitional structure was narrow, competitive, and only stable at the elite level, which at the same time made the provision of public goods less important and much more difficult.

External security demands were not sufficient to discipline internal distributions of wealth and capital. The British withdrawal from the region created a vacuum for power, within which interstate conflict between Malaysia and Indonesia over territory in Borneo, dubbed *Konfrontasi*, erupted. Nevertheless, the conflict was short lived and, with the diminishing communist insurgency, conflict was, and has continued to be, largely internal. KESBAN, or 'Development as Security,' adopted largely to diffuse ethnic rivalries (Tan, 2004, 2006) became Malaysia's key security policy.

Malaysia's combination of rich natural resources, fragmented ethnic groups segmented by industry, and mild external security conditions created preferences for a convoluted coalitional structure. At the elite level the coalitional relationships among the three main ethnic groups was seemingly consociational, with a relatively broad and stable cooperative relationship purchased by resource wealth. Beneath this structure, however, the ethnic groups were fragmented, isolated, narrow and suspicious. Coalitions were characterized primarily by redistributive relationships between Malay political elites and, at least initially, Chinese businessmen. While overall growth was necessary to legitimize mass redistribution, primarily from the Chinese to Malays, no effort was made to compensate for more particularistic redistribution toward privileged, elite-level, patron–client coalitions.

Singapore

In 1819 Sir Stamford Raffles selected Singapore as '[the] station beyond Malacca such as may command the Southern entrance of those Straits' for the British East India Trading Company (Doraisamy et al., 1969). Economically, there was little value to Singapore other than the deep-water port and the entrepôt economy Raffles envisioned. In comparison, Singapore was a key component of Britain's maritime security.

When the British first arrived, Singapore was a sleepy Malay fishing village. To build the port, military installations and community, Raffles imported huge quantities of labor, most of it Chinese. Singapore quickly became a 'large migrant community of . . . hard-pressed peasants who had left their homeland in China, India or Indonesia in search of a better life' (Thomas et al., 1980: 185). Although the Malay, Chinese and Indian ethnic divisions that existed in Malaya also existed in Singapore, the country was overwhelmingly populated with Chinese merchants and laborers.

The type of economic activity on the island accounts for different ethnic concentrations from those found in Malaysia. Since there was little (and ever-decreasing) space for agriculture, few Malays, who were largely farmers in origin, were motivated to move to Singapore (or indeed stay). The Malays that did live in Singapore were mostly fisherman, although there was some in-migration of Malays from Indonesia who were manual laborers. Also, since there was little rubber production, most of the Indians on the island were imported by the British not as laborers, but as members of the civil service (because of their prior experience in the East India Company). Finally, although initially large numbers of Chinese laborers came to Singapore to work as construction and dock workers, subsequently an increasingly disproportionate number of them came as shopkeepers and small-business owners, many of them in support of the newly built entrepôt trading center created on the island.

After World War II the British agreed to a speedy transition to Malaysian independence. Nevertheless, owing to Singapore's strategic geographical position and its outstanding natural deep-water port, its place in the Malay Federation was not assured. Some argue that the British initially had no plans to grant Singapore its independence, either alone or as part of a Malayan Federation (Tremewan, 1994). Domestic and international pressures, however, were calling for the halt of both military and economic imperialism and for Britain's expeditious exit from the region.

Even so, the rise of the cold war and communist insurgency made it difficult for the British to extricate themselves gracefully from the region. The British felt obligated to remain and secure the region from communist infiltrations. But bigger concerns of domestic economic growth and military security in Europe, coupled with local pressure for self-rule and determination, made independence for both territories a matter of time. These same conditions created tremendous external vulnerability for Singapore. According to Lee Kuan Yew shortly before independence, 'Singapore, with its predominately Chinese population would, if independent on its own, become Southeast Asia's Israel with every hand turned against it' (Leifer, 1988: 342).

As a path to independence, competitive elections were first held in Singapore in 1955. For at least two reasons these elections were largely ignored by the general population. First, the two primary contending parties, the Singapore Progressive Party, which represented the tiny merchant middle and upper class, and the Singapore Labor Party, which represented primarily Indian labor interests, were incapable of generating any significant mass support, especially from the dominant Chinese-based organized labor unions. And second, the legislative assembly had no real power before 1959 (hence only two narrowly supported parties contested these elections). Thus, during the time leading up to the 1959 election, parties were scrambling to consolidate and expand their power base.

As Singapore moved closer to independence, its coalitional development diverged dramatically from Malaysia's. In Malaysia, the British supported the Malays' bid for political supremacy partially because they suspected that the Chinese, especially the working class, harbored communist sympathies. In Singapore, however, the Chinese were the overwhelmingly dominant ethnic group, making it nearly impossible for the British to grant political power to anyone else. Within the Chinese population were two distinct elite groups. The first was British educated and worked primarily in the civil service. The second was Chinese educated and represented labor. The British clearly supported the first. Conspicuously lacking, however, was any semblance of a landed or resource-based capital elite.

Without a strong local capital or landed class, labor became the most important political player, and as a result, wielded tremendous political power. Nevertheless, without the support of the British, the organized labor faction, dominated by the Chinese educated elite, could not be successful. At the same time, although the British-educated elites had British support, they lacked the mass-based support of labor. Hence neither group could assume the government alone. In the end, the two factions united in an uneasy partnership to form the People's Action Party (PAP).

Lee Kuan Yew and the other British-educated PAP leaders quickly positioned themselves to assume power upon the withdrawal of the British. Nevertheless, to win the 1959 election the PAP would need to garner and maintain the support of organized labor. In particular, they would need the support of the 'big six' labor unions (Tremewan, 1994; Rodan, 1989). The labor faction, however, was suspicious that the Lee faction would push the party too far to the right. In 1956 the left captured four of the 12 seats of the central executive committee of the party and in 1957 they successfully gained six of the seats. But, utilizing a British effort to quell social uprisings (aimed at communists), the Lee faction implemented a 'communist purge' in which four of the six newly elected members were dismissed (Rodan, 1989: 58). In spite of this back-door power grab, the left continued to support the PAP, presumably because it felt it could contest for power later on. By uniting a broad, cross-class coalition between labor, the civil service and British capital, the PAP was able to ensure a landslide victory upon independence in 1959.

The combination of few resource endowments, potential internal ethnic fragmentation and external vulnerability created an environment in which political legitimacy hinged on economic growth and development, as did the means to pay for military capacity. Once in power, the PAP adopted Israel's 'Forward Defense' or 'Preemptive Defense' strategy, in which a technically advanced military and aggressive posture would serve as an effective deterrent to external aggression (Huxley, 2000). The problem was how to pay for military equipment demanded by such a strategy.

Furthermore, there were few if any sources that could produce revenues or assets that could be redistributed to meet the demands of internal political competition. Although port and financial services might provide a foundation, growth could be assured only through an expansion in manufacturing. Initially it was not at all certain that this expansion of manufacturing would bring with it an increase in technological capability. This was decided only later. Nevertheless, the initial formation of a broad economic and political coalition meant that when decisions were made to pursue technological upgrading as the dominant economic strategy, coalitional structure helped rather than hindered in the effort.

Thailand

Thailand is endowed with a rich natural resource base composed of tin, rubber, natural gas, tungsten, tantalum, timber, lead, gypsum, lignite, fluorite and a land frontier suitable for the cultivation of rice agriculture. Historically, rice production was the most important economic activity in Thailand. Rice exports provided critical foreign exchange earnings, redistributed wealth through export taxes, and provided resources upon which other industries have been developed.

In 1855 King Mongkut executed the Bowring Treaty with Great Britain, effectively opening the country to foreign trade. The Treaty demanded unencumbered market access for foreign powers and specified rules for foreign trade and domestic commerce, thereby 'greatly reducing the scope for an independent Siamese fiscal or trade policy' (Muscat, 1994: 13). At the same time, the encroachment of foreign powers on either side of Siam – Great Britain on the west and south in Burma and Malaysia, and France on the east and north in Cambodia, Vietnam and Laos – applied increasing pressure on Siam for state-building and increasing statecraft. In response, King Mongkut, and later his son King Chulalongkorn, undertook aggressive administrative reforms to consolidate central control over what had previously been a loosely defined group of regions, sultanates, suzerainties, tributary states and nobles; develop central bureaucratic institutions to manage and fund the kingdom, such as tax, education, commerce and agriculture; and, finally, develop local economic capacity and strength.[3]

Reforms, however, require money. The revenue system at the time, based on the Sakdina, or *corvée* labor, system, was unable to generate sufficient capital to meet the needs of the newly developing state.[4] As Brown (1988) argues, the lack of control over fiscal and trade policy severely reduced the options government had to raise money. This, coupled later with world wars and global economic depressions, made it difficult to borrow needed funds. In response, the government instituted sweeping social and economic reform.

The first of these reforms consisted of laws passed to encourage land clearing and paddy cultivation, which dramatically raised the number of freeman farmers and their agricultural output while simultaneously decimating the old Sakdina system (Ingram, 1955). While it is not clear that these manpower reforms were due solely to the major economic changes occurring in the kingdom at this time, it is clear that rice expansion was the major policy objective of the government and that changes in rice agriculture provided significant incentives to form new relationships between the government and newly free farmers (ibid.). Nevertheless, these new relationships, both economic and political, were modeled on the deeply ingrained patron–client relationships fostered under the now dying Sakdina system (Muscat, 1994).

To meet the expanding demands for labor, the government encouraged the immigration of Chinese labor to perform entrepreneurial activities eschewed by the Thais. Many Thai historians have argued that the Thais, like the Malays, were inclined toward agriculture and left other economic activities to foreigners (Skinner, 1958). Ingram (cited in Muscat, 1994: 44) states it well:

> The extension of rice land has been the major entrepreneurial achievement of the Thai themselves . . . they have left most other entrepreneurial functions to foreigners. The cultivation of rice is an ancient and honorable occupation to the Thai, however, and they seem to have preferred it to all others . . . The Thai has preferred the communal life of the village, and it is not easy to break the ties of culture and tradition which have induced him to become a rice farmer . . . This preference has probably been one of the most important determinants of the pattern of the economy which has developed in Thailand.

In industries other than agriculture, the growing immigrant Chinese population quickly dominated. Chinese immigration peaked in the 1920s and by 1950 the Chinese were estimated to make up 15 percent of the population. Most Chinese took up residence in Bangkok, where they quickly dominated the local banking sector. Those who settled outside of Bangkok often ran rubber plantations, tin-mining operations, or rice-milling businesses.

The results of state-building reforms were several. First, from the late nineteenth century until well into the twentieth century the amount of land converted to rice agriculture grew rapidly (Ingram, 1955). By 1905 both private farmers and the government had developed aggressive plans to breed new seed varieties, build locally appropriate machinery, and expand culti-vation by digging new irrigation systems (Feeny, 1982). In addition to rice agriculture's growing importance, teak, tin and rubber were also important to Thailand's economy (Muscat, 1994) and promising economic activity was evident in sericulture, cotton, cement and shipbuilding (Brown, 1988).

Even so, economic reform made it much more difficult for the gov-ernment to collect revenue from the agricultural sector than in the past. Prior to reform, the government collected revenues from the rice industry directly from a small group of Bangkok-based absentee landowners. Elites could extract payments from labor (both free and indentured) that worked the fields, acting as an income aggregation point for the government. As the amount of land under cultivation rose, the size of single farms diminished, and the number of farmers increased, making new revenue collection institutions necessary.

Instead of taxing individual farmers, which would have required the creation of broad political coalitions, the government implemented export taxes and quotas 'at the border' and a rice reserve requirement in which exporters sold a portion of their quota to the government at discounted prices (Christensen, 1993). These policies elevated milling and banking, both owned primarily by Sino-Thai families, as the new aggregation points. Brown (1988) notes how banks would purchase bills of exchange from the millers for shipments of rice to Hong Kong and Singapore for further shipment around the world. By the end of the nineteenth century, exports of rice depended on millers to aggregate supply and on banks to finance shipment and payment. While the government received a direct cut of these transactions through export and *ad valorem* taxes, government officials also formed patron–client relationships with Sino-Thai rice millers and bankers to ensure a personal income from the large revenue stream.

Over time these relationships between Thai politicians and Sino-Thai business families proliferated, engendering a competitive rent-seeking mind-set. Although having no technological expertise in rice agriculture, government officials from numerous ministries recognized the potentially lucrative opportunities of getting involved in the rice business. The Ministry of Commerce asserted its influence through management of canals and irrigation facilities. The Ministry of Agriculture, the Ministry of Finance and the Ministry of the Interior all laid claim to various aspects of the rice industry. Bureaucratic segmentation and competition made it attractive for a vigorous and fairly well-organized private sector led by large industrial and financial conglomerates,[5] many of them family owned, to form narrow, particularistic, competitive, and often very shallow coalitional relationships with these different ministries to seek the rents generated by the rice industry. As Muscat (1994) notes, similar coalitional configurations existed in virtually every resource-intensive sector.[6]

Few pressures existed to reconcile highly fragmented private–public relationships. Although internal conflict emerged between Thai and Chinese during the early 1950s, the threat was quickly smoothed over through assimilation laws. At the same time, the serious demands on resources for external security during World War II quickly diminished as the USA took over military operations during the Indochina conflict. Thus, unlike the situation in Singapore, the level of external military vulnerability never rose to a level that required the state to discipline local capital to meet security needs. Since the Indochinese conflict ended, most of Thailand's conflicts have either been of the small border variety (Tan, 2006), or ethno-religious confrontation, primarily in the southern-most provinces of the country (Smith, 2004). Since there was little pressure to divert government revenues to military purposes, funds could be redistributed to more narrowly favored groups and cronies as a reward for political support, which undermined future policy decisions aimed at technological upgrading.

COALITIONAL STRUCTURE AND PREFERENCE FORMATION

Assuming that coalitional actors are rational, it is reasonable to expect that coalitional structures will be created and maintained to maximize the gains of the parties involved. If they endure, they can be thought of as representing an equilibrium where each actor 'chooses the best action available to him given the signal that he receives and his belief about the state and the other players' actions that he deduces from this signal' (Osborne and Rubinstein, 1994: 26). A critical component of this book's argument is that coalitional relationships influence the formation of institutions, which are formed in large part to perpetuate the current coalitional power structure. Two important questions, then, are: what steps do coalitional actors take to maintain their power advantage *vis-à-vis* other social actors? And are these steps antithetical to technology-led development or do they further innovatory activities?

Distribution or Expansion?

Systemic vulnerability creates incentives not only for particular coalitional structures, but also for the preferences coalitions have for particular issues. Some of these preferences are generated by the coalitional structure itself, and so are an indirect outcome. Others are generated directly. Two of the most important preferences are (1) how coalitions prioritize economic redistribution *vis-à-vis* economic expansion, and (2) how coalitions emphasize innovation and industrial upgrading. While it is true that the latter is at least somewhat a function of the former, systemic vulnerability directly influences preferences for both.

Malaysia

Although the newly forged Malay-dominated government acted swiftly after independence to redistribute public monies to the rural Malay landholders, the proto-consociationalist bargain at the elite level acted to check efforts to create a Malay bourgeois class. The Rural and Industrial Development Authority, which was designed to provide subsidized credit, technical training and equipment to ethnic Malays, accomplished very little (Jomo, 1986). Other affirmative action policies were similarly ineffectual – such as those contained in the 1956 constitution to increase Malay representation in the bureaucracy and give priority to Malays for business licenses, educational assistance and land reservations. The result was that from independence until 1970, the income of the lowest 10 percent of the population dropped over 30 percent (ibid.).

By the late 1960s, ethnic competition and confrontation in Malaysia reached boiling point. In May 1969, economically marginalized Malays vented their economic frustration by killing several hundred Chinese in Kuala Lumpur. In a move to increase ethnic harmony and national unity, the government implemented the New Economic Policy (NEP) in 1971, and the Industrial Coordination Act (ICA) soon afterwards, which had as their stated goal to raise the Bumiputra (ethnic Malay) ownership of productive assets from the current level of 2.4 percent to 30 percent by the end of the millennium (Crouch, 1996).[7] As part of this legislation, Chinese business owners were required to have minority Bumiputra partners, and quotas were established for virtually every aspect of economic life including equity and debt financing, home ownership, education and other public assistance. In short, affirmative action permeated every aspect of economic and political life in Malaysia.

Efforts to expand asset ownership for Malays did not come with a corresponding effort to diversify political power to the non-Malay minorities. Thus, with formal avenues of political participation still limited, but with their economic assets now far more vulnerable, Chinese and Indians (but especially Chinese) sought to strengthen their patron–client relationships with Malay political elites. On the one hand, the move was political: only by linking themselves to political leaders could ethnic minorities maintain some say in economic policy making, even if it was through the back door. On the other, while political influence was important, the relationships were far more valuable economically: well-connected firms were often able to secure steady monopoly rent flows. Monopoly rents, and hence rent-seeking, often subsidized by resource-based sectors, was a far more profitable use of private economic resources than pursuing market-based rents, especially in the short term.

At the same time UMNO worked to transfer resources from the largely urban ethnic minorities (again mostly Chinese) to the rural Malays. As Scott (1985: 57) states, 'UMNO is a well-organized and well-financed political machine providing both individual and collective blandishments that reach into every Malay village.' Between independence and 1975, expenditures on rural development, largely in the form of infrastructure and collective goods, grew more than six-fold (Scott, 1985). Nevertheless, it would be a mistake to say that UMNO represents all Malays equally.

In fact, government spending was geared predominantly toward large landholders, who make up the fundamental base of UMNO (ibid.). Also, rather than actually distribute assets to Malays, the government held assets in escrow in government-owned firms such as Khazanah.[8] UMNO then uses these firms and their assets for its own purposes.

Malaysian society sought to balance redistribution with economic expansion, although redistribution had to be paramount. True, redistribution had to be accompanied by some level of overall growth if the minority Chinese and Indian masses were to tolerate redistribution. At the elite level, public revenue derived largely from resource-based sectors was channeled into large Chinese-owned firms attached to important political figures. Through the use of preferential licensing, subsidization, financing, insider bidding and so forth, these firms established monopoly positions, thereby redistributing and concentrating wealth from the broader population to a few wealthy, well-placed and well-protected cronies. At the mass level, government policies redirected wealth to the Bumiputra population in the form of subsidies, privatization of government-owned firms, and quotas, usually paid for by revenues generated from natural resource sectors.[9]

Singapore

An entirely different set of constraints worked in Singapore to create a set of preferences for expansive economic development. Although initial preferences for a broad coalitional structure were driven primarily by political competition, ongoing preferences were driven by the exigencies of economic development in the face of resource scarcity.[10]

On assuming power in 1959, the PAP called upon the World Bank for assistance in creating a development plan. In what became known as the 'Winsemius report' the Bank encouraged Singapore to pursue an import substitution industrialization strategy built upon private capital. Because of the dearth of local capital and know-how, however, foreign capital was needed. Three things were necessary to persuade foreign capital to invest in Singapore: a professional and efficient bureaucracy coupled with political stability; contained and controlled labor (especially labor costs); and access to captive markets. This last requirement was thought best met through unification with Malaysia.

To improve its image as a business-friendly island for foreign MNCs, the PAP first implemented sweeping reforms in the bureaucracy. The objective was to create a 'developmental' bureaucracy as in Japan, Korea and Taiwan (Doner et al., 2005). These reforms included the elimination of variable expenses, making 'voluntary' weekend service mandatory, imposing new disciplinary measures, and requiring political training for all civil servants (Rodan, 1989). At the same time, the PAP began covertly to undermine its own overt efforts to pursue the labor agenda. Not only was this necessary to induce foreign capital to invest, but also for unification as Malaysia demanded that its labor not be excluded from the Singaporean market.

On 27 May 1961 Tunku Abdul Rahman, the leader of Malaysia, proposed a federation of Malaysian states to include Sabah, Sarawak, Brunei and Malaya (including Singapore). The Lee faction of the PAP believed that its economic plan – on which rested its political legitimacy – hinged on unification. The left faction, however, feared unification because of the vast amounts of cheap labor in peninsular Malaysia. The prospect of merger forced the two factions onto a collision course. The left, backed by the big six labor unions, made their support of the PAP contingent on addressing the perceived threat of the merger. Lee, however, held strong and called for a confidence vote in which he won by the narrowest of margins, with 26 of 51 votes. On winning, the left split from the PAP and formed the Barisan Socialis (BS).

The formation of the BS in 1961 had important ramifications for the PAP's social base, industrial relations and ideology. The bulk of the Chinese working class, intellectuals and students all joined the new BS. To compensate and increase its support, the PAP took several steps to distribute significant side payments in return for political support.

First, the PAP realized that the previous reforms in the civil service aimed at increasing efficiency had also alienated the bureaucracy. The first priority, then, was to regain the support of this constituency. The PAP reestablished the perks of civil service; it transferred significant economic power to the ministry of trade and industry by spending $100 million to create the Economic Development Board in August 1961; it dissolved the City Council and transferred the funds to the national bureaucracy; and it also created the Housing Development Board and the Public Utilities Board, again transferring considerable power and resources to the bureaucracy. In three years the PAP increased public spending by over 20 percent compared to the previous 10 percent (Rodan, 1989).

At the same time the PAP decommissioned the Singapore Trades Union Congress and subjugated all labor to the newly created and government-controlled National Trades Union Congress (NTUC), and then aggressively deregistered unions not willing to become part of the new structure (Deyo, 1989). This action cut organized labor off at the knees by transferring complete oversight control from the big six labor unions to a government-controlled labor congress. As direct side payments to rank-and-file labor, the government immediately began a massive public housing and education initiative, spending S$153 million on low-cost subsidized housing and S$94 million on universal education. Fully 5.4 percent of the GDP between 1960 and 1970 was spent on housing. By 1963, 22 336 new apartments (in just three years) were built, providing accommodation for approximately 100 000 people (Rodan, 1989).

Third, the government made sure that local capital benefited from these investments. The PAP stipulated that only local capital could be used to build government housing and schools.[11] Nevertheless, the building projects would be released only through competitive bidding. Moreover, development funds were issued from a consortium of local banks with government support when needed.

The important point here is that Singapore was not without its political incentives to provide side payments to certain groups of society. At first glance these side payments may appear like those in any other country. But there are several important differences. First, the government provided these side payments not to a narrow, politically and economically connected elite, but to a broad cross-class and cross-ethnic coalition. Second, there was little if any redistribution from one group to another. The payments were implemented more or less equally across the board. In other words, they more closely resembled at least collective, if not public, goods. And third, without a resource base as a source of revenue to pay for these side payments, government, and indeed society as a whole, was forced to look to economic expansion to pay the bill.

Interestingly, at the time these side payments were implemented, Singapore was anticipating its merger with Malaysia. The point of this merger, remember, was for Singapore to be able to pursue import substitution industrialization strategies. This evidence suggests that Singapore was hedging its bets. That is, if the merger worked out, then more side payments could be given as private goods and paid for through more redistributive means. However, if the merger failed, such options would be foreclosed. As preferences for expansive economic growth and technological development became clearer over time, the government was not hamstrung by any previous decisions to implement narrow, patronage-based rents.

Thailand

To appropriate rents from an expanding number of farmers, the state instituted export and milling taxes. Not only were these rents designed to support the newly created state, but they were also funneled from the rural farmers to the urban Bangkok elite in two ways. First, price setting assured that food prices would be low and that the surplus could be used in other commercial and industrial endeavors. Evidence of this transfer of wealth can be seen in the terms of trade, which between 1900 and 1940 ran against rice farmers (Brown, 1988). And second, rather than creating the institutional capacity to deal with myriad farmers, the political elite formed narrow coalitions with ethnic-Chinese rice millers and banking magnates to expropriate the gains from rice agriculture through indirect means, such as kick-backs, buying programs, warehousing and storage plans, financing, export processing and a host of other methods (Muscat, 1994).

But like Malaysia, redistributive pressures in Thailand were also driven by political priorities. By 1925 the monarchy felt growing pressure for additional political reform (Muscat, 1994). Whereas earlier reform under King Mongkut and King Chulalongkorn centered on political consolidation, by 1930 new political groups were demanding representative government – in particular a constitutional monarchy based on the British and Japanese systems. Nevertheless, it was not mass-based groups who were advocating political reform, but a small cadre of military and academic elites who were chafing under a system that severely limited their upward political mobility.

Of general concern to the leaders of the 1932 Revolution was the 'backwardness' of absolutism in a time of modernity and the need for adjustments. To paraphrase Thak, absolutism had served the Thais ably during the past, but its foundations (had) been weakened by the establishment of necessary state bureaucracies based on rationally organized and functionally relevant structures. The expanded modern state bureaucracy absorbed younger and new talents into its structure. These men received good education within the country and abroad. Their growing expertise and professionalism made them uneasy and frustrated with the tradition of royal prerogatives in selecting high-ranking officials based upon ascriptive criteria. Thus this modern bureaucratic organization created its own internal dynamism which eventually agitated and brought about political change (Thak, 1978: 1–2).

Although eventually willing to undergo an orderly transition to representative government, the monarchy mistrusted the general population and felt that the masses were both unready for, and uninterested in, participatory politics. Ironically, those in the democracy movement felt the same way: Pridi, an influential member of the group, characterized the Thai people as 'children,' unready for the demands of democracy (Thak, 1978). This shared attitude may have been one reason why Thai political elites never made any overtures to mass-based groups for political support. Ultimately, political elites, in both the monarchy and the democracy movement, were more concerned with political education and socialization than they were with economic, and especially technological, upgrading.

Unable to wait for the monarch to hand over political power as promised, the Promoters (democracy movement) instigated a *coup d'état* on 24 June 1932. What became immediately obvious after the *coup* was that there was very little support for the Promoters outside of the bureaucracy (Muscat, 1994). Moreover, whereas the Promoters were unified as to immediate ends, they were highly fragmented when it came to purpose, design and pace of implementation for a new government, especially as it impacted economic priorities (ibid.). It did not take long for the split to tear wide open and from 1932 until 1939 Siam was fully engaged in intensive political competition.

Unlike Malaysia, though, Thailand lacked the same ethnically based intensity for redistribution. Instead, political competition further strengthened traditional patron–client relationships. It would be wrong, however, to characterize this aspect of redistribution as formal economic policy comparable to redistributive efforts in Malaysia. Instead, it can be seen as the *status quo* continuation of earlier economic relationships in the absence of any proactive policy or institutional initiatives for change. Indeed, beyond the redistributive efforts in the agricultural industry, it is accurate to describe formal Siamese economic policy as neither redistributive nor expansive. It would be more accurate to say that Siam had *no* economic policy, at least from 1932 until World War II.[12] Although Thailand was able to insulate its macroeconomic policy-making processes from corruption and patronage (Doner et al., 2009), government patrons competed intensely for economic clients and vice versa throughout the early part of the twentieth century. Both economics and politics, then, were primarily about competitive rent-seeking and redistribution away from the masses and toward these narrow coalitions (Doner and Ramsey, 1997).

Innovation and Technology Development?

To what extend did coalitional bargaining in each country influence preferences for technological development? Part of the difficulty of this question is that Thailand started processes of state-building much earlier than Singapore and Malaysia. Also, in later years Malaysia and Thailand almost certainly learned from Singapore. Nevertheless, even though absolute levels of demand for technology were initially lower in Thailand, relative demands for resource-based technologies were comparable to those in Malaysia. Moreover, the case of Galton's problem[13] actually strengthens the case: if Malaysia and Thailand learned from Singapore and adopted and implemented the same policies and institutions with dramatically different outcomes, something else must have been going on.

Malaysia
By the mid-1970s Malaysia had embarked on a dual economic strategy. On the one hand, the government had created a favorable environment

for MNCs to invest. Beginning in Penang and gradually working east and then south, MNCs began to set up operations in export promotion zones (EPZs) that offered extensive tax relief and export promotions. In a relatively short period of time, high-tech manufactured exports in consumer electronics, silicon-chip packaging, hard drives and other electronics dominated Malaysia's exports. The government also created a state-owned industrial complex, which included steel, automobile manufacturing, heavy truck manufacturing, and other related heavy industries.

Nevertheless, as Lall (1999) argues, virtually all of the technology in both the foreign private-owned sector and the domestic public-owned sector was foreign. Moreover, the activities in the foreign MNCs were low-tech and labor intensive. For example, instead of producing silicon wafers, operations in Malaysia cut and packaged wafers produced in Singapore. Hard disk companies set up operations only to assemble drives, head gimble assemblies, and perform other labor-intensive processes (McKendrick et al., 2000). Ultimately there was little technology transfer from foreign MNCs to local industries, nor was there much demand from local industries for these technologies. The situation did not differ much in the state-owned industries. Proton, the national carmaker, for example, derived most of its technology from Mitsubishi and later Lotus.[14] Why were levels of technical capacity in industry so low?

The historical evidence suggests that the Malaysian government needed to balance increasing wealth for the Malays without decimating the Chinese-owned foundation of the economy. At the same time, continued bedrock political support from the agriculturally situated Malays precluded aggressive and overt support of local capital. The government was therefore walking a tightrope and foreign direct investment (FDI) was the safety net. Foreign MNCs provided employment, particularly for the non-Malay population. Second, they provided foreign exchange and the semblance of economic progress and development, including healthy balance sheets. With this arrangement, government could safely ignore local Chinese capital and use resource-based income to pay directly for affirmative action policies. Technological development of Chinese-based local capital, by either the government or the foreign MNCs, would have upset this delicate balance by distorting relative asset ownership levels between Malays and non-Malays. Thus sincere efforts to develop a local technology base would have to wait until a local Malay capital base existed.

But, on the other hand, while Chinese-owned businesses could not get help to upgrade technologically, competing political elites made it difficult for the state to impose any restrictions on rents being supplied by public actors to private business interests, regardless of ownership (Crouch, 1996). Initially, as in Thailand, the majority of these rents were funded by resource-based sectors. Unlike the situation in Thailand, however, intense ethnic competition for resource allocation made monopoly rent provision all the more desirable. Resources and ethnic composition also had a fragmenting effect on business, as Chinese-, Indian- and Malay-controlled firms competed together through patron–client relationships for government-supplied rents. In this environment, rent-seeking was more important than technological development, and where innovation would have been welcomed by the local Chinese-owned capital sector, politics made it difficult to achieve.

In summary, two things made it possible for UMNO to de-emphasize the development of local capital. First, both MNCs and natural-resource-based industries provided foreign exchange, employment and, by extension, wages. Foreign-dominated export industries created an appearance of technological progress, economic growth, export earnings and healthy financial indicators. Second, primarily state-owned resource-based industries, but also non-resource-based industries, provided funds directly to the government to pursue affirmative action policies and patronage-based development projects. In the end, all of Malaysia's ethnic groups were happy: the Chinese were left relatively alone (or were able to avoid connection with the government) and the Malays received real and perceived economic assistance from the government. But, as I show in later chapters, this social bargain is coming under increasing economic and political pressure, as neither Chinese, Indians nor Malays have been able to develop local technical capacity.[15]

Singapore

As in both Malaysia and Thailand, state-building in Singapore entailed extensive political upheaval, turmoil and consolidation of power. Nevertheless, economic and military vulnerability ensured that economic development would be key to political legitimacy. In 1963, after just two years as part of Malaysia, Singapore divorced from the Malaysian Union.[16] By the early 1970s Britain had closed down its military bases in Singapore, which had accounted for over 30 percent of GNP. The government, however, had not been caught flat-footed. Even before independence, it had been clear that eventually the British would leave. Also, even though Singapore desired union with Malaysia, there was no guarantee this would happen, or if it did, that it would last.

Early steps taken by the PAP helped develop indigenous technical capacity. In 1961, the government formally created the Economic Development Board (EDB). Even though not formalized until 1961, the EDB had its beginnings in the 1950s, several years before independence. When it became apparent that Britain was going to withdraw from Singapore and take a significant chunk of the local economy with it, Lee and his close advisors immediately began to chart a course for Singapore's post-independence economic growth. In 1958 Lee sent Goh Keng Swee on a round-the-world trip to learn about different methods of economic development. The model that seemed to fit Singapore best was that of Israel.

From Israel, Singapore learned three very important lessons about how to develop from a position of resource scarcity. First, if none of your neighbors want or need your products, you must 'leapfrog' them on the development chain, making products they don't make.[17] This requires a tremendous emphasis on high-tech and knowledge-intensive industries. Second, it is imperative to engage in industry that not only generates income, but also is relevant to the rest of the world. In other words, industry for industry's sake is insufficient. You must be highly selective of what industries to pursue. Finally, recognize that the only resource you have is your people and their brains and skills. In other words, the road to success passes through education and training (Schein, 1996).

The second step was to overhaul and recreate the education system. Such a transformation was, according to Lee, the most difficult thing about creating a developmentally inclined society. Indeed, he stated that other developing countries have been unable to replicate Singapore's success precisely because they have been unwilling (or unable) to integrate and consolidate their education system with a focus to drive a technically advanced society (ibid.).

Even though the Winsemius report suggested that Singapore pursue an ISI (import substitution industrialization) growth strategy, Singapore's leadership realized that such a strategy depended upon Malaysia as a captive market. Thus they were always prepared to go it alone should something happen to preclude Malaysia as a ready market. When Singapore left the Malaysian union, it rapidly refocused its economic strategy around export industrialization, innovation and technological development. The transformation was relatively painless because the infrastructure for Singapore's technology-based economy had been laid at least a decade before.

The bottom line was that although political priorities for power and position were strong, these were subordinated to expansive economic development (or perhaps, more accurately, dove-tailed perfectly). Ultimately there was no resource-based safety net for Singaporean society to rely on.[18] Both political legitimacy and economic profits depended on technological and quasi-market rents as opposed to monopoly rents.

Thailand
Unlike Malaysia, Thailand has never had to balance ethnic priorities. Although the kingdom underwent a short period of anti-Sinicism during

Phibun's premiership from 1939 until 1957, xenophobia was shallow and short-lived. Instead of leading to alienation and confrontation, government policies restricting the economic activity of the Chinese in Thailand actually encouraged more rapid ethnic assimilation. In Thailand, unlike the Islamic countries to the south, the Chinese easily adopted the Thai language, religion and culture. By 1950 it was difficult to identify pure ethnic Chinese, and today there are few that live in Bangkok that cannot identify a Chinese ancestor.

Rather than ethnicity, the factors driving technology preferences were the nature of the rice industry, a mild external security condition (or at least covered by the USA), preferences for terms of trade, and the demands of political transformation. But while the starting point for technological development in Thailand was very different than in Malaysia, the technical trajectories of the two countries were similar.

To begin with, there was relatively little pressure to upgrade rice productivity, owing in large part to an extensive land frontier. By the early twentieth century, Thailand was one of the world's largest rice producers. But although there was extensive discussion on improving productivity through R&D for equipment, seed varieties and irrigation, from 1880 to 1940 very little technical progress was made (Feeny, 1982). Many scholars studying the early development of Thailand's rice industry bemoan this lack of innovation and the wasted opportunity for technological progress. Why did Thailand drop the ball?

Increasing the productivity of rice agriculture is not without its challenges, the chief one being sufficient water. In the fertile central plains of the Chao Phraya river delta, inconsistent rainfall makes irrigation necessary. In the saline northeast, however, water problems must be addressed with increasingly drought- and disease-resistant seed varieties because digging canals and ditches releases the salinity into the topsoil, thus making cultivation even less productive. In 1902 the Thais hired a Dutch irrigation expert to create an overall irrigation plan for the lower delta. When the plan was finished in 1903, however, funds that were to be used for the project were allocated to building the north–south railway instead (Brown, 1988), to address geopolitical pressures.

The short-term pressure on Siam was balancing two aggressive European powers, France in Indochina and Britain in Malaysia and Burma. Concerns over internal security and national unity elevated preferences for the railway over irrigation (ibid.). And yet, as relevant as security decisions were and even though improvements in seed varieties, machinery and irrigation would have increased productivity and economic rates of return, agricultural technology did not carry the day because survival did not depend on it. Siam's rice production met the food demands of its own people, with tremendous surplus for export. An extensive land frontier meant that any increase in demand for aggregate supply could easily be met by increasing the amount of land under cultivation. To this end the government passed a series of laws in 1908 that gave anyone the right to settle land if that land could be turned to a profit. The result was a tremendous increase in paddy acreage and total production in kind, but without any improvement in productivity (Christensen, 1993; Feeny, 1982).

At the same time that the government was pushing to expand total cultivatable land, the powerful landowning Bangkok elite quashed efforts to expand irrigation in the fertile plains beyond the north of Bangkok because they feared that rising productivity on smaller farms would drive overall prices down and increase competition for scarce labor. The urban Bangkok elite also pressed the government for favorable terms of trade and cheap food. In response, the government took active steps to turn the terms of trade against the rice farmers. Thus, right at the time capital for R&D was most needed, farmers were squeezed for development resources (Feeny, 1982). The evidence of failure of the Thai government's rice policy before 1950 is stagnant incomes and falling productivity (ibid.).

Low priorities for technological development extended to industry. In 1913 the government created two companies, Siam Cement and Siam Steamship Co. In the case of the former, the government felt that the ability to provide basic infrastructure products for a growing economy was important. For the latter, the government recognized that it could save money currently being spent on ships made in Japan. For neither company, however, did the government intervene to assist in technology acquisition, absorption or transfer. Of the two, Siam Cement went on to be hugely successful, while Siam Steamship Co. went out of business in a matter of a few short years. Part of Siam Cement's success was due to the difference in shipping prices between foreign and local cement. The difference of a few cents provided a natural protective barrier while Siam Cement got up and running. In contrast, the ship company did not have such an advantage and without government intervention the project failed (Brown, 1988).[19]

Finally, from roughly 1920 through 1939 government priorities were focused on political transformation and succession of power from an absolute to a constitutional monarchy. Until the revolution of 1932, the focus was on nation-building, political development and socialization (Muscat, 1984). From 1932 until 1939 political upheaval and competition for power dominated (Wilson, 1962). In the early period, government preferred expanding rice farmland as opposed to productivity for two reasons. First, employment was a growing concern. Second, increasing the number of free, landowning farmers increased the number of civically active, taxpaying adults. In the turbulent post-*coup* politics, Field Marshall Phibun was able to achieve power through a combination of public support and ruthless repression of political opponents. Part of the reason we see a shift in the terms of trade for rice agriculture from negative to positive after 1935 may have been attempts to woo the support of these smallholding farmers.

In sum, coalitional preferences were first for political transformation and only minimally for any form of technological development. As Muscat (1994: 43) notes, the Thai government can fairly be described as having had a policy of 'promoting development' in the rice sector – for a good 50 years. As significant as the policy measures were in the context of nineteenth-century Siam, the content and extent of promotion fell far short of what might have been done. During the century before World War II, very little was done to study the problems of rice production or to develop better technology.

Without R&D of irrigation and new seed varieties, and without the transfer, adoption and creation of new equipment and techniques, rice productivity fell dramatically from 1900 onward (Christensen, 1993; Brown, 1988; Muscat, 1994). Evidence from other industries suggests that failed technology promotion was not limited to the rice industry. Promotion of Thailand's other resource-based industries – teak, tin and rubber – was similarly weak and fragmented (Muscat, 1994). Competition between the ministries of finance and agriculture doomed the blossoming cotton and sericulture industries before they could get off the ground (Brown, 1988), suggesting that many of the same coalitional dynamics evidenced in the rice industry existed in other industries as well.

CONCLUSION

Malaysia, Singapore and Thailand, like their Northeast Asian counterparts, emerged as states amid significant conflict of external colonial power struggles and internal ethnic and communal conflict for political power. But once established, different combinations of resource endowments and domestic stability combined with levels of external vulnerability to create preferences for particular coalitional structures. In Malaysia and Thailand, which could rely on large resource endowments to generate foreign exchange, narrow and/or less participative coalitions formed between political and economic actors. The opposite conditions in Singapore led to a broader, more participative coalition.

Different coalitional structures in each country generated preferences for various outcomes with respect to key economic questions. Internal ethnic conflict in Malaysia and urban–rural divides in Thailand encouraged resource payments to be redistributed to favored groups in return for political support. Emphasis on political objectives in the education and training system came at the cost of a focus on technological development. Singapore's coalition focused on economic expansion *through* technological development. Since there were no other ways to generate foreign exchange to pay for military security, Singapore society emphasized upgrading as the mechanism to reduce systemic vulnerability.

NOTES

1. The ethnic breakdown in 1957 was very different from what it is today: 55 percent Malay, almost 30 percent Chinese, 7 percent Indian, with the remainder made up of various groups, including indigenous peoples in Sabah and Sarawak. Over the intervening 30 years, reproductive rates for the Malays have been much higher than for the other ethnic groups and account for the relative increase of Malays as compared to the other ethnic groups.
2. The Federated Malay States (FMS), formed in 1896, consisted of Perak, Selangor, Negri Smbilan and Pahang. The Unfederated Malay States included the remaining states of peninsular Malaya, including the four northern states previously controlled by Siam – Kedah, Perlis, Kelantan and Trengganu, which were given to the British by Siam in 1909 – and Johor, which was transferred by the British from Singapore to Malaya in 1908. In 1948 a new constitution combined all the states on the peninsula except the Straits communities of Penang and Malacca into the Federation of Malaya. In 1957 Penang and Malacca were added to the federation, and Sabah and Sarawak (the latter two from Borneo Malaysia) were added in 1961. In 1963 Singapore was added, but in 1965 left the federation. See Gullick (1981) for a complete history of Malaysia.
3. Much of this early history comes from Muscat (1994).
4. The Sakdina system hierarchically ordered Thai society by assigning 'points' to every individual, with kings and princes at the top and slaves at the bottom of the food chain.
5. See Felker (1998) for an insightful study on the influence of coalitions on technology and development strategy in Malaysia and Thailand.
6. Muscat (1994) notes that the bulk of the resource sector is contained within the rice agriculture industry. But he also argues that the Thai government had also reserved for itself the lion's share of the revenues generated from the rubber and tin industries.
7. By 2000 this figure had increased to 19 percent, well short of the 30 percent goal, but representing significant progress from the original starting position.
8. When measuring total Malay wealth, state-owned companies such as Khazanah are counted as Malay assets. In this sense the actual well-being of the average subsistence farming Malay has changed little, while reported aggregate wealth of Malays has gone from 2 percent to 19 percent since 1971.
9. An interesting example of a natural-resource-based industry underwriting government support is the case of oil and the state of Terangganu. In peninsular Malaysia, the lion's share of oil and natural gas occurs in the northern states of Terangganu (the northern state of Kelantan as well as Borneo in East Malaysia also have large deposits of oil and natural gas). When oil was discovered here, the federal government signed an agreement with the state government of Terangganu to pay a royalty of 5 percent of the cost of all oil extracted from the state and its offshore territory. This money was used to build roads, schools, libraries, and for whatever other purpose the state government saw

fit. However, after the opposition Islamic-based Pan-Malaysian Islamic Party (PAS) gained control of the state government, the national government stopped making the royalty payments and said that the agreement had run its course. The Terangganu government is pursuing the matter in federal court. It would be difficult to be optimistic about its chances.

10. Certainly the PAP had exhibited a past willingness to narrow the coalition. For example, soon after gaining power in 1959, it abrogated many of the significant perks enjoyed by the bureaucracy, arguably the group from which the PAP derived its strongest support at the time (Tremewan, 1994).

11. The Housing Development Board confirmed this for me in a personal interview, August 2000.

12. This is true only up to World War II. After this period Thailand makes a concerted (and successful) effort to maintain a very conservative macro fiscal and monetary policy. Nevertheless, microeconomics remained largely unstructured and informally based on personal relationships between economic and political actors.

13. Galton's problem refers to the methodological conundrum where variation is not caused by hypothesized causal variables, but by simple learning processes and knowledge diffusion.

14. Proton acquired Lotus, the British car manufacturer, and uses the new company to produce new engines. This R&D, however, is taking place mostly in the UK. Also, in spite of these technology acquisitions, most believe that Proton will not survive liberalization of the auto industry demanded by AFTA (ASEAN Free Trade Area) agreements unless it can merge with a larger, foreign automaker.

15. As I noted in the example on Penang, there have been some locally owned companies that have in fact developed significant technical capacity. But these are the exceptions that prove the rule.

16. There is some debate as to whether Singapore took its ball and went home or whether the rest of the Malaysian team left Singapore alone with its ball.

17. See Hobday (1995) on the feasibility of such 'leapfrogging.'

18. Some might argue that Singapore could rely on entrepôt or financial services to survive, *à la* Hong Kong. This comparison, however, is unfair given that Hong Kong also retained its colony status and could always rely on the British Parliament for support if necessary. As an independent country, Singapore had to develop an economic base outside of ports and banks, which it could do only through technological development.

19. Some might argue that Siam's hands were tied: if it implemented tariffs it would almost certainly have borne the wrath of the foreign countries on its borders. While it is not clear what the ramifications of such a move might ultimately have been, the argument suggests that Siam would have been colonized by Britain, France, or both.

5. Coalitions and initial decisions during state-building

Beginning with the invasion of China in the early thirteenth century, Genghis Khan and the Mongolian army conquered a vast territory that extended across Persia, Russia and into much of Eastern Europe. But while possessing great equestrian and military skills, Genghis Khan was less adept at state-building. Instead of building institutions that would perpetuate Mongolian language, politics, economics and culture, he established tributary mechanisms to extract wealth from the existing societies. Without underlying Mongolian institutions, the territories quickly returned to former or new forces soon after Genghis's death.

Forming institutions associated with building states is, as Genghis discovered, difficult. And yet creating institutions as part of state-building is necessary and has far-reaching impacts on subsequent capacities and performance of the state. The conclusion is that initial policy decisions as the precursor to institutions are critical to subsequent outcomes.

In Malaysia, Singapore and Thailand, coalitional bargaining and interactions impacted four important policy decisions made during the formation of education and training systems during periods of state-building. These four decisions were: language of educational instruction; level of fragmentation in the education and training bureaucracy; the extent to which labor is included in education and training; and the level of focus on technology and science in the education and training system.

All four decisions depended heavily on how coalitions prioritized economic expansion as opposed to political or redistributive outcomes. In Thailand, narrow, patronage-based coalitions bent on consolidating political power preferred an education and training system that reinforced social and political norms and behavior. In Malaysia, broad but non-participative coalitions preferred an education and training system that could be 'morseled' out in patterns of ethnic patronage and politics as a reward for support of political objectives. In contrast, broad and participative coalitions in Singapore preferred a technically oriented education and training system to support generally expansive economic development as a means of social survival. These preferences and the legacies of the choices that followed influenced the creation and change over time of the institutional systems surrounding education and training. Institutional systems, in turn, have directly impacted society's ability and desire to resolve key collective dilemmas inimical to the formation of technical intellectual capital.

EDUCATION AND TRAINING BEFORE STATE-BUILDING

Before we can understand how coalitions have influenced institutional formation in education and training at the point of state-building, it is necessary to understand the beginning points of education and training in each country so that we can determine what components are new and which ones 'carry through.'

Malaysia and Singapore

Before the British arrived, education and training in both Malaysia and Singapore, to the extent that it existed at all, was religious in content and form and conducted mainly at the mosque by Islamic leaders. The little bit of vocational training that existed in the villages was oriented to subsistence agriculture and local handicrafts (Loh, 1975). When the British arrived, they implemented education as the East India Company had done in India. That is, not much. British education was mostly focused on the children of a small group of elites that the British hoped to prime for service in the bureaucracy. Nevertheless, the British did support the rise of vernacular education, at least to some degree. Unlike Malaysia, Singapore had Sir Stanford Raffles, who, though an employee of the East India Company, felt it was the British responsibility to give all the inhabitants a Western, liberal education. As a result, Singapore did much more than Malaysia to develop an infrastructure and system to make this happen.

By 1906, education in the Straits Settlements[1] was vested in a director of education. However, a formal ministry of education was not established until after independence in 1963. The first technical institute was established in Kuala Lumpur in 1957. The Technical College was opened in 1955 and subsequently made a federal institution under the Ministry of Education. Technical education, however, was initially focused on improving natural rubber production, developing synthetic rubber and increasing agricultural efficiency. It wasn't until the Third Malaysia Plan (1976–1980) that industrial science and engineering technology were elevated to a similar level of importance with unity and citizenship.

Nevertheless, national unity remained the overarching priority (Aziz and Chew, 1980).

Although the Straits Settlements were administratively distinct from the Federated Malay States, the educational system was similar at the lower levels and integrated at the higher levels (Loh, 1975). Nevertheless, since Britain's main educational goals were first to create a sufficiently large pool of English-educated bureaucrats to administer the territory and second to develop adequate skills to exploit the territory's natural resources (Bedlington, 1978: 50–53), they never created a comprehensive educational system capable of sustained economic development. In place of a centralized system, four distinct, ethnically based systems emerged (Chinese, Tamil, English and Malay) and were later formalized by the British into 'streams' (Francis and Ee, 1971). Each stream served a different segment of the population, and as Loh (1975) points out, fostered a feeling of ethnic division among the principal ethnic groups living in Malaya and Singapore.

Thailand

Unlike Singapore and Malaysia, Thailand has a very long history of educational development (Buripakdi and Mahakhan, 1980). However, like Singapore and Malaysia, religious (Buddhist) and apprentice (vocational) instruction characterized most early education and training (Cleesuntorn, 1987). It wasn't until the late nineteenth century that a public education system capable of technical instruction began to develop. In 1887 King Chulalongkorn established the Thai Department of Education. The department was later upgraded to the ministerial level and called the Thammakan Ministry. Education during this period produced primarily civil servants. General education was provided to the public but focused on manual, occupational training (ibid.).

During the reign of King Wachirwut, Thailand began consolidating and formalizing its educational facilities, curricula and programs. The Educational Scheme of 1902 divided education into two categories: general and special or technical. In 1909 the two streams were renamed academic and vocational. In 1916 Chulalongkorn University, the first university in Thailand, was founded. This was followed in 1921 by the first Compulsory Education Act, making Thailand the second country in Asia, behind Japan, to implement universal compulsory primary education (Cleesuntorn, 1987; Sukontarangsi, 1967). Thus, just prior to the worldwide depression, Thailand appeared to have developed a solid education and training foundation equal to any other country in Asia.

The technical depth of the system, however, was extremely shallow.

Instead of innovation and technical development, the education and training system in this early period focused on 'the virtuous life' and how to achieve it (Cleesuntorn, 1987). Issues such as citizenship; Thai literature, culture and religion[2] and political socialization and training dominated curricula. The system was ill suited to educate and train a sufficient pool of agricultural scientists capable of improving high-yield seeds, agricultural equipment, fertilizers and productive cycles of planting and harvesting (Brown, 1988). To address this lack of agricultural training, the government established the Bureau of Agricultural Science in 1923. But by 1930 the new agricultural school, modeled after the Japanese, had failed miserably.[3]

The reasons the new school failed are instructive. First, it was not simply that farmers needed to be educated in solely Western agricultural technology. The bigger problem was training people in both Western methods *and* the conditions and practices in Siam itself. But young ministers with knowledge of new practices were unable to teach them to established farmers. Old ministers, with long-standing connections to the villages, lacked any real knowledge of rice agriculture and blindly implemented economic policy, usually leading to failure. Second, fusing foreign and local knowledge required, to degree, that agricultural technical education and training be bilingual to be most efficient. But, since secular education was so limited, only a very small pool existed from which to draw people capable of delivering or obtaining a specialist, bilingual technical education. Third, there were major differences between the landowning elite in Japan and Siam. Unlike the Siamese landowning elite, the Japanese landowning aristocracy, the Gono, worked their land. As a result, the incentive to develop high-yield seeds, cultivation cycles and agricultural equipment was much higher than found in the absentee Thai landowners. In response to these incentives, the Gono formed agricultural societies and associations to disseminate information and facilitate training and technology development. The Thai agricultural elite, in comparison, was interested simply in the rents generated by tenant farmers (Brown, 1988). Fourth, those in the bureaucracy responsible for agriculture, especially Chaophraya Wongsanupraphat, the Minister of Agriculture, were convinced that the farmer's plight was due to gambling and poor foresight and saving rather than the cycles of monsoons and water. Thus no attention was given to irrigation or favorable access to credit (ibid.). Finally, although both farmers and consumers would have benefited from technological development, demand was extremely low.

CRITICAL JUNCTURES: INDEPENDENCE AND POLITICAL TRANSFORMATION

During the transition to independence, the countries of Southeast Asia initiated institutional reform of their inherited education and training systems. In Malaysia, ethnic divisions and conflict forced the government to implement all policy, including education, on a communal basis (Crouch, 1996). Accordingly, the primary goal of the Malaysian education system evolved toward the unification of diverse peoples (Francis and Ee, 1971; Aziz and Chew, 1980). Nonetheless, to appease all parties, the government allowed the vernacular streams to continue. Educational reform quickly settled on the smaller goal of improving education within the various streams. But although separate, the system was anything but equal. As with much else, the Chinese system was far superior to the Indian and Malay systems.

By the late 1960s, confrontations between the various ethnic groups were occurring more frequently, culminating in the May 1969 ethnic riots. Realizing that the current educational system perpetuated a fragmented, suspicious and, as the riots revealed, hostile ethnic environment, in 1971 the Malay government consolidated the four ethnic educational streams into one at the secondary level and above, and designated Malay as the official medium of educational instruction.

Singapore gained its independence in 1959, two years after Malaysia. However, to ensure a large and captive domestic market for its import substitution industrialization (ISI) economic strategy, Singapore joined the new Malaysian Federation in 1963 (Rodan, 1989). As part of the integration, Singapore and Malaysia merged their educational systems.[4] But when the PAP opted to contest national Malaysian elections, they upset the delicate balance of Malay political power.

In 1965 Singapore left the federation. At roughly the same time, the British withdrew its military forces from Singapore, which had accounted for over 30 percent of the economy (Schein, 1996). Suddenly Singapore was extremely vulnerable, both economically and politically. Without Malaysia's hinterland as a domestic market, ISI strategies were no longer practical. And without the income from the British military bases, survival demanded an extremely rapid economic transition away from ISI strategies. Finally, without the British military presence, Singapore was vulnerable to Indonesian *Konfrontasi* and Malaysian political hostility. In response, the government made it a priority to reform the education system to facilitate a rapid transformation to export-oriented industrialization and technological development.

Unlike Malaysia and Singapore, Thailand was never colonized. Thus the Thai education system was free to develop organically without the imposition of foreign institutions or control. Initial results were promising. But as part of the dramatic political transformation in 1932, the government revamped the education and training system to foster nationalism, social unity and political socialization (Cleesuntorn, 1987). High demand for political education and manipulation as well as efforts to consolidate political power combined to create education and training institutions that furthered primarily political ends.

THE DECISIONS

State-building at or around the critical juncture of independence in Malaysia and Singapore, and political transformation in Thailand created pressures for institutional creation and/or change. Unique pressures during the critical juncture in each case resulted in policies and institutions that addressed (or failed to address) four issues that have proven critical to developing technical intellectual capital: language of instruction, bureaucratic structure, the role of labor in development strategies, and the relative focus on technology. Choices in each issue area were driven largely by the level of demand for innovation- and technology-led development during the period of institutional formation.

Language of Instruction

Language and development strategy are intimately linked insofar as technological progress depends on the ability of a country to absorb and disseminate exogenous technology, especially in its explicit forms, e.g. blueprints, equipment, codes and so forth. When technologies are created in the local language, there is little to hinder widespread dispersion, comprehension, utilization and improvement. On the other hand, processes of transfer, dissemination and absorption become much more difficult when technologies are framed in foreign languages.

Northeast Asian countries pursued developmental strategies that centered on creating world-class technological capacity in local firms. Even though much of the technology was initially foreign, government and the private sector worked together through organizations and institutions, such as the Ministry of International Trade and Industry (Japan), the Economic Planning Board (Korea) and the Council for Economic Planning and Development (Taiwan), to quickly localize the technology and then facilitate its widespread transmission and adoption (Weiss, 1994; Johnson, 1986).[5]

In contrast to the Northeast Asian developmental economies, the countries of Southeast Asia pursued more techno-globalist development strategies. Smaller market size and majority ownership, however, made foreign multinational firms less willing to share technologies with local firms. Moreover, these states lacked the institutional capacity to extract, centralize, organize, translate and disseminate technology. Hence the ability to bridge the technological gap between foreign and local firms was initially limited and largely ineffective.

Persistent mismatches between language and technology hinder the transmission and absorption of technology in three ways. First, in techno-global developing economies, technology resides almost exclusively in foreign firms. To the extent that technology is available, it is accessible only to a select few in local firms that can speak the foreign language. And third, it is difficult to link foreign firms to the local education and training infrastructure, including the components of the institutional system responsible for R&D.

Malaysia's choice of Malay as the language of instruction made great sense politically, despite being questionable from an economic perspective (especially given the population's inherent ability to speak English). It distanced the new country from its previous colonial master and developed national pride in a national language. Moreover, the Malay political base on which UMNO depended was largely agricultural, illiterate and uneducated. Education was therefore an important component of the government's new affirmative action policies. And yet if education were to do anything for these people in the short term, it would have to be conducted in Malay. Finally, although technology was in high demand, there was no incentive for the British to diffuse any of this technology to the local economic sector. Both the demand for, as well as the ability to develop, technical human talent among the indigenous population was virtually non-existent during this period. Thus there was little pressure for immediate technological development that would have overridden the political issues for making Malay the language of choice for education and training.

Economically the decision was more problematic. Malaysia's early developmental strategies stressed internal development and import substitution (e.g. Mahatir's Hi-Com initiative), a strategy was largely underwritten by foreign technology partnerships.[6] By the mid-1970s, the government had begun to turn away from nationalistic development strategies and instead embraced export-oriented, and largely foreign-owned, manufacturing. In 1975 the government implemented the Industrial Coordination Act to begin soliciting FDI. In a relatively short period of time Malaysia successfully encouraged a wide range of multinational high-technology firms – which produced semi-conductors, hard disk drives, consumer electronics and so forth – to set up local manufacturing operations.

Recognizing the need to develop a labor force with a new set of skills, in the early 1970s the Ministry of Science, Technology, and the Environment (MOSTE) developed plans to work with the Ministry of Education and the Ministry of Human Resources to ensure that education and training curricula were sufficiently infused with appropriate technical and scientific content. However, the number of Malaysians possessing technical skills was extremely small and language barriers made it difficult for foreign-speaking technologists to effectively participate in a Malay-language-based education and training curriculum.

As in Malaysia, political demands to unify the country during political transformation made the Thai language a priority. At the same time, initial demand for technological skills and knowledge in Thailand was low. As we noted in Chapter 4, early economic focus on improving rice yields by expanding the cultivatable land frontier rather than improving productivity reduced the emphasis on innovation and technological progress (Brown, 1988). Subsequent government efforts to create state-owned import-substituting firms and then protect these industries from outside competition further reduced incentives for industrial upgrading. In spite of several government-to-government initiatives to create industry-targeted research institutes, poor linkages with academia and the private sector ensured that these institutes would be marginally successful at best. Without a strong demand for technology acquisition, transmission and absorption, pressure to adopt a more technology-friendly language as the language of instruction was low. The result, as in Malaysia, was that language barriers hindered efforts to expand linkages between local firms, education and training institutions, and multinational firms.

Singapore's separation from Malaysia provides a quasi-experimental research design from which to evaluate coalitional preferences. Before independence, the education and training system in both countries was, to all intents and purposes, one.[7] When Singapore joined the new Malaysian Federation in 1963, in an effort to impart, as Bedlington (1978) puts it, a veneer of 'Malayness,' Singapore adopted for its official educational system the objectives and language of the Malay stream. On separation in 1965, however, both the government and economic actors quickly realized that further reliance on the Malaysian hinterland as a captive export market was no longer possible.

In response to this new economic and military vulnerability, a broad developmental coalition between the state, labor and foreign MNCs provided a base of support to reform the education system around English (Schein, 1996). From an ethnic standpoint, English was not the natural choice. The bulk of the population spoke Chinese, although this was further divided into numerous dialects including Teochow, Cantonese, Mandarin and others. Economically, however, it made perfect sense.[8] Singapore had created the Economic Development Board in 1961 to encourage FDI. Even though this export-oriented strategy was replaced with an import substitution strategy for the two years that Singapore was part of Malaysia, from 1965 on it was the main industrial strategy.

The decision to make English the medium of education and training instruction had immediate consequences. By choosing English, the government defused potential ethnic tensions by focusing education around business and technology rather than supporting the dominant ethnic group and social class (Thomas et al., 1980). But even more important, whereas linkages between foreign capital and the education system in Malaysia and Thailand were very weak (with the exception of Penang), Singapore was able to create a training system incorporating the direct participation of MNCs; in many cases training facilities were created and operated within the multinational firm and produced labor, with industrial skills in precision engineering, advanced welding, tool and die, plastic injection and molding, and machine operation and repair. Such high levels of interaction and cooperation were possible only in the absence of language barriers.

Bureaucratic Fragmentation

The second key institutional arena impacting processes of technology-led development is bureaucratic fragmentation. Bureaucracies are most effective for technological development when they are centrally coordinated, foster decentralized implementation, and are tightly connected with the private sector (Ritchie, 2005a). Fragmentation works against all three of these goals.

At first glance it seems odd to suggest that politicians *choose* levels of fragmentation. Is not this, some would argue, more of a result? Yes and no. On the one hand, political actors often take purposive steps to *segment* the bureaucracy. Such has regularly been the Malaysian government's response to meeting the demands of an ethnically driven polity. On the other hand, political actors may passively allow the bureaucracy to fragment, taking no determined steps to halt or correct bureaucratic divisions. In either case, actively pursuing fragmentation or passively allowing it to occur constitutes a policy 'choice' that is both driven by a set of preferences and results in a set of outcomes pertaining to technological development.

Since bureaucracies often control or provide access to government resources, politicians often use the bureaucracy as a reward for political support. The more a ministry can generate some amount of surplus, the more valuable it is as a reward. Surplus is most easily maximized and extracted when bureaucratic operations are opaque and complicated. Distributing bureaucratic responsibilities over a large number of ministries, agencies and departments maximizes potential revenue opportunities by increasing the public budget while allowing greater access to these funds by clouding operating practices, hiding corruption and minimizing accountability. The natural response is for bureaucrats to focus on expanding their turf and accumulating resources. Quickly the game degenerates into a zero-sum competition for resources with an incentive to create ministerial empires. Duplication, waste and lost opportunities for scale economies are the immediate consequence. But over time the technocratic ability of the bureaucracy also suffers as positions are filled by political appointees with no ability in the area they are supposed to be leading.

Contrast this with rational and cohesive bureaucracies, which are much better positioned to pursue broad-based cooperation with the private sector. High demand for innovation and technological development requires responsiveness, flexibility and credibility, which are best furthered through transparency, accountability, trust and technocratic capacity. Instead of turf and accumulation, the bureaucracy must be focused on accomplishing market-based objectives.

Singapore has come much closer to this ideal type than has either Malaysia or Thailand. Responsibility for education and training in Singapore was initially divided between the Ministry of Trade and Industry, the Ministry of Labor (later changed to the Ministry of Manpower), and the Ministry of Education. The EDB was given primary control to coordinate manpower development with the needs of potential and actual foreign investors. In its broad overarching role, the EDB was able to coordinate education and training activities for the entire Singapore education system (see Figure 5.1), including budgets, curricula and forecasting. But perhaps most importantly, the EDB was able to link the bureaucracy with private MNCs.

Within the government, however, the role of the EDB was primarily one of direction. Actually formulating and implementing education- and training-related policies fell to the line ministries. Instead of acting unilaterally, a multitude of coordinating bodies was formed to create and implement policies to reach the objectives outlined by the EDB (Kwong and Sim, 1990).

Bureaucratic development in Malaysia has been very different. Before 1971 and the NEP (New Economic Policy), responsibility for education was the purview of the Ministry of Education and training the Ministry of Labor (later changed to the Ministry of Human Resources).

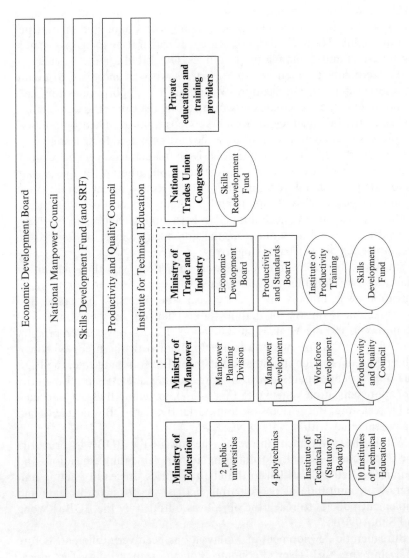

Figure 5.1 Singapore's technical education and training system

102

After the NEP was introduced, however, two additional ministries – the Majlis Amanah Rakyat (MARA), which later was incorporated into the Ministry of Entrepreneurial Development and the Ministry of Youth and Sports – were created to oversee education and training specifically for Bumiputras, or 'Sons of the Soil'[9] (see Figure 5.2). But although these latter two ministries were set up specifically to deal with ethnic issues, the original two ministries have become racially politicized over time. As an example, an elite-level bargain exists wherein the Minister of Education will always be Malay and the deputy Chinese. To compensate minority coalition members, the head of the Ministry of Human Resources will always be Chinese and the deputy Malay.[10]

Also, unlike either Singapore or Thailand, Malaysia has a federal political system. Thus, in addition to national initiatives, virtually every state has created a skills development center. These centers often receive financial assistance from the national government. These additional training centers increase the amount of people the country is able to train. But they also add yet another layer of fragmentation to an already fragmented system. Except in the case of the Penang Skills Development Center (more on this below), these centers lack coordination with other training facilities and suffer from problems of poor teacher quality and scarce equipment and resources.[11]

In comparison to Singapore, one is struck by the absence of cross-ministerial and organizational committees and connections within the education and training system in Malaysia, especially at the middle to lower levels. Each ministry, department and agency is in effect an isolated stovepipe. In the late 1960s the government created the Economic Planning Unit (EPU) as a department in the prime minister's office to oversee economic functions in the line ministries. While it is true that the EPU was responsible for coordinating all education and training policy, it did so only at a financial level. That is, each ministry, agency and department developed and operated its own self-contained programs, policies and plans.

In Thailand, education was initially the purview of the Ministry of Education. But almost immediately the Ministry of the Interior assumed responsibility for education in the municipalities. The Ministry of Education concentrated on general education while the Ministry of the Interior developed a separate education infrastructure for the villages.[12] Virtually every ministry, in some fashion or another, immediately took up vocational training. Thus the Ministry of Agriculture began offering vocational training in areas relating to agriculture, the Ministry of Industry (MOI) set up industrial training programs for manufacturing, the Ministry of Labor and Social Welfare for general vocational studies, and so forth (see Figure 5.3).

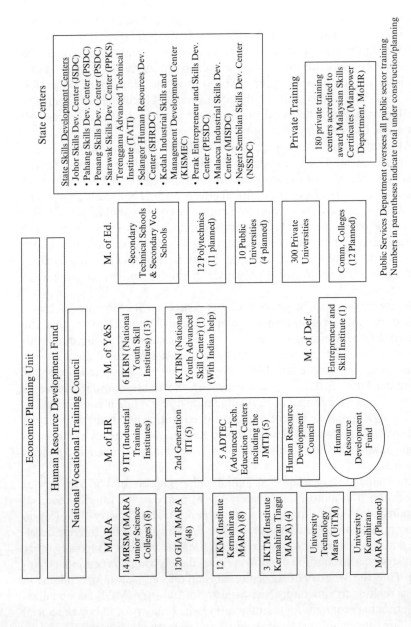

Figure 5.2   Malaysia's technical education and training system

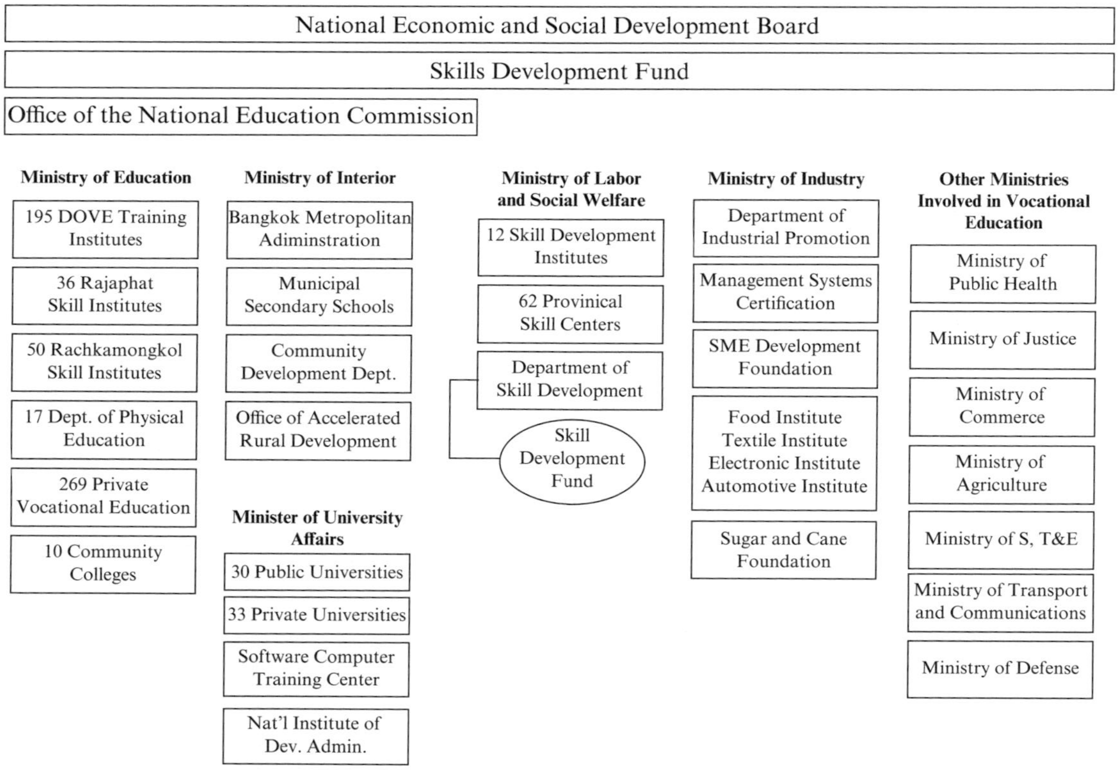

National Economic and Social Development Board

Skills Development Fund

Office of the National Education Commission

Ministry of Education

- 195 DOVE Training Institutes
- 36 Rajaphat Skill Institutes
- 50 Rachkamongkol Skill Institutes
- 17 Dept. of Physical Education
- 269 Private Vocational Education
- 10 Community Colleges

Ministry of Interior

- Bangkok Metropolitan Adminstration
- Municipal Secondary Schools
- Community Development Dept.
- Office of Accelerated Rural Development

Minister of University Affairs

- 30 Public Universities
- 33 Private Universities
- Software Computer Training Center
- Nat'l Institute of Dev. Admin.

Ministry of Labor and Social Welfare

- 12 Skill Development Institutes
- 62 Provinical Skill Centers
- Department of Skill Development
- Skill Development Fund

Ministry of Industry

- Department of Industrial Promotion
- Management Systems Certification
- SME Development Foundation
- Food Institute
- Textile Institute
- Electronic Institute
- Automotive Institute
- Sugar and Cane Foundation

Other Ministries Involved in Vocational Education

- Ministry of Public Health
- Ministry of Justice
- Ministry of Commerce
- Ministry of Agriculture
- Ministry of S, T&E
- Ministry of Transport and Communications
- Ministry of Defense

Figure 5.3   Thailand's education and training system

Like Malaysia, however, Thailand was unable to effectively develop intra-bureaucratic linkages. Early preferences for politicization and segmentation of the bureaucracy meant that those responsible for education and training often had no technocratic capacity to successfully discharge their responsibilities. Moreover, each agency, department and ministry was responsible for its own infrastructure, budget, curricula, teachers and so forth. Like Malaysia, peak-level coordinating bodies existed, e.g. the Office of the National Education Commission and the National Economic and Social Development Board,[13] but while they pursued macro-level policy initiatives, they did little to foster coordinated implementation or cooperation across bodies.

Without an entity like the EDB to help coordinate policy creation *and* implementation, fragmented bureaucratic structures in Malaysia and Thailand operated individual budgets, developed stand-alone infrastructure and disconnected curricula, and otherwise pursued separate objectives, or no clear objectives at all. The result has been tremendous duplication, waste and lost advantages of scale and coordination. Fragmentation also hindered the formation of linkages between the bureaucracy and private economic actors in both countries. As I show in Chapter 6, in Singapore the EDB initially acted as a 'one-stop shop,' becoming the linkage nexus between private firms and the government and involving appropriate departments and ministries in the government as necessary to foster industry-relevant education and training. In Malaysia and Thailand, public–private linkages could be formed only with small sub-sets of the bureaucracy at a time. While it was possible for private firms to establish bilateral relationships with multiple bureaucratic actors, a lack of coherence among government actors ensured that these relationships would be narrow, particularistic and based on rent-seeking priorities.

Including Labor in the Developmental Alliance

Preferences for technological development are also influenced by the decision to include or exclude labor in the education and training system. Including organized labor in developing and implementing education and training processes, programs and initiatives can dramatically influence worker participation and productivity. Labor in most countries recognizes the importance of training. Nevertheless, without government support and some level of corporatist recognition, it is difficult for labor to be involved. When labor is excluded, the training that does exist tends to focus on the upper end of the workforce, especially management training for executives. Historically this has been a significant problem in all three countries, but one that Singapore effectively addressed by working with and through organized labor.[14]

In Malaysia, labor has been actively suppressed. Without financial resources and government support, efforts to train have been minimal (Jomo and Todd, 1994). By the time the British granted Malaysia its independence, ethnic Indians, primarily those working on the rubber plantations, dominated organized labor. Although the number of Malays in organized labor would rise dramatically over the next three decades, organized labor has always represented a political threat to the Malay-dominated government as well as an economic threat to development strategies based on low-wage labor. Thus, while development strategies focused on reducing unemployment, labor elites were not involved in the education and training system, either formally or informally.

In Thailand a formal tripartite arrangement was designed to provide a channel by which labor, government and business can coordinate developmental strategies. In practice, however, the Thai government has taken a strong anti-labor stance (Anderson, 1998), and little bargaining between the three groups takes place (Deyo and Doner, 2001: 111). To the extent that early economic strategy relied on low-wage labor to fuel manufacturing-led growth, rising wages, collective bargaining and work stoppages needed to be controlled, if not eliminated. When government offers labor concessions in wages and benefits, it does not focus on technological or productivity improvements. As in Malaysia, the early developmental focus was on creating new jobs, not upgrading skill levels in existing jobs.

As in Malaysia and Thailand, labor in Singapore has also been suppressed (Deyo, 1989). But unlike in Malaysia and Thailand, labor in Singapore plays an important political role. Lacking a large base of domestic capitalists, labor is the only mass social group with pivotal political power. To successfully maneuver itself into political power, the PAP created the National Trades Union Congress, a government-designated corporatist body representing all organized labor on the island as a way to weaken the political power of organized labor as well as create institutional mechanisms to control labor's influence in the future. As Deyo rightly argues, labor's initial influence in this tripartite bargaining structure was weak and often marginalized by the interests of foreign MNCs. Particularly stark is the example of labor pushing for increased wages and collective bargaining rights in the early 1970s. When foreign MNCs threatened to leave the island in response, the government quickly suppressed the movement.

But despite government's ability to extract concessions from labor, it had to pay for these concessions with side payments or risk losing labor's important political support. Initially these side payments included subsidized housing and financing and universal education (Rodan, 1989; Doner et al., 2005). But an additional side payment given to labor has been the increasingly important responsibility for policy leadership on matters concerning training and skills upgrading.

Technological Focus: Match or Mismatch?

The supply of technical intellectual capital must match industrial demand to maximize economic growth (Birdsall et al., 1997).[15] When countries pursue techno-nationalist development strategies, incremental innovation and technological progress is possible through a symbiotic relationship among private firms, public research institutes, the education and training system, and labor.[16] Industrial transformation marked by technological deepening requires that each of these actors interacts. Firms derive technical talent from the education and training system, the public research institutes provide technology and training, the firm provides technology, equipment and trainers to the education and training system, the research institutes and firms share technology, labor ensures technology gets driven deep within the labor force, and so forth. When this process is relatively incremental, technical advances can be shared among the various actors, each leading the process when necessary. The state makes the equal and incremental improvement possible by protecting the entire system from the demands of the global economy until industries can compete as an equals.

On the other hand, when countries pursue technological upgrading through more globalist strategies, especially through foreign multinational firms, as all three countries eventually did, the aggregate technological capacity of the foreign business sector is discontinuously much higher than other public and private actors. In this 'dualistic' economic structure, technical knowledge and skills in the public research institutes, the education and training system, and the labor force remain focused on traditional, often commodity-based industries, while technical knowledge and skills in the manufacturing sector increasingly center on electronics, software, chemicals, biotechnology, advanced materials, robotics and so forth. As the gap between private sector demands and public sector supply grows, the likelihood of productive education and training and R&D linkages between the two diminishes.

Two scenarios are possible, both equally detrimental. First, foreign firms usually have radically more advanced knowledge and skills than the local education and training system, making cross-fertilization between the two difficult: the education and training system lacks the faculty, equipment and systems to support education and training in advanced skills. Rather than participate in a drawn-out ramping up of the domestic education and training system to meet increasing technical needs (and these processes are fraught with collective dilemmas and uncertain return on investment), foreign firms simply import needed intellectual capability or set up knowledge-intensive operations in other locations where such skills and knowledge are already in abundance.

Assuming indigenous firms are exposed to the international market-place, local firms demand technical knowledge and skills to either compete with or supply the locally situated MNCs. The education and training system, however, can offer expertise only in traditional handicraft, and commodity and agricultural skills, making it extremely difficult for the local firms to develop world-class technological capability to compete in the global marketplace, or alternatively to become embedded in the global production networks of the MNCs. To survive, these local firms usually seek government protection from the market.

At the critical juncture Singapore bridged the gap between technology-rich MNCs and a backward education and training system in three ways. First, the government provided temporary incentives to foreign MNCs to establish training centers inside their firms. The firms became the most important component of the training system. But, at the same time, the government completely overhauled the education and training system to bring it in line with the demands of industry. Doing so entailed a great deal of short-term social and economic upheaval. Nevertheless, such extensive reform reflected the government's commitment to long-term growth based on technological upgrading even while focusing initial efforts on improving employment through labor-intensive industries.

Second, without the low-hanging technological fruit frequently found in resource-based industries, Singapore was forced to bite the bullet and develop internal bureaucratic capacity to develop more technologically complex skills demanded by multinational manufacturing industries. In 1968 the government formed the Ministry of Science and Technology to focus on technological upgrading. By 1970, sophisticated manpower evaluation techniques were developed to assure that the educational system output matched the manpower needs of the economy (Thomas et al., 1980). These early manpower evaluations illuminated the need for technical education, and particularly skill development efforts focused on precision engineering, welding, materials handling, electronics and other industrial skills. Between 1965 and 1978 the emphasis in education shifted dramatically toward technology. In 1973 the Industrial Training Board was created, and in 1976 the Shelly Committee was established to further ensure the development and improvement of technical education.

Additionally, in 1978 Singapore created the National Industrial Council (comprising the Ministers of Education, Finance and Labor), and the Technical Education Department within the Ministry of Education to manage technical education throughout Singapore. Finally, in 1979 the Vocational and Industrial Training Board (VITB), and the Council on Professional and Technical Education (CPTE) were created to enhance technical education for those already in the workforce (Kwong and Sim, 1990).

Third, Singapore developed a system of industry- and technology-based public research institutes to both respond to the needs of high-technology firms in manufacturing and services as well as drive cutting-edge technology development. With R&D initiatives in communications, data storage, materials handling, biotechnology, imaging, petrochemicals and so forth, linkages between technically advanced firms, academia and the research institutes are far more likely as well as more productive.

Unlike in Singapore, there was no connection between firms and the education and training system in Thailand at the critical juncture. Decisions made for technological capacity in the education and training system focused on agricultural and traditional technologies and science, and matched the needs of most firms. Any forgone technical capacity in Thailand was only due to some amount of intellectual Dutch disease (Auty, 1998). Indeed, Christensen (1993) observes that Thailand successfully developed technologically leading-edge, high-yield strains of rice.

Nevertheless, over time Thailand's development strategies began to bend toward FDI-led development, albeit never to the level of Singapore or Malaysia. But rather than push for dramatic reform in the local education and training system or in raising technical capacity in local industry, the government sought to protect local manufacturing industries with trade tariffs while choosing to deepen technological capacity in resource-based industries, particularly rice agriculture.[17] Thus there was little effort or need to link the education and training system to foreign MNCs. Both the government and local industry viewed FDI as an easy source of foreign exchange and jobs, but also as a source that could be held at arm's length and operated independently of traditional or import-substituting industries.[18] MNCs could provide temporary balance-of-payments relief while the country developed technological capacity in traditional industries.

The bigger immediate problem, however, was that the government made little effort to support technological development in local industry outside a few commodity, usually state-owned, ventures, including sugar milling, distilling and cigarettes (Muscat, 1994: 45).[19] In many cases Thailand is a story of 'roads not taken.' Promising initial progress in rice, rubber, sericulture, cotton and ship building, among other things, rapidly attenuated without concerted and focused government intervention to nurture fledgling technologies (Brown, 1988).

In most respects Malaysia was similar to Thailand. In general, efforts to develop technologically were limited. Before independence, industrial strategy as well as knowledge and skills development was focused on primary products. In 1925 the British created the Rubber Research Institute to further the development of both natural and synthetic rubber. The focus placed on rubber production throughout the 1950s, 1960s and 1970s, encouraged the education and training system to develop scientists in this area. In 1969 the Malaysian Agricultural Research and Development Institute was created. And in 1979 the government established the Palm Oil Research Institute of Malaysia (PORIM). All three are well staffed and well funded. Significantly, many believe that Malaysia's Rubber Research Institute and PORIM are conducting R&D on the technological frontiers of their respective industries (Rasiah, 1996).

And yet, at the same time, the Malaysian government was actively soliciting investment from foreign MNCs as well as implementing an aggressive infant-industry development program in automobiles, construction and construction materials, and heavy equipment. But despite rising demand for industrial skills in both the foreign and local industry sectors (most of it driven by foreign technology), to the extent that the education and training structure focused on innovation and technology, it did so for commodity-based sectors, primarily rubber, palm oil and agriculture (and later petroleum). Although institutes, research and educational institutions, and public agencies capable of training engineers and scientists exist, they have been much more successful in primary commodity industries than in manufacturing sectors (Kassim, 1995).

The Case of Penang

By the early 1990s it was clear that Penang Malaysia was a hotbed of technological development. Electronics manufacture, especially for hard disk drives, had moved from Singapore to this small island state virtually overnight. What accounted for this rapid development? Why did it happen here and not in Petaling Jaya or Kuala Lumpur? A comparison between Penang, a small island state with few natural resources, a majority Chinese population (60 percent), and the only local Chinese government in Malaysia, and the Klang Valley in Selangor near Kuala Lumpur, which is more representative of Malaysia as a whole, provides some insight.[20]

When the Malaysian government implemented the New Economic Plan (NEP) to restructure the economy along ethnic lines, Penang was suffering from severe unemployment due to the oil-induced economic downturn of the early 1970s. As part of the NEP, the Malaysian government transferred the country's two primary port facilities from Penang and Malacca to Klang, just outside of Kuala Lumpur, thereby exacerbating Penang's economic woes. Almost as compensation, the federal government granted Penang export-processing-zone (EPZ) status. Responding to this opportunity and heightened levels of vulnerability, the Chinese-backed Gerakan Party formed the Penang Development Corporation (PDC), an organization based on a broad coalition of business and government leaders to encourage increased foreign investment in the island. The PDC met with early success and persuaded a number of high-tech firms to set up shop, including Texas Instruments and Intel. But the government wasn't content simply to locate foreign technology firms on the island for employment purposes. Instead, they tasked the PDC with developing an ambitious plan to upgrade the technical skills of the workforce and transfer foreign technology to local firms.

The PDC approached this challenge in three ways. First, it was able to minimize fragmentation by coordinating government policy and linking it to private firms. Functioning much like the EDB in Singapore, the PDC was given the lead role in organizing and leading the government's approach to economic and technological development.[21]

Second, it harmonized technological focus between the local and multinational firms and these firms and the education and training system in two ways. First, it persuaded the Chinese purchasing agents for these MNCs to give contracts with the appropriate technical specifications to local companies, especially precision engineering and electronic components shops. The PDC would then work with these firms to ensure world-class output. And second, in 1989, the PDC established the Penang Skills Development Center (PSDC) to develop a pool of industrial skills that matched the needs of both foreign multinational technology companies as well as aspiring local technology firms.

The PSDC worked in tandem with the local universities to create workers skilled in basic industrial skills. Significantly, however, all of the courses were taught in English, even though courses with similar content at the universities and colleges were taught in Malay. Without a language barrier, the PSDC successfully solicited cooperation and input from the foreign multinational firms to provide mid- and high-level vocational and engineering training. This training was often accomplished with the latest equipment and foreign technologists. Moreover, because the PSDC was a state organization, it was not beholden to national affirmative action policies. The rate of participation was phenomenal.[22]

Finally, although the PDC did not take any formal steps to include labor in its skills upgrading efforts, several factors encouraged at least neutral and often harmonious relations among labor, the government and business. First, even though labor was repressed, as in the rest of Malaysia (Jomo and Todd, 1994), formally established labor unions, typically associated with rubber and tin, were weak. To the extent that labor was organized at all, it tended to be within the new foreign corporations.[23]

A lack of open hostility or confrontation made it possible for labor to participate in the education and training system at least as a consumer, even if not initially as a provider.[24] Importantly, early relationship patterns with labor paved the way for future collaboration on skills development in Penang that would be significantly higher than those in the rest of Malaysia.

The Klang Valley experience was different. Firms dominated by ethnic Chinese enjoyed little support from the Malay-dominated UMNO state government. The intermediary coordinating role played by the PDC in Penang was absent in the Klang Valley. MNCs in the valley reported they were unmotivated to use local firms. The Selangor Human Resource Development Center (SHRDC), modeled after the PSDC, has been unable to attract the same level of local firm participation as has the PSDC.[25] Rasiah (1999a) summarizes the condition as follows: 'Ethnic divergence in the Klang Valley – between the small and medium business community and UMNO dominated political leadership, both at the state and federal levels – blocked political support for the ethnic Chinese controlled small and medium scale businesses' (10). Without government support to both encourage and sanction the MNCs, there was little incentive to participate.

This comparison between Penang and the Klang Valley suggests that key decisions have a dramatic impact on institutional formation and economic output. But assuming that once 'correct' policy choices are identified it is possible to rapidly and radically alter the existing national innovation system in general and the education and training institutions in particular to match changing industrial needs is to ignore the power of increasing returns. Although there has certainly been change over time, choices in each of the four areas outlined above continue to influence education and training in these countries. Subsequent decisions have been built on the foundation laid by these early choices, which in turn have influenced still later decisions. Thus the development of technological capacity, especially in education and training, is a path-dependent process and is vulnerable to both economic and political increasing returns.

CONCLUSION

As the experience of Penang shows, decisions made on language, bureaucratic fragmentation, labor participation and technological focus have a great impact on the ability of the education and training system to inter-act with foreign and local firms to produce technical intellectual capital. Political considerations at the point of institutional reconfiguration in Thailand and Malaysia led to education and training institutions that were focused on political objectives of domestic unity, nationalism and cultural connections. In Singapore and Penang, demands for economic survival encouraged otherwise unpopular decisions, but these decisions led to eco-nomic productivity, technology and knowledge transfer, and the capacity to generate future intellectual capital.

The next chapter explores the legacies of these decisions. Whereas deci-sions can often be easily made, perhaps with just the stroke of a pen, it can be far harder to reverse course or start over. As decisions create returns, future decisions are made to maximize increasing returns, both economic and political. Evidence of economic increasing returns can be seen in growing returns to scale. Evidence of political increasing returns can be seen in vested interests.

NOTES

1. Singapore, Malacca and Penang.
2. Even now, as the education infrastructure is reformed, religion has been reunited with education and culture as the three pillars of society (see the Education Act of 1999).
3. Brown (1988) argues that some of the failure was due to the untimely death of its patron, Prince Phenpat. This may have been true, although saying so simply reinforces the argument that there was little demand for the services of the school in the general population, as little was done after his death to continue or resurrect the school.
4. This was not as difficult as it first might appear, as the British administered the same educational system for both countries.
5. The development literature is replete with excellent studies on how the countries of Northeast Asia successfully created internal technical capacity. Cf. Johnson (1982) (Japan); Wade (1990) (Taiwan); Amsden (1989) (Korea); Weiss (1995) (all three).
6. For example, Petronas, the national oil company, depended heavily (and still does) on technology from Exxon and Shell. But perhaps the most famous of these partnerships is the involvement of Mitsubishi as the technology partner in the national car company, Proton.
7. The inhabitants of both countries could access the education and training institutions of the other as if they were in their own country. For example, the people of Malaya could register at the National University of Singapore and receive resident tuition.
8. Many argue that the decision was also politically prudent. Lee Kuan Yew's faction within the PAP was closely allied with the British. Politically the English educated elites of the Lee faction were pitted against the Chinese-educated elites of organized labor. Even after the labor elite was removed from power, it was in the best interest of the Lee faction to further distance organized labor from its traditional Chinese roots.
9. Initially Bumiputra referred to Malays. The classification of Bumiputra was subse-quently enlarged to include all 'indigenous' peoples of Malaysia (everyone except those that had immigrated after British colonial control was established).
10. Author interview at the Ministry of Human Resources, December 2000.
11. This said, when they work, the state-run training centers have a distinct advantage over

other training facilities in Malaysia. This is because they draw heavily on their private sector partners, usually foreign MNCs for trainers, equipment and other resources. Unfortunately, only Penang has experienced unqualified success, while the Selangor Human Resource Development Center has experienced more modest success. It remains to be seen whether the rest of the centers will be able to build the private sector linkages needed to succeed.

12. Actually the Ministry of the Interior focused on education at the village level. Ironically, that meant that the Ministry also oversees education run by the Bangkok Metropolitan Area.

13. Both bodies are part of the prime minister's office, like the EPU in Malaysia.

14. Author interview. See Chapter 6 for more details.

15. On another level, when countries choose to emphasize technological development in primary commodity industries, intellectual capital is drawn away from potentially higher-productivity manufacturing industries, resulting in an intellectual 'Dutch disease.' This problem, however, does not result in a mismatched allocation of intellectual capital. Although the country forgoes some level of productivity gains associated with manufacturing, demand for skills and knowledge matches supply. Nevertheless, there is evidence that intellectual capital needed for the manufacturing sector is prone to stronger externalities from learning by doing than skills used in the primary resource sectors (Sachs and Warner, 1997). As Auty puts it, 'the East Asian combination of a more intensive agricultural system and a larger and also initially less capital-intensive manufacturing sector makes greater demands on skills than does the combination of primary product exports and import substitution industry of Latin America' (1998: 20).

16. This is a necessary but not sufficient argument. In other words, while technological development requires the interdependent participation of these actors, a techno-nationalist strategy does not guarantee such interaction.

17. This differs from the traditional view that tariffs were implemented primarily to generate revenue for the government. See Nipon and Fuller (1997).

18. Author's interview with a former Minister of Science, Technology, and the Environment, April 2001.

19. Ironically, when it became clear that the government did not have the expertise to run the ventures, they invited the Chinese who had previously owned them to return and run them (Crouch, 1996). Afterwards, instead of venturing into the market themselves, political elites chose to partner with Chinese–Thai economic mavens, much as in Malaysia.

20. Much of this analysis is taken from Rajah Rasiah's 'politics, institutions, and flexibility: microelectronics, transnationals, and machine tool linkages in Malaysia' (forthcoming), a comparison of institutional structure in Penang and the Klang Valley.

21. Author interview, PDC, 1998.

22. Author interview, PSDC and PDC, summer 1998. By 1998 there were 80 board-level companies, all large multinationals, that participated in the Center's education and training programs. From an initial small building the PSDC had grown to three large buildings and trained over 10 000 people per year by 1998.

23. Author interviews with various private firms and the PDC.

24. From an interview with the PSDC I learned that labor groups were active supporters of training programs at the PSDC. This support, however, was more moral than financial or knowledge-based.

25. Author interview, SHRDC, November 2000.

6. The legacies of initial choices

Since 1995, children in the USA have made significant gains in math scores. This is good news to many, as it is widely believed that proficiency in technical subjects like math and science are key to sustaining innovative economies. But as the scores of the children in the USA climb, so too do those of the children in some of the countries in Asia, only faster. The edge that these Asian countries, notably Singapore and Taiwan, have in math and science keeps growing.[1]

This growing gap between education and training outcomes is due, in large part, to early decisions made decades ago during periods of institutional formation and change. The point is that institutions for education and training created in response to preferences generated by coalitional politics are vulnerable to both economic and political increasing returns.[2] Large set-up costs, learning effects and adaptive expectations make coordinated and interconnected activities and institutions more effective than fragmented and isolated efforts (Ritchie, 2005a). As important, the collective nature of education and training systems, the density of its policies and institutions, its vulnerability to politics, and the complexity and opacity of its operations mean that interests can easily become vested over time and that paths once chosen are not easily changed.[3] Once formed, institutional systems feed back into coalitional politics. In the case of Malaysia, Singapore and Thailand, early decisions regarding language, bureaucracy, labor and technology have all influenced increasing returns from both an economic and a political perspective.

The other important observation stemming from increasing returns is that outcomes turn on decisions and choices, many of which often seem small and insignificant at the time, and which are made often long before the observed outcome. These critical decision junctures are critical precisely because they spawn legacies. In other words, the range of future choices is constrained by past decisions. This concept, known as path dependence, is a pattern of change wherein outcomes during a crucial transition establish distinct trajectories (Collier and Collier, 1991).[4] Or as Paul A. David says somewhat more concisely: 'one damn thing follows another' (quoted in Collier and Collier, 1991: 27).

This definition of path dependence, however, is overly broad and simply 'refers to the causal relevance of preceding stages in a temporal sequence' (Pierson, 2000: 252). After Pierson, I adopt a narrow definition of path dependence[5] in which path dependence is accompanied by increasing returns (ibid.). That is, prior events do not simply lead to particular outcomes with the option of changing paths at any time. Rather, preceding steps down a certain path induce future movement in the same direction. As one moves along a certain path, the relative benefits of remaining on that path increase compared to other options.

Education and training processes are subject to both economic and political increasing returns. Economists describe increasing returns as virtuous cycles of increasing capacity and endogenous growth (Buchanan, 1994). Increasing political returns, on the other hand, can be accurately depicted as increasing 'vested' interests (Pierson, 2000). First I shall examine the influence of increasing economic returns on education and training systems, after which I shall analyze the effects of increasing political returns.

INCREASING ECONOMIC RETURNS

Decreasing returns have long been utilized in economics to search for unique equilibria. If one can determine existing factor endowments and preferences, a single, optimum outcome, or equilibrium, can be determined. Decreasing returns generate negative feedback, making each step away from the equilibrium harder than the last. New economic research, however, is increasingly focusing on path dependence and increasing returns. Particularly important for this research has been the work of new growth theorists who argue that economic growth is endogenously driven, especially when it comes to technology (Romer, 1994). Increasing returns are evident in intangible investment, particularly in R&D and education and training. These 'knowledge intensive' activities generate positive rather than negative feedback. Feedback effects are strongest when set-up and fixed costs are large and where there are significant learning effects, coordination effects and adaptive expectations. Policies, processes and institutions designed to develop technical intellectual capital exhibit each of these tendencies in spades.

Large Set-up or Fixed Costs

Education systems require a tremendous amount of fixed costs. Buildings, libraries, phones, computers, teacher training and so forth require significant resources. In 1998, Malaysia spent 19.51 percent of its total government expenditures and almost 5 percent of total GNP on education alone (not including training) (Malaysian Ministry of Education, 2000). By 2005 those figures had increased to 25.2 percent and 6.2 percent respectively (UNESCO). The mean for education expenditures in Organisation for Economic Co-operation and Development (OECD) countries for the late 1990s was 5.9 percent of GNP (Malaysian Ministry of Education, 2000). By 2005 the average across all countries reporting was 4.9 percent (UNESCO). Singapore spent 3 percent of GNP on education in 1999 and 4 percent in 2005, with 28 percent of per capita GNP spent on tertiary education in both years (World Bank, 2000). Thailand spent 4.14 percent of GNP on education, placing it between Malaysia and Singapore. Large set-up costs and long and often uncertain investment maturities virtually require that governments be involved in the initial creation as well as ongoing maintenance of some portion of the education and training system.

Learning Effects

Those involved in operating education and training systems learn by doing. As the system begins to educate and train people in priority fields of study, innovations, expertise and advancements are made in these areas. Expertise, innovations and advancements feed back to the system, improving capacity in certain areas while diminishing it in others. Learning effects either reinforce the match between skills developed by the education and training system and the demand of private sector firms, or they exacerbate the mismatch.

In Thailand the modern education and training system was oriented around proper citizenship, democratic participation and traditional economic activities, primarily rice agriculture and handicrafts (Muscat, 1994; Cleesuntorn, 1987). Those educated in the system were those available to become new trainers. Thus Thailand was able to develop respectable agricultural scientists. Over time Thailand has pursued a more foreign-investment-led development strategy. As the number of manufacturing and service companies has grown, agriculture, and especially the rice industry, has consistently declined as a percentage of overall GNP. And yet, as late as the mid-1990s, agricultural R&D still made up, by one estimate, over 50 percent of all R&D (Arnold et al., 2000).

The problem is that without linkages to the private sector, the education and training system lacks the expertise to develop the technical intellectual talent needed by the new industries. For example, Thailand underwent an education boom in the early 1970s in which hundreds of thousands of new vocational school and university graduates matriculated into the labor force. Nevertheless, only about 25 percent were able to find jobs in the rural areas and 50 percent in Bangkok (Anderson, 1998: 156). While aggregate levels of demand certainly influenced these numbers, the bigger problem was that graduating students did not obtain the skills and knowledge needed by the manufacturing sector.

Twenty years later, the situation had not improved. In 1995 Thailand graduated 61 students with advanced degrees in science and engineering. From this number, two were engineers of any type, seven were agricultural scientists and 23 were doctors. In 1996 two were engineers, 13 were agricultural scientists and 21 were doctors. In 1997 the numbers were three, 10 and 11, and in 1998, two, 11 and 23. Enrolment data don't promise any quick changes. In 1995, 54 percent of tertiary students were enrolled in science and technology fields and 46 percent enrolled in social sciences. In 1996 the ratio was 40 percent to 60 percent. Although the numbers recover in 1997 and 1998 to 42 percent to 58 percent, and then 51 percent to 49 percent, the bulk of the increase in science and technology enrolment is in medicine and medical related fields (NSTDA, unpublished data).

Even within NECTEC (National Electronics and Computer Technology Center), which was created to do industry-relevant science and technology research, the priority focus is on lobbying and politics. A well-respected researcher at the Thailand Development Research Institute explained how NECTEC was the most active science and technology policy-making body within the Ministry of Science, Technology, and the Environment. Ironically, all of the top researchers at NECTEC are involved in lobbying and spend the bulk of their time sitting in policy-making and deliberating councils. This researcher lamented that the 'best brains' in Thailand were not engaged in scientific and technological research.[6]

As in Thailand, Malaysia's education system continues to focus on primary commodities, especially palm oil and rubber. Industrial focus, however, is now on industrial development. As part of the Promotion of Investments Act in 1986, the Malaysian Industrial Development Authority (MIDA) was formed with a mandate to aggressively solicit foreign investment through tax and other investment incentives. As Malaysia increasingly promotes technological development through high-tech MNCs, the demand for technologists has shifted and is now heavily concentrated in electronics and other manufacturing industries.

And yet Malaysia has also not been able to meet this new demand. In 2001 only 39.8 percent of first-degree enrollment at private institutions and 41 percent of first-degree enrollment in public institutions are studying technical subjects. Graduation figures are similar. A total of 63.7 percent of first-degree graduates in 2001 were in the humanities and social sciences. Master and doctoral degree enrollments favor humanities and social sciences by 62.6 percent and 54.5 percent respectively.[7] A study by the Ministry of Education in 2000 found that only around 28 percent of those in primary and secondary education are electing to take science and technology courses.[8]

For both Thailand and Malaysia the problem has become one of transitioning the social knowledge base away from primary products and toward more technology- and science-based industries. However, while physical capital is readily reallocated to new industrial ventures, learning effects make reallocating intellectual capital much more difficult. How, for example, does one rapidly undo a lifetime of learning as an agricultural scientist and then reform oneself as an expert in chemical or electrical science and processes? Technologies have trajectories: scientists and engineers continue with their area of expertise, and people can teach only what they know. Ultimately, new technical expertise, knowledge and skills must be absorbed into or developed within the system before they can be transferred to students.

Unlike that in Thailand and Malaysia, Singapore's system has been built to create industrial skills and technical capacity. Here, 61.4 percent of first-degree enrollment is pursuing technical subjects (unlike Thailand, Singapore counts medical students separately from scientists and engineers). Likewise, 51.5 percent of first-degree graduates graduate with a technical degree (Singapore Ministry of Education, 2000). Thus there are tremendous learning effects between the education and training system and public and private economic actors.

Coordination Effects

The benefits of a chosen path are enhanced when individual or organizational activities are integrated with those of other individuals or organizations. Although this coordination can be formally designed, created and nurtured, just as often it is informal. That is, certain choices will maximize the return for one group of actors precisely because it builds upon a set of choices made by a different group. These groups may never formally coordinate their activities. Nevertheless, each group's choices are based, at least in part, on the decisions of the others. Increasing integration amplifies feedback effects of initial institutional and policy choices.

Coordination effects, with both positive and negative outcomes, are especially obvious in all three countries between the education and training system and public research initiatives, research initiatives and private firms, and private firms and the education and training system. Every actor within this triangular relationship participates in a self-reinforcing cycle of technological development on the one hand or stagnation on the other. The way these relationships interact is instructive.

To begin with, public research initiatives are constrained by the intellectual capacity developed in the education system. Simultaneously, public sector research and development initiatives feed back to the education system. Thus early decisions to conduct research in a particular field create demand for researchers in these fields. Increasing expertise within the research institutes leads to educators trained in these fields. The coordination effects magnify technological gains in the chosen industries. When technological capacity in education, training and public research match the demand of private firms, society is in a position to maximize innovation and technological development.

Singapore has planned for and continues to nurture coordination between its public research institutes and its education and training system, thereby amplifying the development of manufacturing process and product technology demanded by the private sector. In Malaysia and Thailand the coordination has been much more *ad hoc* and perpetuates a technological mismatch between the education and training system and the public research agenda on the one side and private firms on the other.

To illustrate, leading up to the Asian financial crisis, public research and development initiatives and expenditures in Malaysia closely matched the output of the education and training system. In 1998,[9] 77.8 percent (4072) of public sector R&D personnel were involved in primary commodity research. But, by comparison, only 11.4 percent (475) of R&D personnel in the private sector were similarly involved in primary commodity research. Investment in R&D broken down by public and private sector tells a related story (see Table 6.1). Comparing the private sector's 81.59 percent of total investment in manufacturing, science and technology compared to the public sector's 49.19 percent puts this disparity in sharp relief. Indeed, the figures for 1994 and 1996 paint an even starker picture. For example, in 1996 the Malaysian Institute for Microelectronic Systems (MIMOS) had 21 R&D personnel and spent just over RM 4 million on R&D. To Malaysia's credit, in 1998 this same organization spent over RM 93 million and increased its personnel to 216. Nevertheless, there is still some way to go before matching the 1793 researchers at the Malaysian Agricultural Research Institute.[10] Also, there are still few if any *formal* linkages between public research institutes and the education system. The end result is that neither local nor foreign firms are linked significantly to the education and training system. And, without a sufficient base of technical intellectual capital, foreign technology has been slow to transfer into local companies.

In an effort to increase the capability and value-added of local manufacturing, the Thai government created several government-to-government research institutes in the early to mid-1950s, the most visible being with Germany and Japan. Linkages between the institutes and the private

Table 6.1 *Malaysian R&D expenditures*

R&D objective	Total expenditure (millions of RM)							
	GRI*		IHL*		Total Public Sector		Private	
	RM	% of total	RM	% of total	RM	% of total	RM	% of total
Agriculture	75.20	30.00	29.90	22.30	105.10	27.58	30.90	4.100
Animal prod.	6.40	2.00	2.50	1.80	8.90	2.30	0.00	0.000
Mineral resources	0.30	0.12	0.36	0.26	0.66	0.17	0.05	0.006
Energy resources	0.42	0.16	1.14	0.85	1.56	0.40	76.00	10.100
Other nat. resources	7.30	2.90	1.80	1.30	9.10	2.38	0.04	0.005
Total primary products	89.62	36.20	35.70	26.71	125.32	32.89	106.99	14.300
Manufacturing	28.80	11.64	48.80	36.51	77.60	20.37	506.00	67.820
Infocomm	92.00	37.20	4.40	3.30	96.40	25.30	83.00	11.120
Natural sci., tech., eng.	4.90	1.90	8.50	6.30	13.40	3.50	19.70	2.600
Total mfg, tech. and sci.	125.70	50.82	61.70	46.17	187.40	49.19	608.70	81.590

Note: *GRI = government research institute; IHL = institute of higher learning (public).

Source: 1998 Malaysian Science and Technology Indicators Report, MASTIC.

sector in the area of training as well as research were minimal, however, and foreign support for the institutes was dropped when they were combined into the King Mongkut Institute of Technology.[11]

In 1991 the Thai government created three technology research institutes under the National Science and Technology Development Agency (NSTDA): the National Electronic and Computer Technology Center (NECTEC), the National Center for Genetic Engineering and Biotechnology (BIOTEC) and the National Metals and Materials Technology Center (MTEC). These centers conduct direct research and training as well as provide incentives for local firms, especially SMIs (small and medium industries), to conduct research and training. Unlike their counterparts in Malaysia, these centers are marginally more connected to universities, with several research laboratories located in various university departments. Still, the number of researchers and research projects focused on these new cutting-edge technology industries is disappointingly small. In one striking example, the Thailand Institute of Scientific and Technical Research (TISTR) has 31 high-profile research initiatives of which 25, or 80 percent, are based on primary commodity industries.[12]

As Table 6.2 shows, coordination effects have led to a large mismatch of technical intellectual capital between the public and private sectors in both Malaysia and Thailand, especially for the computer and electronics industries during the financial crisis. In both countries the number of public sector researchers focused on primary commodity industries outnumbers those in electronics and computers by as much as a factor of 10. Mismatches in technical talent between the public and private sector have made coordination effects through technical liaisons between the two unlikely.

For example, the Innovation Development Fund overseen by the NSTDA, which was initially funded with 100 million baht for between 90 and 100 projects, received 62 proposals of which it initially funded three with between 5 and 8 million baht per project.[13] Similarly, the World Bank, in its Country Economic Monitor for Thailand, reports that only 3–5 percent of industrial firms have used the services of any of a range of public-sector science and technology programs (World Bank, 2002).

While the emphasis on IT technology is much more visible in Malaysia, the underlying outcomes are similar. In 1999 the government earmarked 300 million RM to fund promising R&D. One year later, Maybank, the bank designated to evaluate proposals and distribute funds, approved no projects and made zero investments. When asked why, the director of the program cited insufficient capacity to evaluate technical proposals. Although the ratios are better for the Multimedia Development Corporation's investment arm and investment funds at the Malaysian

Table 6.2   Congruence between public and private intellectual capital investment before the crisis (%)

	Malaysia	Singapore	Thailand
GERD (% of GDP)	0.69 (2002)	2.25 (2004)	0.26 (2003)
Public sector RSEs in primary commodity research	77.80	0.92	47.88
Private sector RSEs in primary commodity research	11.4	0.14	24.6 (1997)
Public R&D expenditure on primary commodity research	32.89	2.2	39.69
Private R&D expenditure on primary commodity research	14.3	0.23	7.19
Primary commodity exports (% of exports)	24 (1995)	14 (1995)[a]	26 (1995)
Private sector RSEs in electrical and electronics industry	18.08	28.2	7.9[b]
Public sector RSEs in electrical and electronics	6.49	26.1	0.7[c]
Total R&D expenditure for electronics industry	28.37	45.25	33.2[d]

Notes:
[a]   Virtually 100% of this number consists of re-exports.
[b]   Computer and communication technologies.
[c]   Computer and communication technologies.
[d]   Private sector only.

Sources: Singapore National Science and Technology Board, *National Survey of R&D in Singapore*, 1999. MASTIC, *1998 Malaysian Science and Technology Indicators Report*, 2000. National Science and Technology Development Agency, 1999, *Thailand Science and Technology Profile, 1999*. World Bank Development Indicators, various years.

Technology Development Corporation, in no case was more than 50 percent of allocated funds invested.[14]

By contrast, Table 6.2 shows that in Singapore, public and private sector researchers are evenly matched by research agenda. In Singapore, public research institutes, institutes of higher learning and the private sector are closely integrated and coordinated in their development activities. Instead of functioning as stand-alone research facilities, the government-designed public research institutes operate in conjunction with institutes for higher learning and the private sector. Between 1992 and 1998 the National Science and Technology Board (NSTB) created 13 public research institutes. Because the universities were already developing the human resources in areas needed by these institutes, logistically it made sense to locate these institutes on or near to the university campuses. To ensure tight linkages between the institutes and the universities, researchers at the universities, primarily university professors, were assigned to the research institutes, thus emphasizing research as the core of the university system. Then, although the government initially funded the public institutes, private firms were offered 'memberships' to participate in the research activities. Membership dues and joint development projects formed the foundation for the institute's ongoing revenues.

Technological capacity developed within the research institutes is also effectively transferred back to the education and training system through the institute-based university faculty. But technology is also transferred through students. Students doing research in the areas covered by these institutes are assigned to the appropriate institute for their junior- and senior-year projects and for masters and PhD. theses. Through the institutes many of these students are placed at member companies for internships. After completing their degree, the students often go to work for the firms for whom they were interns. It is not unusual for these new employees to find themselves back at the research institute on a regular basis working on joint projects.[15] These intertwining relationships reinforce the technological trajectory that is shaped by complex interactions between public and private actors.

When education and training systems are highly coordinated with public research initiatives, either intentionally or by default, and these do not match R&D priorities of the private sector, then by extension linkages between the education and training system and private firms are also likely to suffer. Without these coordinating linkages, government often misunderstands the human resource needs of the private sector. Three examples from Thailand and one from Malaysia demonstrate this.

In the first, at a local seminar to further the hard disk drive industry in Thailand, the president of a local firm supplying high-precision parts to the multinational hard disk drive firms needed master tool and die craftsmen. Unable to find such skills in the local economy, the firm created an in-house apprenticeship training facility and hired a master craftsman from India to run it. Over time the firm began to build internal capacity for training master tool and die craftsmen. But the effort was expensive. The company therefore approached the government about expanding the in-house training facility into a national Thai tool and die institute. In this way the firm would receive government support for skills development in an area it needed and, like Singapore, workers with highly sought-after skills could be developed for other firms and other industries. In spite of the benefits, the government was unresponsive. Later, when confronted at the industry seminar, a representative from the Ministry of Labor claimed that a training facility was already developing such craftsmen in Thailand, whereupon the firm's president trenchantly noted that if this were true, only two, equally damning conclusions, could be drawn: either the government was unable to communicate to the private sector the availability of these trained craftsmen; or, more likely, the government was not producing master craftsmen that met his firm's needs. In the end, the only reasonable conclusion to be drawn was that when it came to the industry's needs for master tool and die craftsmen, there existed a complete disconnect between business and government.[16]

In an extremely similar case, an official at the National Economic and Social Development Board explained how the Thai Productivity Institute had been assisting the development of the local furniture industry. According to her, one of the most pressing needs of this industry was for training programs that could produce much higher-skilled master craftsmen, especially those that could operate new high-tech shaping and forming equipment. To this appeal, an official at the Ministry of Labor and Social Welfare responded that such training programs already existed in her department. The conclusions drawn by the president of the hard disk drive company also apply here, except that this disconnect is also within government as well as between government and the private sector.[17]

Third, the Ministry of Labor and Social Welfare spends US$153 million on new training programs and infrastructure, a significant portion of which is targeted to developing IT-related skills. Nevertheless, the private sector has not been hiring the graduates. According to one report, not one employee at Seagate, the largest IT employer in the country, had been through the training.[18] Officials at the ministry concede that the courses are not sophisticated enough to be useful to technologically intensive firms.[19] And yet there is virtually no communication with those firms that might potentially hire the graduates of the new program as to how the initiative might be usefully modified.[20]

In the fourth example, matching skills to development initiatives has also hindered technological development in Malaysia. Taking the very visible Multimedia Super Corridor (MSC) as an example, several anchor 'world-class technology' firms have expressed concern over the amount and level of technical talent. The company presidents of these firms, in town for the advisory panel meeting, revealed that their decision to invest in the MSC was as much political as economic, and that currently the technical capacity did not exist to do any serious R&D. All stressed that this did not mean that such capacity would never exist and that the venture would not be successful, but that increasing investment, innovation and technological progress would depend on large quantities of technical human resources being available in the very near term.[21]

Unfortunately, the ability of the flagship university in the MSC, the

Multimedia University (MMU), to develop this talent seems to be declining rather than improving. For example, one visiting US professor in the Department of Creative Multimedia reports that only three of 50 professors have PhDs and two of these are in fields unrelated to the department. He also observed that in the last year, three or four other professors with PhDs, all foreign nationals, have left MMU for other positions. Other sources reveal that the intellectual credentials in the other departments at the university are similar.[22] Indeed, the Dean of Social Sciences at the Universiti Kebangsaan Malaysia (National University of Malaysia) revealed that after 30 years of trying to build a base of faculty with PhDs at the public universities, the very best departments' faculties have less than 50 percent PhD holders.[23] But even when faculty have PhDs, the universities do not emphasize research, nor create an environment where meaningful research is possible. The same is also true in Thailand.

Finally, language continues to obstruct coordinating linkages between private firms and the education and training system in Malaysia and Thailand. To illustrate, by the early 1970s, Thailand had reoriented its economic growth strategy toward export-oriented industrialization. But rather than upgrade its existing industrial structure, the government chose to pursue FDI to operate in geographically circumscribed export manufacturing zones. In 1977 the Thai government passed the Investment Promotion Act, which reoriented the Board of Investments to provide investment-oriented tax incentives for both foreign and local capital. Foreign firms soon dominated whole industries, especially automobiles, electricals and electronics, and petrochemicals.[24] With this rise in foreign ownership, language as a barrier to moving technology from foreign to local firms also rose. Since few, if any, foreign technologists were able to participate in the local education and training system, the country has been able to transfer and absorb foreign technologies only to the extent that it can train local engineers who are fluent in English. Even then, however, the process of translation before diffusion is time-consuming and difficult.

Two examples illustrate the problem. First, the Software Park of Thailand partnered with the Ratchamongkol Institutes for Technical Education to develop badly needed software engineers through a series of advanced software engineering courses. However, it is unclear whether a sufficient number of technically trained, English-speaking instructors can be found. Even if this first hurdle can be overcome, there is concern that the students, primarily upper vocational level, do not have sufficient English language skills to make the courses successful. Preliminary tests were encouraging, but even if these students have the comprehension capacity to learn the technology, few have the speaking skills to become teachers themselves.[25]

And second, the Thai–Japan Technology Promotion Association was created to help transfer technologies from Japanese MNCs to local Thai firms. However, the institute reports that the bulk of its training focuses not on technologies, but on Japanese language training for Thai workers in Japanese companies and Thai language training for Japanese executives managing Thai-based Japanese companies.[26] Before any technology can be transferred between foreign and local firms (or between foreign firms and the education and training system), language barriers must be removed.

Malaysia struggles with similar problems. As one senior director at MOSTE lamented, it is still virtually impossible to link foreign firms and the domestic education and training system together to provide technical training as there continues to be a tremendous deficit of competent Malay-speaking teachers and trainers.[27]

Adaptive Expectations

Closely associated with both learning and coordination effects are adaptive expectations. If the risk is high that decisions made today will fail to win broad approval in the future, the tendency is for actors to 'pick the right horse.'[28] Put simply, expectations about future outcomes lead actors to adapt their behavior in such a way as to make those expectations come true.

Adaptive expectations are also clearly evident in education and training. In Singapore a clear and rational structure of education and training institutions and processes provides a reasonable expectation that long-term education and training success is most likely to be achieved from working within, or in harmony with, the system. Singapore has a single, well-integrated education and training system that starts with the Institute of Technical Education (ITE) and moves through the polytechnics and then to the university. For those already in the workforce, the National Trades Union Congress (NTUC), Productivity and Standards Board (PSB) and private corporations are the primary providers of training. Nevertheless, these organizations primarily rely on the ITEs and the polytechnics to actually do the training. All of the certificates, diplomas and degrees are standardized throughout the system, making it desirable and easy for actors to make choices that reinforce the cohesiveness and interrelated nature of the institutional system.

In Malaysia and Thailand, however, there are no clear-cut patterns. Fragmented bureaucracies and marginalized labor groups make it difficult to choose the 'right horse,' indeed even the 'right stable,' which perpetuates fragmentation within the education and training system in both countries.

In Malaysia training opportunities have mushroomed in the last few

years. Over 600 private education and training institutions are now registered with the government. In the public sphere one can, especially if
one is Bumiputra, opt for training at MARA's advanced government-
to-government training institutes,[29] the Ministry of Human Resources'
Advanced Technical Training Centers, the Ministry of Youth and Sports
IKTBN (national youth and sports higher skills training institute), or
the Ministry of Education's planned community colleges or polytechnics.
Although MARA, the Ministry of Youth and Sports and the Ministry
of Human Resources all subscribe to the standards set by the National
Vocational Training Council, the Ministry of Education does not.
Furthermore, all are either awarding tertiary-level degrees, or plan to do
so soon.

The same level of confusion and overlap exists in Thailand. Among
options for vocational education, for example, one can choose from the
Thai Ratchamongkol institutes which have recently also begun to offer
four-year bachelor degrees, the Ratchapat Institutes, the Department
of Vocational Education training institutes, and the community colleges, all of which reside within the Ministry of Education. Confusion
increases when one takes into account the vocational and diploma training programs that exist in the Ministry of Industry, Science, Agriculture,
Commerce and so forth. The point is that the standards of these education
and training programs vary and private firms are often confused about the
relative worth of the various certificates, diplomas and degrees.

INCREASING POLITICAL RETURNS

In addition to being prone to economic increasing returns, early decisions made in the education and training system are also prone to political increasing returns. Four characteristics of the education and training
system make it especially vulnerable to increasing returns of a political
nature, including the collective nature of education and training politics,
its institutional density, political authority and power asymmetries within
the education and training system, and the complexity and opacity of
politics and policies related to education and training. Unlike increasing
returns in economics, these conditions make it difficult to find a single
equilibrium outcome. Instead, many outcomes are possible.

Collective Nature of Education and Training Policies and Institutions

The preferred outcomes of government policy are very often collective, if
not public, goods. Although most education and training policy demands

some level of collective action, initiatives to develop technical knowledge and skills are especially demanding, since to succeed they require the active participation of groups outside of government, especially business, but also academia and labor. When nationalization, ethnic harmony or citizenship is the focus of education and training systems, fewer formal and informal linkages are required with groups outside of government. Therefore societies that prefer education and training systems to be organized around economic development choose to create institutions that foster dense institutional public–private linkages. Such has been the case in Japan, Korea, Taiwan and Singapore, although the organization of these linkages in each country varies dramatically. In particular, the linkages in Singapore are much broader than those in the Northeast Asian countries and include linkages between education and training institutions, private business, academia, labor and the government. On the other hand, those that organize education and training around political priorities need fewer such linkages. Without a collective effort to rationalize the institutional structure, it tends to develop in fragmented and disconnected ways that inhibit future collective action when it becomes necessary to enhance the provision of public goods associated with technological development.

To demonstrate, the Malaysian government has been emphasizing a transition to a knowledge-based economy since the mid-1990s.[30] The Third Outline Perspective Program specifies that, to reach this goal, a significant number of people must be educated and trained in technology-related knowledge and skills. Nevertheless, ethnic quotas in the public education and training system have inhibited this drive. In spite of a tremendous deficiency of technical skills, the 55:45 ratio of Bumiputra to non-Bumiputra quota still exists for university placement. Yet, owing to the insufficient number of qualified Bumiputra students, there were 7168 places at the country's 14 public universities that went unfilled in 2000. This means that the Ministry of Education has rejected almost 169 000 qualified secondary school graduates, even though places were available at the university.[31] Equally troubling, many of these Chinese and Indian students were from low-income families and could not afford to continue their education overseas or in the private sector. The government, however, is paralyzed to address the problem. If it acts to remedy the problem it upsets the agreed-upon ethnic contract and guarantees itself the loss of a significant proportion of ethnic Malay political support. By not acting, short-term political unrest can be averted, but long-term economic success is jeopardized. Unless the contract is rewritten, which can only be done successfully with input from a broad range of social actors, the result will be continued economic mediocrity.

The output of the education and training system also impacts actor's preferences for collective action in other, but related, areas. Although the connections are often difficult to discern on the surface, education and training has a particularly strong influence on a country's trade regime. In Thailand and Malaysia, low quantities of technical intellectual capital have made it difficult for MNCs to upgrade labor-intensive industries to technology-intensive ones. Harder hit, however, has been the innovative capacity of local firms. Meager levels of technical knowledge and skills severely restrict the ability of local firms to compete in the global economy. To survive, local firms in both countries have had to secure ongoing government protection in the form of trade tariffs and subsidies.

To illustrate, in the early 1970s, government officials implemented steps to attract export-oriented foreign investment to address balance-of-trade and unemployment problems. But, at the same time, the state increasingly sought to protect local industry through trade barriers. Nipon and Fuller (1997: 480) describe this condition in Thailand as 'export-oriented protectionism.' By 1985 the nominal rate of protection for Thai manufacturing was 52 percent. As import-competing firms became increasingly dependent on government protection, and as the ministries of Industry, Commerce and Finance became accustomed to tariff-generated revenue, a vicious cycle of declining technical competence and rising revenue dependence made reforming the tariff structure increasingly difficult. The result has been an intensifying of 'de-linked dualism.'

Protecting local industry without requiring that it upgrade technologically in return has had at least three negative consequences. First, rents associated with trade policies lessen the pressure local firms feel to upgrade technologically. As one official at the NSTDA in Thailand put it, 'tariffs designed to protect domestic industries have done nothing to help these firms develop technological capabilities.'[32] As technical capacity stagnates, local firms are less likely to forge productive relationships with technology-rich MNCs. Second, tariffs often increase the costs of product inputs for local firms. Thus protection makes it difficult for local firms to compete on either cost or quality. Finally, as possibilities for productive linkages between local and MNCs dim, the gulf between them grows and local firms become ever more dependent on, and become more aggressive in seeking for, government protection.

Politicians can also benefit from tariffs and subsidies, especially where a narrow coalitional structure favors personal, crony-promoting relationships. Consider the historical penchant of Thai firms to provide politicians with an economic annuity, usually in the form of a board or advisory position, in return for protection from foreign and domestic competition.[33] In the end, neither firms nor politicians have any incentive to change the system.[34]

Finally, collective dilemmas have made reform difficult. Although some bureaucratic reform has been initiated in both Malaysia and Thailand, it centers on the prime minister, with little rationalization of the line ministry structure. Coordination between the various ministries on education and training also remains low. In one stark case, the Malaysian government created a National Vocational and Training Council to establish standardized vocational training courses and certificates. Although both MARA and the Ministry of Youth and Sports opted to participate, the Ministry of Education refused to submit to the council and stubbornly championed an alternative system of standards and courses. In the words of a high-level official at the Ministry of Education, 'Let the consumer decide between the two standards.' The problem is that the 'consumer' is paying little attention to the training coming from either camp and has little means to distinguish between the two.[35] Finally, even though many within the government argue that fragmentation is not a problem since a proliferation of training centers is necessary to meet demand,[36] increasing numbers of training and education centers are stretching an already thin layer of technically competent instructors even thinner.

Although Singapore faces many of the same obstacles, the outcomes here differ from those in Malaysia and Thailand. First, protecting the local market for indigenous firms was never a viable economic strategy, especially after separation from Malaysia. Instead, economic and political vulnerability put tremendous pressure on the education system to develop the technical intellectual capital necessary to compete in the global economy. Thus the government took proactive steps to link the bureaucracy to the MNCs and the MNCs to local capital. Because of its unwillingness to protect local industry, the Singapore government was initially seen as hostile to local capital. In fact, however, the government took early and extensive measures to assist local firms, not through trade protection, but through technology transfer, education and training, technology diffusion and technological upgrading. Since there were no rents generated by the trade regime, politicians secured political legitimacy and economic actors made profits by forming broad coalitions to develop public goods that would most efficiently expand the overall economic pie. Despite the fact that foreign capital was initially favored in these relationships, over the last two decades government has increasingly emphasized the development of indigenous firms.[37]

Institutional Density of Education Policies and Institutions

Education and training systems are institutionally dense for several reasons. First, as mentioned above, they must often deal with issues of collective action, such as capital accumulation, risk aversion and free-riding, which requires capacity to coordinate, monitor, evaluate, reward and punish. Second, education is one of the great social equalizers and has ramifications for social hierarchies. Both those interested in equality as well as those who desire *status quo* or increasing inequality must manipulate education and training policies and institutions to achieve their ends. The more political and social interests that must be served by the system, the more dense are the policies and institutions. The degree to which societies focus on political versus economic outcomes dramatically influences the density of political institutions within education and training. Third, education and training systems must deliver products and services to meet a wide range of economic demands, interests and activities. Again, as the number of these demands, interests and activities increases, so does institutional and policy density.

Once created, either intentionally or by default, policies and institutions are incredibly durable (North, 1990). As Pierson states, 'policies, grounded in law and backed by the coercive power of the state, signal to actors what has to be done and what cannot be done, and they establish many of the rewards and penalties associated with particular activities.' Moreover, he goes on to explain that institutions '[discipline] expectations about the behavior of others,' making them increasingly prone to feedback and path dependence (2000: 259). But perhaps the most important cause of path dependence among political policies and institutions is that they are created to be resistant to change, resulting in a strong bias for the *status quo*. But to the extent that stand-alone institutions are durable, dense systems of institutions can be virtually impervious to change.

For example, in Thailand the entire education system was initially constructed as part of the civil service. Kindergarten teachers up through university professors are considered career bureaucrats. As such, they are extremely difficult to remove when they underperform. Indeed, until recently there was no performance system attached to promotion within the Thai university system except 'seat time.' Once hired, professors are considered to have immediate tenure, with virtually no requirements for research or excellence in teaching. In response, professors often spend little time at the university campus and instead moonlight in the private sector.

For almost 30 years now reform-minded politicians have tried to de-link the education system, at least at the university level, from the civil service. Nevertheless, persistent vested interests throughout Thailand's institutional system have repeatedly torpedoed the efforts. In 1996, the Asian Development Bank (ADB) and the Ministry of University Affairs developed a plan to 'corporatize' the universities. Instead of funding the universities with line-item budgets, the government would give a yearly lump-sum grant budget. These funds could be used as the university saw fit. Additional funds, however, would need to be secured from the private sector in the form of joint research or other profit-making activities. The ADB would provide bridge funding as the universities got up and running on the new system. But when it came time to implement the plans for university autonomy, university professors desiring to remain part of the civil service as well as intense bureaucratic turf battles between the Ministry of Education and the Ministry of University Affairs scuttled these attempts.[38] The places where autonomy has been most successful is in the institutions, such as the King Mongkut Institute of Technology campuses, that were never part of the government and, hence, whose professors were never civil servants.

In an attempt to end-run the vested interests, constitutional framers included a mandate for educational reform in the new constitution. As part of this initiative, the government passed the Education Reform Act of 1999, which specifies that all universities must be autonomous by the year 2003. Some have already done so. Others, including Chulalongkorn and Thammasat, are moving much more slowly. Even when transition has been mandated by law and constitution, there are still people – academics, politicians, analysts and journalists – who have been down this road enough times to know that interconnecting vested interests from myriad sources may still win out.[39] Indeed, ten years later in 2009, only a handful of the country's universities are completely autonomous.

Intertwining policies and institutions surrounding the New Economic Plan (NEP) in Malaysia have similarly resisted reformation. Although the plan was replaced with the New Development Plan (NDP) in 1990, Jomo notes that the NEP has continued to function despite being officially replaced. UMNO has even called for its return.[40] While it is clear that the NEP has not achieved what was initially hoped for (both in general economic terms as well as in education and training), it is difficult to deny that the education and skill levels of the majority Bumiputra population have not risen dramatically, and that even though Bumiputras do not own 30 percent of economic assets as originally targeted, the 20 percent they do own is a far cry from the 2 percent they began with in the early 1970s. Nevertheless, it is becoming increasingly clear that NEP-era policies and institutions are becoming a drag on economic development. Many within and without the system report that ethnic Malays feel entitled to the assistance they receive and do not perform as they might if affirmative action assistance were not available.[41] Also, as shown in the above quota example, the country is wasting key human capital it can ill afford to do without. But in addition to unfilled university positions, quotas also impact academic positions: highly skilled Chinese and Indians PhDs are leaving to work in Singapore and other countries. In what is by no means an isolated example, one of the deans in the Faculty of Engineering at the National University of Singapore is a Malaysian-born Chinese.[42] Yet, in spite of their increasingly negative economic impact, their embedded nature as well as their importance to social stability makes NEP policies and institutions difficult to change.

Singapore's education and training system is also institutionally dense. At first glance it even appears to be somewhat fragmented. Three ministries have responsibility for education and training – the Ministry of Trade and Industry, the Ministry of Education and the Ministry of Manpower. Nevertheless, here the density of institutional linkages acts to coordinate and complement the activities of each ministry while encouraging participation from the private sector. Particularly important is the coordinating role played by the EDB and the Ministry of Trade and Industry. The EDB identifies critical technological needs in society and then works within the formal education and training system and with private actors to ensure the supply of skills to meet those needs.

The important point is that increasing institutional density leads to structural inertia. Where institutional systems 'lock in' to developmental trajectories, they are difficult to derail. Likewise, where 'lock-in' occurs on distributional trajectories, it is difficult even to get the train on the track.

Political Authority and Power Asymmetries in Education and Training

Feedback from dense institutional systems magnifies power asymmetries while at the same time rendering these relationships less visible (Pierson, 2000).[43] The nature of the education system in all three countries allocates power to certain actors and then reinforces that power in a self-perpetuating way. Education and training systems are a source of power for a number of reasons.

First, they are useful for disseminating political and social ideology. In other words, education is a tool for maintaining political power and social identity and can be the battlefield on which groups vie for influence. This conflict can be seen clearly in Malaysia, where the Malay-dominated education ministry is pushing for ethnic assimilation and control while at the same time Malaysian Chinese, and to a lesser extent Indian, education leaders push for autonomy and distance from the government. On the other hand, since the Singapore government derives its legitimacy primarily from economic expansion, education is designed to further political power through economic development. Thus it is not that education in Singapore is apolitical, but rather that political aspirations coincide with economic development, and these aspirations are broadly shared by both public and private actors. Indicative of this prioritization is the Ministry of Trade and Industry's aegis over the education system.

Second, because of the pervasive influence education has on the lives of a country's inhabitants, leadership positions within the education system carry significant power and influence. Thus contending social groups place a high priority on controlling some aspect of the education and training system, preferably for the entire country, but at least among its own. In Malaysia, for example, MARA provides pre- and post-employment training and formal education for Bumiputras. The Ministry of Youth and Sports concentrates on training youth, but because of its strong Islamic foundation also focuses primarily on the Bumiputra. Control of the two main ministries, the Ministry of Education and the Ministry of Human Resources, is shared between the Malays and Chinese. The necessity of sharing power among these ministries speaks to their social and political power and influence.

The struggle for control is equally evident in class-based politics. Although labor in Thailand is formally included in a tripartite bargaining arrangement, its power remains weak. Without any real influence, 'workers' organizations revert to wildcat actions such as organized sick leaves and pre-work/post-work rallies. Management in turn frequently reacts with selective lockouts, in which union leaders and supporters are kept out of the workplace while operations continue with non-unionists and new hires' (Deyo and Doner, 2001: 111). Even so, according to the Ministry of Labor and Social Welfare, labor is free to bargain collectively, strike, or otherwise pursue its purposes and agenda. Nonetheless, labor has not engaged in extensive training and education. In what is an especially telling situation, organized labor is not even included in the training programs developed and implemented by the Ministry of Labor and Social Welfare, which is the state organ for managing labor relationships and the development of the labor force.[44] In the government's recently released policy statement, nowhere in the labor development policy section is there any mention of improving labor's tie with technical education and training.[45]

Relationships with labor in Malaysia are even more dismal. Labor is largely uninvolved in the federal- and state-level education and training centers. And while the Malaysian Trades Union Congress does have its own training facility, it is very small and technical courses are very few.[46]

In contrast, although labor in Singapore has been traditionally weak in areas such as collective wage bargaining, it is very involved in the forming and implementing of human resource development policy.[47] As I show in the next chapter, labor is exhibiting increasing political power in issues surrounding education and training.

Finally, since education systems redistribute both economic and political power, vested interests are high and change is difficult. When Suqiu, the Malaysian Chinese Organizations' Election Appeals Committee, suggested that current affirmative action policies, including those for education and training, be changed to apply on a per need basis, dramatic opposition erupted, especially from Malay students. Rather than being seen as a catalyst for change, the group was accused of violating the social contract reached during independence and members of the group were labeled as political extremists.[48] Nevertheless, high-ranking government officials privately admit that to be competitive in a global, knowledge-intensive economy, the education and training system must be reformed away from ethnic imperatives.[49]

Yet rather than implement reform from the ground up and negotiate the rock-strewn coastline of ethnic redistribution, government officials have found it easier to create new systems on top of old, which has further exacerbated fragmentation. The prime minister has created a mini-bureaucratic structure within his office that operates above the constraints of the affirmative action system. This dual system makes it possible for the government to act quickly and decisively, unconstrained by previous bureaucratic institutions and policies, while at the same time maintaining a focus on ethnic redistribution at the lower line-ministry level.

Centralizing policy-making in the prime minister's office, however, has not been accompanied by policy-making responsibility and capacity at the line ministries. This tendency is especially clear with respect to the development of science and technology capacity. The chief science and technology policy-making body is no longer the Ministry of Science and Technology, but the Science and Technology Advisor to the Prime Minister. Likewise for technical education and training. Although the multitude of line ministries responsible for education and training implement individual strategies and programs, strategic education and training policy is carried out by the EPU, again a member of the prime minister's office. Instead of reforming bureaucratic fragmentation at the line level, these ministries play a diminishing role in strategic policy-making.

Also, whereas the line ministries are obligated to implement policy within their existing institutional structure, which is subject to previous NEP laws and regulations, the prime minister's office increasingly implements policy through wholly or majority-owned government corporations. In this way the prime minister's office maintains control of the implementation and exempts itself from the drag of redistributionary laws, all the while seeming to maintain support for the same redistributionary laws it is avoiding. Thus the Multimedia Development Corporation is elevated over the MIDA as the investment coordinating body for all high-tech investment in the country. The Malaysian Technology Development Corporation takes the lead in venture capital startups and technopreneur incubation projects over the Ministry of Science, Technology and the Environment. And so forth. Ultimately, reform is *ad hoc* and patchwork, and does not address the underlying issues that are hindering further economic progress in other sectors.

In a particularly striking example, the flagship university around which the MSC was initially conceived and developed was not a government public university, but rather a private university. A private university was chosen because it would not be subject to the affirmative action policies of the NEP. To ensure control of the university, however, the government had Telekom Malaysia, a corporation 70 percent owned by the government, build and run it. This way the government can exercise direct control for economic purposes without being beholden to (or seen as betraying) the very policies and institutions it created for other political purposes.[50]

A similar pattern of centralizing bureaucratic power in the prime minister's office has occurred in Thailand. Hundreds of advisors to the prime minister are slowly accumulating power and influence, especially in areas such as science and technology, where the line ministries have not been traditionally strong. In Thaksin's government, the chief science advisor was a former employee of NECTEC. After assuming power, he declared that the Software Park of Thailand, NECTEC and the national Internet project would be moved out from under the NSTDA and the MOSTE and placed under his purview. Needless to say, others had different objectives and ideas. Turf battles erupted that diminished cooperative capacity and left initiatives underfunded and undersupported. Interestingly, bureaucratic initiatives in Thailand are most highly sought after when they prove successful. An official at the Software Park of Thailand explained that when the idea to develop the software industry in Thailand was first suggested, representatives from the ministries of industry, commerce, education, interior, finance and so forth – virtually every ministry – were invited to participate. No one came. But after the project received initial funding, several ministries, including industry and commerce, stepped forward and laid claims to the project. The future and ownership of the project was then debated among the Ministry of Science, its subsidiary organization NSTDA, the Ministry of Industry, the Ministry of Communication, and the office of the Chief Science Advisor in the Office of the Prime Minister.

Again, Singapore's approach has been different. Rather than create additional bureaucratic layers, it has increasingly pushed responsibility for both policy creation and implementation away from the center and out to the line ministries. Ironically, the system encourages government to share decision-making power and influence with private actors. With skills development, overall policy direction and objectives are created in committees comprising representatives from government, business, labor and academia. The Manpower 21 initiative to recreate policies and institutions to develop world-class human talent, skills and knowledge is a good example. There are five committees: the Steering Committee; the Manpower Development Committee; the Manpower Industry Committee; the Manpower Unlimited Committee; and the Workplace Environment Committee. Members of the Steering Committee chair the other sub-committees. Private business leaders chair two of the sub-committees, while representatives from labor and academia chair the remaining two sub-committees. The membership of each committee is made up of representatives from business, academia, government and labor. In addition, there are working groups, study missions, focus group consultations, dialogue sessions, tripartite consultations (management, labor and government), and consultations with business associations that incorporate hundreds of firms, unions, business associations, government and bureaucratic officials, and educational and training institutes in order to develop relevant direction for useful human resource policy. After direction is established, lower-level working committees throughout the government develop the policies and coordinate their implementation.[51] Within the Skills Development Fund (SDF), for example, power to develop and implement policies that respond to the Manpower 21 initiative resides in the working committee.

Other government ministries and agencies have their own versions of Manpower 21, such as the EDB's Industry 21 plan. These high-level plans reference one another and are tightly integrated, evidencing a tight interconnection within government agencies and the committee structures they create to facilitate the policy creation process.

Complexity and Opacity of Education and Training Policies and Institutions

Elaborate procedures to handle collective choice dilemmas, institutional density, and political authority and power asymmetries necessarily increase the institutional complexity and opacity of education and training systems. Much of this convolution and murkiness is possible because it is difficult to measure the performance of the education and training system. Although numbers of degrees and certificates indicate raw quantities of those educated and trained, the quality of that training, or changes in quality, is difficult to ascertain immediately. Further complicating issues of measurement is the relatively long lag time between acquiring skills and their actual use in the marketplace. Finally, it is not often clear what metric society prefers to use when judging its education and training system. Since politicians, and indeed even firms, come and go in the interim, learning effects are often minimal and *status quo* biases are strong. Measurement difficulties lead to reduced monitoring and outside checks and balances. Again, vested interests in the existing system can easily develop, often resulting in debilitating corruption.

Insofar as both domestic and international actors scrutinize macroeconomic policies and procedures, when corruption does occur it is usually discovered, albeit often in grand and spectacular scandal. On the other hand, education and training systems offer myriad ways to channel resources from one group to another so that it is difficult to detect. Large budgets for property development, building construction, school maintenance, and ongoing equipment and materials purchasing requirements provide opportunities for kickbacks, favoritism and other forms of corruption.

Four institutional characteristics influence corruption and inefficiencies born of complexity and opacity: aggregate levels of bureaucratic fragmentation; duplication of activities; cross-organizational management; and top-down coordination. Whereas bureaucratic divisions and duplicative operations encourage separate budgets and infrastructures, cross-organizational management and top-down coordination add transparency to institutional structures.

Lack of transparency born of fragmentation has made it easy for political leaders in Malaysia and Thailand to use bureaucratic leadership posts as political rewards and sinecures. In both countries, ranking positions in the ministries responsible for education and training are filled according to political considerations, with little attention to previous education and training experience. In Malaysia, rising young political stars usually orbit through the Ministry of Education. In fact, virtually every prime minister and deputy prime minister in Malaysia's history has at one time or another been Minister of Education. As opposed to the political fast track in Malaysia, Thailand uses its education positions as safe-pasture rewards for political cronies. Appointment processes are rife with nepotism and cronyism: choice plums that provide economic pickings in compensation for political favors.[52] In the end, although the purposes differ, the outcomes are similar in both countries: appointments based on nepotism, cronyism or political power with little regard to expertise. Finding or creating spots for such people provides political 'perks' and creates a base of political support within the bureaucracy, but little focused, technocratic expertise on education and training.

In Thailand, institutional complexity and opacity, heightened by bureaucratic fragmentation, have caused education and training policy to be mired in corruption, patronage and cronyism. This corruption, however, was not always so evident and appears to be a legacy of bureaucratic politicization and segmentation where political appointees responsible for the education and training system lacked technocratic talent.

Traditionally it has been the powerful Ministries of Finance, Industry, or Communications that were often at the center of extravagant corruption scandals. But Pasuk and Sungsidh (1994) note that the Ministry of Education is fast closing the gap. In 1970–72 the Ministry of Industry accounted for 55 percent of all corruption cases while the Ministry of Education accounted for only 5 percent. But between 1981 and 1987 the number of corruption cases in the Ministry of Education climbed to 17 percent. By 1989 the Ministry of Education had become the fourth most corrupt government agency in Thailand, misusing or misappropriating over 12 billion baht (1994: 30–31).

Specific examples abound. In one case, the Counter Corruption Commission in Thailand uncovered an operation where millions of baht were being stolen when government officials colluded with suppliers to pocket the difference between high-quality products being ordered and low-quality products being delivered (Pasuk and Sungsidh, 1994). In another, a high-ranking official at the Office of the National Education Commission (ONEC) explained how politicians in the prime minister's department required that the ONEC purchase outdated computers for local schools from a preferred and politically connected vendor at premium prices.[53]

Unfortunately, since the education and training bureaucracy remains highly fragmented, the expectation is that such practices will continue. Nevertheless, the Education Act of 1999 stipulates that all education-related activities, and the associated budgets, will be centralized under a new Ministry of Education, Religion and Culture. Indications from ONEC, however, are that the Ministry of the Interior will likely resist any divesture of its budgetary control.[54]

Opacity and complexity in the Malaysian education and training system, again driven mainly by fragmentation, also results in misallocation and questionable activities. In what is fast becoming the mantra for education reformists, Malaysia's education system is a lesson in contrasts. On the one hand, the new 'smart schools' MSC initiative is putting computers in many of the primary and secondary schools. Initially rolled out in 90 schools in 1999, the program was scheduled to complete all schools over the next few years. At the same time, however, thousands of secondary and primary schools still lack basic infrastructure services, especially electricity. But even those schools that have computers complain that few are connected to the Internet and productive software is scarce.

Singapore's education and training system, although equally complex, is much more transparent than that of either Malaysia or Thailand. In particular, the extensive interconnections within the bureaucracy and between the bureaucracy and private actors foster rationalization, transparency, and checks and balances. Since most education and training initiatives are designed and implemented in multiple ministries and with significant (and often leading) help from private actors, the budget information behind the project must be accurate and easily accessible.

Transparency is fostered in two ways. First, the entire education and training system is characterized by high-level, cross-cutting committees and groups designed to coordinate, facilitate and direct projects. Most of these committees are *ad hoc* and temporary, and include members from academia, business, labor and government. Second, a dense committee structure also characterizes the lower levels of the education and training system. Here, however, the committees are permanent (members revolve but the structure remains) and while lower-level committees plan and direct in conjunction with higher-level committees, at the lower level they are primarily concerned with implementing, monitoring, evaluating and disciplining participants.

The important point is that the lower-level committee structure in Singapore is cross-organizational. Thus, at the point where corruption can occur most readily, multiple groups monitor behavior. The SDF technical committee, for example, is made up of three labor representatives, nine representatives of private industry, and one government employee, and is chaired by two chief executive officers from the private sector. This committee works under the supervision of the board of directors for the PSB, which has a similar makeup.

This system of interacting committees facilitates interdependent cooperation and coordination. Rather than create separate infrastructures to pursue topic-specific training, ministries in Singapore must work within existing programs and frameworks when they exist. The coordinating ministry is the Ministry of Manpower. For its part, the Ministry of Manpower does not design any specific training programs, but works with the submitting agency to develop feasible training plans, both within private firms and in the ministry, depending on the need and capabilities of the various actors. But beyond this, the proposing ministry often finds it advantageous to partner with other ministries and agencies to achieve its own ends. For example, the Infocomm Development Authority (IDA), a statutory board under the Ministry of Communications and Information Technology, which was created through a merger of the National Computer Board and the Telecommunication Authority of Singapore, recently undertook an ambitious project to increase the number of IT workers in Singapore.

To accomplish this objective the IDA established the critical IT resource program (CITREP).

CITREP is at its core a long list of partnerships with existing programs tailored to fit the needs of the IDA. First, the IDA works with the NSTB and Contact Singapore in the Industrial–Academia Partnership Program to work with institutes of higher learning to attract top infocomm professors and lecturers to work in Singapore. The priority is to develop local teaching staff skilled in infocomm technologies. Second, the IDA partners with the PSB to encourage corporations to adopt the PSB's People Developer Standard, an in-house training program run in conjunction with the MoM (Ministry of Manpower), and implement annual training plans that train employees in core infocomm technologies. To help transition employees from non-infocomm-related jobs into the infocomm sector, the IDA has teamed up with the NTUC to participate in its Skills Redevelopment Program (more on this in Chapter 7) and the Strategic Manpower Conversion Program. Fourth, the IDA, the Singapore Computer Society and the Singapore IT Federation established the Infocomm Skills Recognition Framework, with guidance and funding from the IDA, PSB and the MoM, to set benchmark standards for infocomm related skills.[55]

High-level coordinating committees for technology development in general and technical education and training in particular have also mushroomed over the last decade or so in Malaysia. The National Vocational Training Council, the Malaysian Business Council (MBC), the Malaysian Industry Group for High Technology, and the K-economy master plan committee (now the 3rd Outline Perspective Program) all provide top-level, functional connections. Nevertheless, although functionally connected at the top, there is little participation at the mid- to lower levels from firms and academia, and virtually no connection with labor. These bodies solicit input, but do not institutionalize direct participation in the decision-making process. In other words, the government extracts information, but gives no opportunity for private actors to embed within the government. When firms do participate, it is usually local, often government-owned firms who lack the technological expertise to provide reliable input on issues of technological upgrading.

In Thailand, the National Economic and Social Development Board, the Office of the National Education Commission and the National Technology Committee, as well as numerous other top-level committees, function very much like those in Malaysia. In both Thailand and Malaysia inter-ministerial committees are fairly durable, becoming over time yet another component of the bureaucracy; in Singapore, however, those same high-level coordinating bodies are rapidly constructed and dismantled according to changing needs. On the other hand, it is the lower- to mid-level committees in Singapore – those that have so successfully integrated a wide range of private economic actors into the process of forming and implementing public policy – that are more permanent, precisely those bodies that are missing in Malaysia and Thailand. Without coordination and oversight among multiple groups at the point of implementation, corrupt and inefficient policies and initiatives are far more likely.

CONCLUSION

Arguments based on a framework of increasing returns are easily criticized as being deterministic: events, once set in motion, are impossible to stop. But as difficult as change might be, it is always possible. As North (1990) observes, mechanisms of reproduction erode or are swamped, making possible new, often dramatic, directions. Even so, this change is bounded, and institutionally dense systems, such as education and training, are prone to inertia.

The central finding of this chapter is that key decisions, made within an existing coalitional and institutional structure, molded preferences and capacities for an institutional system that in turn encouraged or hindered in a path-dependent way the formation of technical intellectual capital. I have argued that four of these decisions – language of instruction in the education and training system; the level of fragmentation in the bureaucracy; whether or not to include labor in the policy creation and implementation process; and the direction and emphasis of technology development – had an especially far-reaching impact on the institutional makeup of each country's education and training system.

In Thailand, pressure to adopt languages other than Thai as the medium of instruction or to emphasize manufacturing technologies in the education and training system did not exist. Also, purposive decisions were made to expand and segment the bureaucracy, leading to politically motivated bureaucratic fragmentation.[56] Just as often, however, bureaucratic fragmentation resulted because the government was unwilling or unable to make choices to consolidate and rationalize the bureaucratic structure.[57] Bureaucratic fragmentation within the education and training system made it easier for state actors to pull a curtain across an inefficient and corrupt stage of state processes and practices that underlay distributionary policies and institutions. Equally problematic, without a pressing need to develop technical skills in the general workforce, relationships with labor were based on political priorities, primarily containing communism, but eventually also creating a compliant workforce that was MNC-friendly.

And finally, choices for technological focus centered on primary products even though exports were growing most quickly in high-tech products, which led to a mismatch of skills (see Table 6.3 for a comparison of growth rates for different sectors leading up to the Asian financial crisis).

In Singapore, English was chosen as the language of instruction throughout the education and training system. A rational and technocratic bureaucracy was established with dense interconnecting linkages throughout the state. Through high pay and an informal linkage-based system of checks and balances, corruption was virtually eradicated.[58] Labor was formally included in the political system and, although initially weak, has gained influence and power over time, especially in areas regarding education and training. Lastly, without a natural resource endowment to rely on, industrial technology quickly became the country's economic focus.

In Malaysia, preferences for both ethnic domination and ethnic harmony led Malaysia to select Malay as the language of instruction. Although at the higher levels of the state the institutional structure is relatively cohesive, at the line-ministry level the bureaucracy is fragmented, duplicative and inefficient. Much of this bureaucratic segmentation was intentional, to meet the needs of both ethnic redistribution and political patronage. Examples of government bailouts of politically connected economic cronies, such as Malaysian Airlines, Putra and Star Rail, Time.com, Renong and others, provide evidence that such practices are still in favor. Third, as in Thailand, organized labor has been completely disconnected from the formal education and training system. And lastly, technological focus remains mired in commodity product industries despite the tremendous transition of the economy toward manufacturing industries, especially electronics.

Unlike either Thailand or Singapore, Malaysia's institutional structure was created to balance the needs of a narrow elite-based coalition with the minimal demands of distinct, ethnic-based mass groups. Today, this balancing act has resulted in a disjointed, somewhat schizophrenic combination of state autonomy, rationality and foresight, coupled with fragmentation, corruption, inefficiencies and ineffectiveness. When compared to Thailand, such features as technical development, innovation, improved skills and knowledge, and industrial transformation are all much more top-of-mind, top-of-press and top-of-rhetoric. Institutional infrastructure development seems to match the verbal commitment: dramatic increases in technical university, vocational and secondary education and training schools and programs; R&D initiatives including technology parks, incubators and university labs; and thoughtful planning and foresight initiatives to map future technological development.

Nonetheless, education and training and R&D initiatives focus almost

Table 6.3 *Primary exports – Thailand*

Principal exports	Major export items (Millions of baht)					Growth rate (%)			
	1993	1994	1995	1996	1997	1994	1995	1996	1997
Textile products	116670	133471	142441	118521	147402	14.4	6.72	-16.79	24.37
Computers and parts	62745	92059	128432	165240	227738	46.72	39.51	28.66	37.85
Integrated circuits and parts	35550	45307	58149	58483	75741	27.45	28.34	0.57	29.51
Precious stones and jewelry	41031	44684	49946	51494	52847	8.9	11.78	3.1	2.63
Footwear	27935	39256	53751	33508	35243	40.53	36.92	-37.66	5.18
Electrical appliances	62634	88126	102848	106569	134865	40.7	16.71	3.62	26.55
Canned food	42986	50308	53291	57125	73659	17.03	5.93	7.19	28.94
Rice	32947	39187	48627	50737	65088	18.94	24.09	4.34	28.29
Tapioca products	21736	18733	18253	20649	22457	-13.63	-2.77	13.13	8.76
Rubber	29181	41821	61261	63370	57447	43.32	46.48	3.44	-9.35
Shrimps	37842	49156	50302	43400	47184	29.9	2.33	-13.72	8.72
Frozen fowl	9295	10223	10047	9398	11272	9.98	-1.72	-6.46	19.94
Telecommunications equipments	9648	9898	10746	12814	15888	2.59	8.57	19.24	23.99
Vehicle parts and accessories	13226	19980	16341	18848	33581	51.07	-18.21	15.34	78.17
Plastic products	39453	30350	62156	31591	49643	-23.07	104.8	-49.17	57.14
Total principal exports	582879	712599	866591	841747	1050100	22.26	21.61	-2.87	24.75

Source: World Bank Development Indicators, 2004.

146

exclusively on bricks-and-mortar development where opportunities for cronies and clients remain high. Technical capacities of university and vocational faculties has not significantly changed, nor has the number of research-capable scientists, engineers and technicians graduating with technical and scientific degrees.[59]

In the next chapter I extend the institutional argument to show how institutional legacies within the state hinder or encourage the formation of dense and frequent public–private linkages. The focus of the chapter is on the operation of institutions rather than their formation. Specifically, I show how dense and frequent public–private linkages are able to resolve key collective dilemmas to develop high levels of technical intellectual capital.

NOTES

1. 'US students improve in math, science, but some Asian countries have edge in math that keeps growing.' Associated Press, 9 Dec. 2008.
2. Economic increasing returns are described by Buchanan (1994) as virtuous cycles of increasing capacity and endogenous growth. Political increasing returns can be characterized as 'vested' interests and path dependent phenomena (Pierson, 2000).
3. A common criticism of path-dependent theoretical frameworks is that they are overly deterministic. But as much as path dependency matters in my analysis, the reality is that at each step in the causal process social actors had the possibility of choosing to alter their trajectories, even if only slightly. Nevertheless, it is often the case that prior conditions create powerful preferences for particular outcomes, rendering decisions to change trajectories increasingly difficult to make.
4. See also Steinmo et al. (1992) for an excellent review on the place of path dependence in historical institutional analysis.
5. This section is structured around and draws heavily on Paul Pierson's excellent theoretical treatise on increasing returns (2000).
6. Author interview, May 2001.
7. Malaysian educational data come from MASTIC (2006).
8. Author interview, Ministry of Education, Department of Higher Education, November 2000.
9. The year 1998 was the last occasion on which MASTIC organized R&D statistics around specific industries and sectors in this form.
10. Malaysia is already spending significantly more per researcher at MIMOS than at the Malaysian Agricultural Research Center. All these figures come from MASTIC (various years).
11. Both the Germans and Japanese have since re-established joint training and technology institutes with the Thai Ministry of Industry. Nevertheless, while the institutes are fairly well connected to the foreign MNCs, there are few if any linkages with local firms or the education and training system (author interview, Thailand Development Research Institute, April 2001).
12. www.tistr.or.th
13. 'Innovation fund to ask state for B2bn' *Bangkok Post*, 9 May 2001.
14. Author interview with MTDC, MDC and MOSTE. See also 'Maybank yet to give out VC funds.' *Sunbiz*, 30 October 2000.
15. Author interview, Data Storage Institute, August 2000.

16. Thai Hard Disk Drive Industry Conference, 1998, Queen Sirikit Convention Center.
17. This happened while I was presenting a paper at the NSTDA in Bangkok, 20 April 2001.
18. 'Laboring under a misapprehension,' *Bangkok Post*, 17 June 1998.
19. Author interview, Ministry of Labor and Social Welfare, 2001.
20. Ibid.
21. 'Compaq, SGI chiefs: IT staff shortage in MSC a concern,' Malaysia.CNET.com. Monday, 27 November 2000. I am also indebted to Rajah Rasiah and several anonymous sources at the MDC for similar information from other, Japanese-based, multinational firms.
22. Author interviews at MMU, October 2000 and April 2001.
23. Author interview with the Dean of Social Sciences, University Kebangsaan Malaysia, November 2000.
24. On the political economy behind these industries, see Doner (1992) (automobiles), Felker (1998 dissertation) (electronics), and McKendrick et al. (2000) (hard disk drives).
25. Author interview, Software Park of Thailand, 2001.
26. Author interview, TDRI, June 2001.
27. Author interview at the Ministry of Science and Technology, December 2000.
28. This is the phrase Pierson uses to describe the impulse to adapt to the option that appears most likely to succeed in the long term.
29. These include institutes that have been set up with help from the UK, Germany, Spain, France and the USA.
30. All three countries are emphasizing the need for an economic shift to a 'knowledge-based' economy (I prefer the term knowledge-intensive economy). Interestingly, Malaysia and Singapore seem to be equally focused on the task, if government rhetoric is used as the metric. In contrast, not nearly so much is being said in Thailand, although the issue is still clearly important.
31. 'Quota System Doesn't Add Up,' *Bangkok Post*, 15 May 2001.
32. Author interview, NSTDA, May 2001.
33. Doner and Ramsay (1997) have argued that if competition exists among patron–client groups, then monopoly rents can be avoided. Even so, there is no reason to expect, *ex ante*, that the groups will cooperate or that through competition broader productive linkages will emerge between government actors and local firms.
34. Becoming a member of the WTO, which was necessary to ensure that foreign markets remain open to Thai products, is putting external pressure on Thailand to reform its trade policies. Recently, the government lifted the requirement that carmakers source at least 54 percent of their products locally. Local parts manufacturers 'don't have the technology or volume' to compete with international suppliers and are not likely to survive ('Out of the Driver's Seat,' *Far Eastern Economic Review*, 17 August 2000, p. 46).
35. Author interview, Ministry of Education, January 2001.
36. Demand, however, may not be what the government thinks it is. The government's measure of demand is simply the number of those eligible to enrol in education and training facilities and the number that actually do. This, however, does not measure the true demand of the population for such services. The actual number wanting to enroll in education and training facilities is most likely much smaller than the government thinks.
37. Author interview, NSTB, September 2000.
38. Author interview, Brooker Group, 1998 and TDRI, May 2001.
39. Even as I write this, the Education Reform Office is under siege by the Ministry of Education to reform the reform plan. Rather than see the Ministry's 14 departments cut to five as planned, the Ministry is fighting to keep at least eight. Also, rather than agree to 295 municipal education zones, the Ministry wants 142. The Education Reform Office accuses the Ministry of Education of trying to cling to power by undermining reform efforts to decentralize power to local bodies. Ironically, the reform plans have

only been approved by the opposition Chart Thai and Democrat Parties. The Reform panel still seeks the approval of the ruling Thai Rak Thai and Chart Pattana parties. Clearly the reform efforts are anything but battened down; political gales could still blow the goods off the ship. 'Ministry attempt to alter reform plan runs into opposition,' *Bangkok Post*, 20 May 2001.

40. Romen Bose, 'Racial tensions on rise in Malaysia,' *Al Jazeera*, 17 November 2006.
41. Author interviews, especially MFI, October 2000.
42. Author interview.
43. See Gaventa (1980) for an insightful analysis of the faces of power and the transition from the obvious to the less obvious implementation of that power.
44. Author interview. Ministry of Labor and Social Welfare, Skills Development Department, April 2001.
45. Policy of the government of H.E. Prime Minister Thaksin Shinawatra, delivered to the National Assembly on Monday, 26 February 2001 (unofficial translation).
46. Author interview, NTUC, 7 September 2000.
47. Ibid.
48. See 'Government will fight all kinds of extremists: Najib,' *The Sun*, 13 December 2000.
49. Author interview.
50. Author interviews.
51. 'Manpower 21: Vision of a Talent Capital,' Singapore Ministry of Manpower, 1999.
52. Ministerial leaders in both countries often have no relevant experience and do little to advance needed reform or performance. For example, in Thailand a recent prime minister's daughter, who had no relevant experience or qualifications, was appointed Deputy Education Minister. When Thaksin was elected, he was widely praised for finally appointing a minister of education who had at one point been an educator himself. Nevertheless, all but two of the 43 advisors to the minister are Thai Rak Thai (the Prime Minister's Party) cronies, most of them failed election candidates of the party from the Northeast. To a person, none has any credentials that lends themselves to an advisory position in the ministry ('Minister's army of advisers draws flak from academics,' *Bangkok Post*, 3 May 2001).
53. Author interview, ONEC, April 2001.
54. Ibid.
55. See www.ida.gov.sg
56. For example, tertiary education was divided between the Ministry of University Affairs and the Ministry of Education. Also, vocational education was divided between the Department of Vocational Education, the Ratchamongkol Institutes, and the Community Colleges.
57. For example, when the Ratchapat Institutes were decommissioned as teachers' colleges they were set up as yet another vocational education training structure rather than being folded into one of the existing systems.
58. Transparency International gives Singapore its highest transparency score: 10. To give one an idea of salary levels, a mid-level bureaucrat at the Singapore Department of Statistics revealed to me that his salary was higher than the official salary paid to Malaysia's prime minister, Dr Mahatir Mohammad. Whereas beginning professors in Thailand and Malaysia earn about the same as a hardworking taxi driver, in Singapore they earn the same as an entry-level manager in the private sector.
59. There is some evidence that the quantity of output is changing slowly. One encouraging data point is the self-reported rise in technical researchers in Malaysia from around 80 to more than 400 per million capita between 1994 and 1998. If true, the figures give rise to optimism and suggest that perhaps new policies and institutions simply need more time to work. These measurements, however, are notoriously difficult to make, and a more reliable source, like the World Bank or UNESCO, report no such increase. Also, even if the new figures are accurate, they still pale beside the more than 3000 researchers per million capita in Singapore or the more than 6000 in Japan.

7. Institutional formation and skills development

Development theory suggests that institutions that foster 'embedded autonomy,' create capacity needed to upgrade technologically (Evans, 1995). This chapter explores how institutions in Malaysia, Singapore and Thailand operate to create the tight, integrated linkages within the public sector and between public and private actors needed for embedded autonomy to function. As earlier chapters explained, institutional formation during critical junctures led to particular orientations of intra-bureaucratic processes and operation. At the same time, initial decisions of language, bureaucracy, labor and technology led to the creation of institutions that shaped the degree to which the education and training system was able to operate with tight integrated linkages to the private sector. Where bureaucracies were highly linked in rational operation and also tightly connected to the private sector, technological upgrading flourished.

While it is possible to see the impact of the types of connective relationships described above in many different economic policies and initiatives associated with upgrading, three in particular reveal clearly the differences among the knowledge creation systems in Malaysia, Singapore and Thailand. What makes the comparison in the three areas particularly useful is that all three countries aggressively pursued each initiative. The first initiative is the formation and operation of a 'skills development fund' designed to overcome 'poaching' dilemmas by subsidizing the supply of technically skilled and knowledgeable workers. The second initiative is the creation of a government investment promotion agency to create agglomeration economies of high-tech firms. Incentives aimed at upgrading the technological content of investment drive demand for technical intellectual capital by increasing technical sophistication of products and processes within foreign MNCs and then by increasing the rate at which those technologies are transferred, adopted and absorbed into locally owned, indigenous firms. The third initiative is the formation of jointly funded and operated public–private collaborative research institutes. These collaborative institutions are important insofar as they promote early-stage (pre-commercial), basic, de-risking and scale-up R&D.[1]

The importance of these initiatives reflects changing global economic realities in which developing countries must form capacities to leverage technological assets and resources of MNCs. While globalist strategies are often conflated with economic liberalization and thought to justify the dismantling of non-market economic institutions, this is true only if countries abandon completely the objective of developing indigenous technological capacity. Ironically, creating, nurturing and maintaining indigenous technological capacity through techno-globalist strategies in the face of increasing liberalization is in fact *more* institutionally challenging, especially as it demands coordinating both market and non-market institutions to develop technical intellectual capital.

The remainder of this chapter first evaluates how connections do or do not operate within the state bureaucracy and then between the state and private economic actors. It then compares efforts in each country to implement a skills development grant-levy fund to encourage increased supply of technical intellectual capital. Next, it contrasts mechanisms targeted at fostering demand through investment incentives, local industry upgrading initiatives, and efforts to create agglomeration economies.[2] Finally it examines how public research institutes operate to weld together supply and demand for technical knowledge and skills. The analysis runs up until roughly the mid- to late 1990s, before the impact of the Asian financial crisis. The evaluation of subsequent development after the crisis remains for the final chapter.

CONNECTIVE LINKAGES FOR DEVELOPMENT

Linkages within the State

The capacity of the state to coordinate its internal activities is a critical first step before any effective embedding with the private sector can occur. Bureaucracies are most effective when they minimize redundancy and waste while facilitating economies of scale. Functionally differentiated ministries that have decentralized decision-making power but are also tightly coordinated to an overall development strategy are most effective in working with private actors to overcome investment appropriation dilemmas. Whether bureaucratic institutions were formed with this capacity in mind depended greatly on whether elites preferred political over economic objectives or vice versa.

Singapore
The Singapore bureaucracy is highly coordinated and interconnected, giving it a high degree of flexibility and responsiveness. This coordination

makes it possible for the state to provide (1) a national technology strategy that is congruent with and complementary to overarching economic objectives; and (2) 'pay for play' incentives that apply only as firms take concrete steps toward technological capacity and progress.

Integration and coordination happen in a number of ways. First, cross-ministerial connections are widespread throughout the government. Although initiatives designed to improve technical intellectual capital are always assigned to a lead agency, three ministries are virtually always involved in education and training: the Ministry of Trade and Industry (MTI), the Ministry of Manpower (MoM) and the Ministry of Education (MoE).

Within the MTI, the EDB assumes lead responsibility for industry-specific education and training. The MoM is responsible for the Skills Development Fund (SDF), which extracts a levy from firms that can then be used for firm-initiated training. The MoM has two additional responsibilities related to training, including overseeing the manpower development department, which conducts human resource projection and planning previously performed by the EDB and developing training facilities within private firms. The MoE manages, maintains and operates the education system, including a simple but powerful three-tiered tertiary system. The three tiers include the Institutes of Technical Education (ITE), which provide entry-level and basic to mid-level vocational education; four polytechnics that offer mid-level to bachelor-degree-level technical, vocational and management education; and two main universities.

The government ensures that all three ministries work together. Funds for education and training are regularly budgeted to one ministry with the stipulation that the funds can be used only for projects and initiatives jointly specified and implemented with other ministries and departments. For example, funds allocated to the MoM to create internal company training programs have been used by the NTUC for their Skills Redevelopment Program (more on this below), the IDA Ministry (as detailed in Chapter 6) for their Infocomm Skills Development program, and the PSB for their People Developer Standard program.[3] Forcing multiple ministries, departments and agencies to share resources eliminates duplication and corruption, and improves monitoring and evaluation.[4] Ultimately, it is in the interest of these 'responsible' agencies to monitor and evaluate the job that the 'implementing' agencies are doing. Since the implementing agencies often utilize resources allocated to a different, responsible ministry, the incentive is not to jeopardize future opportunities for joint initiatives with shoddy performance on existing programs.[5]

A second way in which the bureaucracy is internally integrated is through the regular rotation of civil servants throughout the bureaucracy.

Civil servants learn certain skills and develop certain contacts within a particular bureaucratic position that are often also useful to other bureaucratic agencies and departments. In one case, a director-level employee of the SDF was loaned to the MoM's Department of Manpower Development for two years to head up projects already being shared by the two agencies and to search for other potentially synergistic projects. Instead of being surprised by this move, the employee expected it as a necessary component of career development within the MTI. The employee also fully expected to be returned to the MTI at some point in the future, although perhaps only after a stint in one or more additional ministries or departments.

The employee pointed to several benefits of such a system. First, having worked at the MTI for over five years, the employee knew the right people, the systems, and the strengths and weaknesses of the agency. Armed with this knowledge, the employee could see where coordinative linkages would be most productive and easily created. Second, linkages were more than just formal committees and meetings. Instead, according to the employee's estimate, 80 percent of contact was informal over lunch and other social activities. Finally, being aware of the budget and monetary systems for both departments made it easy for the employee to detect duplication and waste, and they thus became an outside monitor on the way the PSB's funds were being used.[6]

Thailand

Unlike Singapore's tightly integrated bureaucratic system, Thailand's state bureaucracy is weak and fragmented. Some argue that this weakness is due to the increasingly democratic nature of the Thai political system. Thais point to the focus on technological development when a strong dictator is in power. Examples include the formation of the National Research Council and government-to-government research institutes under General Sarit in the 1950s; the creation of the Ministry of Science and Technology under General Kriangsak in 1979; and the formation of the National Science and Technology Research Institute under the military-supported government of Anand in 1991. Some look wistfully across the border and attribute Malaysia's seemingly more advanced technological progress to the strength of the Malaysian government. The immense popularity of the recent Prime Minister Thaksin Shinawatra was due in large measure to his effective consolidation of state strength through the parliamentary majority of his Thai Rak Thai Party.

But despite Thaksin's consolidation through ministerial rearrangement, bureaucratic linkages are few and weak. Compared to Singapore, there is little resource-sharing, employee-sharing, or cross-monitoring or evaluation. Instead, initiatives are designed and implemented by single agencies. In education and training, various agencies develop independent infrastructure, recruit and train instructors, create curricula and implement programs. In the best cases, the duplication, overlap and waste that follows obscures and frustrates opportunities to cooperate, but in worst cases causes initiatives to work against each other and leads to perverse incentives and distorted outcomes. For example, poor linkages, fragmentation and ministerial rivalries throughout the bureaucracy frustrate coherent and effective technology policy for R&D, technology acquisition, and technology transfer (Doner and Ritchie, 2003). High levels of fragmentation cause the public research institutes to founder under a combination of bureaucratic controls and political interference (McKendrick et al., 2000).[7]

Most efforts to address stovepipe functionality within the bureaucracy have been addressed through coordinating committees, commissions, councils and advisors, most often established in the Prime Minister's Office. For example, to foster technology and innovation, the government created the Ministry of Science, Technology and the Environment (MOSTE) in 1979. Even though on paper the MOSTE is responsible for fostering R&D and creating sufficient scientists and engineers, policy-making related to both functions was increasingly developed in the Prime Minister's Office during Thaksin's time in power and then sent to the line ministries for implementation.[8] Until 2009, The National Information Technology Council (NITC) was the lead agency for both R&D and scientific and technical education and training.[9] Rather than develop coordination with the Ministry of Education (MoE) for education and training, coordination is done through the National Education Commission, another agency in the Prime Minister's Office. The problem is that neither the NITC nor the NEC has any meaningful connections with the line ministries that must ultimately implement, maintain and monitor the policies.[10] Realizing that the current system does not actually link bureaucratic agencies, the government announced a new National Information Bureau to coordinate the activities of the coordinating NITC. The government then split the MOSTE into a ministry of science and technology and a ministry of natural resources and environment.[11] In 2009 the government announced a new innovation coordinating body working through the National Science and Technology Development Agency (NSTDA).

Malaysia

Malaysia, like Singapore, has aggressively attempted to promote and direct technological development; nevertheless, despite the high priority placed on technology policy by the state, outcomes have been mixed.

Malaysia has long been thought to have the most autonomous and capable bureaucratic state in Southeast Asia after Singapore (Crouch, 1984; Jesudason, 1989). A strong bureaucratic state transformed the structure and content of the country's science and technology policy in an attempt to centrally coordinate and support technology development (Rasiah, 1996). Coordination and direction of the country's technology policy was entrusted in 1984 to a science advisor who was appointed as part of the Prime Minister's Office. Under his direction, the Intensification of Research in Priority Areas (IRPA) program was created in 1986 and the Action Plan for Industrial Technology Development (APITD) in 1990. Whereas the first program was designed to consolidate all public R&D funding in one location, the purpose of APITD was to consolidate national technology policy direction in the hands of the prime minister. Other significant policy initiatives during this period included tax incentives for R&D and new public research institutes for specific industrial sectors (Felker, 1999: 20).

Nevertheless, in many ways the reform has been superficial. Rather than directly address underlying problems of line ministry fragmentation, the government continues to add to an already top-heavy structure by concentrating duplicative bureaucratic power in the Prime Minister's Office. For example, the government created peak planning committees, such as the National Science Council, the Malaysian Business Council (MBC), and the Malaysian Industry–Government Group for High Technology (MIGHT) to coordinate private sector participation and involvement in technological development. These activities were previously the responsibility of MOSTE and MITI. Indeed, when these new agencies were set up, no directive to stop performing the same functions has ever been issued to the line ministries previously involved.[12] The Cabinet also formed a new Committee on Science and Technology under the Prime Minister's Office to coordinate and authorize all new technology direction, plans, policy and legislation. In addition, high-profile projects, such as the Multimedia Super Corridor (MSC), conspicuously reside within the prime minister's purview. Here they are allowed to develop free of the normal policy and institutional encumbrances associated with the social contract of special Malay rights.

But while the supra-agencies can avoid ethnic sensitivities, they have conferred little benefit on the traditional line ministries, which remain fragmented and duplicative.[13] Instead of rationalizing and coordinating the activities of the various line ministries, extra bureaucratic layers around the prime minister marginalize the traditional bureaucracy and concentrate power over technological development in the hands of the prime minister. Nevertheless, the infrastructure and budgets to implement policies made by the Prime Minister's Office continue to exist in the line ministries. Thus, rather than coordinating the activities of the line ministries, the new structure increasingly divorces policy-making from policy implementation. In the end there is little coordination either between the top and bottom of this dualistic bureaucratic structure or among the line ministries at the lower level. As in Thailand, each agency, department and ministry responsible for education and training functions independently with stand-alone infrastructures, budgets, curricula and programs.

Linkages between the Public and the Private Sector

Successfully developing and implementing policies designed to further technology development hinge both on state cohesion, capacity and initiative, and on increasingly broad and dense linkages between the state and private actors. In other words, without private participation, the state can no more overcome collective dilemmas associated with innovation and technological development than can a competitive market without the state. To overcome collective dilemmas, informational and cooperative linkages must be bi-directional and exist at the point of implementation. That is, in addition to autonomous states being embedded in the private sector, firms, organized labor, academia and other economic actors must actively participate in the formation, implementation, monitoring and evaluation of public policy. Bi-directional linkages ensure both that government actors are well informed about the needs and desires of economic actors and also that private interests become 'vested' through high levels of participation. Both lead to credibility for both policy creation and implementation.

Singapore

Dense linkages exist at multiple levels between public and private organizations in Singapore. As early as the late 1970s the Singapore government explicitly tied education and training to foreign MNCs. Many early firms investing in Singapore needed skilled precision engineers, of which there were few, if any. Yet instead of shouldering the burden exclusively, the EDB entered into a training partnership with Rollei, a German precision manufacturing company that had located on the island to produce optical and camera products. The Singapore government compensated Rollei for the costs of space, equipment and staff to create a precision engineering training center at their company site. In return, Rollei trained twice as many precision engineers as they needed. Additional engineers could either join the general workforce, or were recruited into the education and training system to produce more optical engineers. The Singapore government then aggressively advertised to foreign firms that Singapore had human resources with skills in optical engineering.

The benefits of this plan were numerous. Through external linkages, the state effectively initiated a transfer of technology from Rollei to the Singapore education and training infrastructure and the workforce. It did so by establishing a pattern of cooperative linkages between the government and private firms. Rollei was also able to recoup the entire cost of its training, thereby eliminating its investment appropriation dilemma. Over time this pattern was followed many times to increase other specific skills needed to further technology development in priority areas identified by the EDB. Eventually these company training centers were absorbed by the government and converted into industrial training centers.[14] In 1992 these training centers were subsumed by the Ministry of Education and converted into institutes of technical education (ITE). Significantly, the early linkages with private firms had become embedded into the culture and remain at the nucleus of the ITEs.[15]

However, as technology and the global economy have evolved, linkages only between just the state and business are no longer sufficient. Connective linkages must be broadened to include labor, academia, research institutes, business associations and so forth. The relationships among these actors must also change from one of strategic state-led intervention in the economy to more balanced load-sharing and interaction.

Singapore has made this transition in a number of ways. First, peak-level linkages are ubiquitous among the various government agencies and academia, business and labor. Singapore's efforts to create a 'knowledge-based' society in the twenty-first century are instructive. Driving the initiative is an overall National Science and Technology Plan (NSTP). The National Science and Technology Council wrote the plan with help from sub-committees on R&D manpower; R&D environment enhancement; technology infrastructure; technology commercialization, entrepreneurship and investment; and international strategy to enlarge R&D space. A total of 32 percent of the 66 representatives on the various councils and sub-committees that made up the initiative were from the private sector and 23 percent from academia. Members of the council and sub-committees also included representatives from every major government ministry. In turn, each government ministry and many departments and boards developed plans to support the NSTP. For example, the EDB created an Industry 21 plan, the MoM a Manpower 21 plan, and so on. For each of these sub-plans, committees were established that again featured membership from a wide cross-section of government, business, academia and labor.

As important as these macro-linkages have been for planning and vision, very little policy gets made at this level. Peak-level committees tend to be epiphenomenal and focus on providing broad objectives and direction. Most policy is formulated and implemented in permanent and semi-permanent boards, committees and councils that exist in each bureaucratic ministry, agency and department. Like the peak-level committees, these working committees comprise representatives from government, business, labor and academia. For example, the Manpower 21 plan, designed to meet the human resource needs of the new technology-based economy comprises a steering committee and five sub-committees. Of the 27 members on the steering committee, 10 (37 percent) were from business, 2 (7 percent) from academia, 2 (7 percent) from labor, 1 (4.5 percent) from a business association, 1 (4.5 percent) from a private think tank and 9 (41 percent) from the MoM, Ministry of Finance, EDB, MTI, MoE and the Prime Minister's Office. In addition, the input of over 450 individuals from government, business, labor and academia, both inside and outside the country, participated in the sub-committees, advisory programs, study missions, consultations, dialogue sessions and tripartite consultations.[16]

These meso- and micro-level linkages have been the key to overcoming collective dilemmas hindering cooperation and participation. High levels of trust within these committees allow public actors to derive mission-critical information from private actors. Economic actors are able to directly influence public policy, often dominating the actual policy formation, implementation and monitoring processes. The breadth of these cross-class and cross-functional representative linkages (1) encourage initiatives to be implemented as public rather than private goods and (2) provide a set of checks and balances that curb waste and inefficiencies.

Thailand
In Thailand, broad cooperative linkages between government and economic actors are extremely rare. Although strong linkages exist between the Ministry of Industry (MoI) and protected local firms, these linkages are narrow in scope, patronage-based and particularistic. Political and economic fragmentation has made it difficult to address the problem of low capacity in science and technology, and, hence, innovation. Policies and institutions designed to improve Thailand's technological capacity through R&D and education and training have often foundered for lack of integrated and coordinated planning and support.[17]

And yet, like Singapore, Thailand is good at including private sector representatives on peak committees and planning bodies. There are, however, several key differences. First, labor is not included. Second, to the extent that private firms and academics participate, they do so primarily in a consultative rather than participative role. These differences do not adversely impact direction, vision and high-level objectives, which at this level are not radically different from those of Singapore, at least in substance if not in form. But, unlike the situation in Singapore, much more policy is made at the peak level and then handed down to the line-ministry level to implement. Here the differences do matter. Without broad-based participation in policy formation (as opposed to only consultative input), private sector ownership of and responsibility for these policies is very low and does not extend to a cross-class or cross-function coalition.

Equally troublesome, the same pattern of consultative linkages exists at the meso- and micro-level. Government agencies spend a tremendous amount of money on consultants to help direct policy formation and implementation. Again, however, there is no participation from the private sector actors for whom the policy will have the most direct impact.[18] Moreover, many of the advisors and consultants at all levels, many with dubious credentials to begin with, are eventually subsumed and adopted into the bureaucracy.

Malaysia

Although the public–private linkages in Malaysia appear to be somewhat more advanced than in Thailand, they are still weak. Malaysia has done a better job than Thailand in formally soliciting the input of the private sector for policy-making processes. Both the MBC and MIGHT were created to coordinate government initiatives with the needs of private firms. Of the 84 members of MIGHT, businesses make up 79 percent (66), with approximately 11 percent (9) foreign. Nevertheless, among the influential permanent members, only one (5.5 percent) represents business, with the rest representing academia, public research institutes and the government.[19]

Although more formalized, these bodies operate much like the high-level committees in Thailand. First, neither includes labor. Second, they do not engage in direct policy-making themselves, but act as consultative bodies to the ministries, agencies and departments that do. In fact, MIGHT is actually a wholly owned government corporation and therefore does not engage directly in policy-making. Instead, it must funnel input from its members to internally insulated policy-making bodies.

At the line-ministry level, Malaysia has been unable to develop the same linkages that exist in Singapore. In most cases, where committees exist to promote technology policy, they are most often populated by the department's own people with a smattering of representatives from the private sector.[20] However, in one very relevant case, the Human Resource Development Council (HRDC), the number of private sector representatives actually outnumbers the public sector representatives (Malaysia HRDF, 2004). Even so, the report does not specify where these representatives come from, making it difficult to tell whether they truly represent private sector constituencies or not. But in addition to having broad representation, these bodies must have policy-making capacity. Whereas policy-making power in Singapore is being pushed out to the line ministries, the reverse is true in Malaysia and Thailand.

The Multimedia Development Corporation (MDC), which has been touted by the government as a new model of public–private cooperation, helps clarify the differences among the countries. First, more so than Thailand, Malaysia is making a concerted effort to formalize the linkages between the public and private sector.[21] For example, as in Singapore, Malaysia has solicited the input and advice from numerous foreign and local technology firms in a technology advisory panel. High-ranking executives from foreign technology firms, often the CEO, MD, or president, offer input, advice and direction to the MDC, the group responsible for the development of the MSC.[22] But none of these people are actually involved in the policy-making process. Indeed, neither are the officials at the MDC, another wholly owned government corporation under the Prime Minister's Office (PMO). Instead, input from the advisory panel is funneled through the MDC to the PMO, where actual policy-making takes place.[23] Thus, unlike Singapore, where the heads of companies not only participate but in many cases actually lead the policy-making process, in Malaysia only a small group of private sector actors play any role, and then only at the margins.

DEVELOPMENTAL LINKAGES AND SUPPLY

Developmental public–private linkages, both within the state and between the state and private economic actors, influence both internal and external supply of human resources. The role of private actors is pivotally important to the success of these programs. Probably the most effective tool developing countries have used to address collective dilemmas associated with the supply of training and education is a grant-levy training investment scheme. Internal supply, however, must also be matched with external demand, especially when the economic strategy emphasizes the importation, adoption and diffusion of foreign technologies.

Skills Development Funds

Grant-levy skills development schemes are aimed squarely at the collective dilemmas that hinder firm-level training and education. Firms are assessed for a training levy, which is then aggregated into a training fund. Firms can then draw on these funds to conduct approved training and education. In theory the fund addresses both investment appropriation and free-riding dilemmas. Free-riding is minimized by making participation in the fund mandatory. Investment appropriation dilemmas are resolved by requiring firms to contribute funds regardless of whether they use them or not.[24] But not all funds are equal. Depending on the way the fund is designed and implemented, firms' preferences for skill types, levels, quality and intensity of training can vary remarkably.

Singapore

One of the key tasks facing Singapore after independence was to create a sufficient number of jobs for the growing working class, many of whose members were unemployed. Although separation from Malaysia forced the government to adopt an export-oriented strategy, it was also a labor-intensive industrialization strategy. As a result of a robust world economy, liberal investment incentives, reformed labor laws and expanding educational achievement, a rising number of foreign MNCs set up operations in Singapore during the early 1970s. During 1970–79 Singapore experienced 8–9 percent GNP growth per year. Unemployment also fell rapidly over this period, from 6 percent in 1970 to 3.3 percent in 1979, with the manufacturing sector generating almost half the new employment (Singapore Skills Development Fund, 1999b).

By 1972 the Singapore economy had reached full employment. Nevertheless, firms did not voluntarily respond to the tight labor market by upgrading productivity through training and education. Instead, they imported foreign workers to meet demand, but did not substantively alter their labor-intensive business strategies. While this was not a problem for the current wage-based economic strategy,[25] the government realized that this strategy was unsustainable. Singaporean industry would need to upgrade its industrial capacity and value added, or the country would not survive.

In response, the PAP launched a second industrial transformation initiative in 1979 to transition the economy away from labor-intensive activities and toward more capital- and skill-intensive industries. To enlist the participation of the private sector in this transition, the government passed the Skills Development Levy Act, which stipulated that every employer, both foreign and local, was required to pay a monthly skills development levy amounting to 2 percent of every employee's monthly salary less than or equal to S\$750.[26] The money goes into a general fund from which companies can claim reimbursement for training expenses, usually up to 50 percent of the cost of the training, but, depending on the type of training, up to 100 percent or more. While the main objective of the Act was to increase the pool of technical intellectual capital in the country, there were several other secondary priorities.

First, the Act was designed to increase wages through increased skills. The National Wages Council had recommended a three-year wage correction policy to bring Singapore wages to a level comparable to those in Korea, Taiwan and Hong Kong. Nevertheless, prior attempts to do so through government fiat had seriously affected FDI. By increasing the skill levels of the workforce, it was thought that wages would increase naturally as productivity rose. Second, the government sought to discourage firms from relying on labor-intensive operations or from using labor excessively or inefficiently. Thus the levy was designed as a tax on low-skilled labor: labor-intensive industries end up funding the training efforts of capital- and skill-intensive industries.

Finally, the Act aimed to create a culture of education and training within companies in a number of ways. First, the government matches contributions to training initiatives. Broad government subsidies, available to both foreign and domestic firms, reduces the time between training and profitable return, making net present value analysis immediately positive. Second, all the levy funds are pooled. Funds that firms can access for training are not limited by the amount they contribute, but by the number of approved training courses they are willing to provide for their employees. Thus firms that do no training end up funding the training efforts of firms that do.[27]

To manage the levy funds, the government created the Skills Development Fund.[28] Initially the administration of the Fund was entrusted to the EDB. During this early period the Fund was used to establish industry-training centers in conjunction with business associations. From the original Hotel Association Training and Education Center and the Textile and Garment Industry Training Center, there are now 16 such centers, established with initial funding by the SDF at 90 percent of the start-up costs as well as 90 percent of the salaries of the center directors for the first three years. It was also through the SDF that the EDB funded the initial in-house training centers in companies such as Rollei.

It is important to pause here and note that the initial design of the program was made with little private sector involvement. Indeed, the government implemented the SDF in the same unilateral fashion as the previously failed wage correction policies.[29] This was probably necessary, however, to ensure that private firms did not block the initiative before it could be implemented (see Thailand below). Even so, the government was forced to modify the program multiple times to achieve its current efficient design. But this is exactly the important message: an internally coherent, tightly linked bureaucracy was able to learn and quickly modify the plan by directly incorporating a broad range of actors directly into the policy-making and policy-implementing processes *after* initial implementation.

Further tracing the history of the Fund's development illustrates this trend well. In 1986, responsibility for the Fund was transferred to the National Productivity Board (NPB), which was also transferred at the same time from the Ministry of Labor to the Ministry of Trade and Industry. With this transfer, the focus of the Fund shifted from training infrastructure to worker-based training. The NPB recognized, however, that effective worker training would require the participation of private firms. For example, in 1987, the SDF, IBM, the National Computer Board (NCB) and Singapore Telecoms jointly designed and implemented the IT Program for Office Workers (IT POWER). The program aimed to develop transferable technical skills in junior-level office staff.

In 1992 the focus again shifted somewhat as the Fund emphasized workers in small and medium-sized enterprises (SMEs). Nevertheless, the main focus remained on lower-skilled workers throughout the economy. By this time, however, successful implementation of skills development initiatives, especially those aimed at the middle to lower levels, required extensive input from labor. In July 1993, subsidiary legislation was added to the SDL Act at the behest of the NTUC to allow the NTUC, the Association of Muslim Professionals, the Chinese Development Assistance Council, the Eurasian Association, the Singapore Indian Development Association and Yayasan to utilize SDF funds to sponsor skills development training for their members. The purpose was to provide an avenue for training to people who were denied training from their employers.

Incorporating private economic and social bodies outside of business dramatically increased the amount of influence these groups, especially labor, had within the SDF. The result was education and training focused on a much broader cross-section of society. To illustrate, in 1995 the SDF combined with the NTUC's Women's Program Department to prepare women to return to the workforce. Other participants in the program included the Ministry of Labor, the NPB and the Singapore National Employers Federation (SNEF) (Singapore SDF, 1999a and 1999b).

On 1 November 1996, the SDL Act was amended again, effecting two important changes. First, the NPB and the Singapore Institute of Standards and Industrial Research (SISIR) were merged to form the Productivity and Standards Board (PSB). The new thrust of the PSB was to raise total factor productivity. The primary mechanism by which the new board planned to reach this objective was education and training.[30] And, second, the Ministry of Finance transferred the Fund and its operation from the government to the new PSB. Within the SDF, one department, with help from the Ministry of Finance, disburses the funds, while another department, more closely tied to the PSB, decides where the funds should be spent. The Central Provident Fund Board, which is part of the

Ministry of Manpower, collects the levy when it collects the provident fund contributions. Thus those who collect and distribute SDF funds do not determine where they go, and those that determine where they go do not distribute them.[31] With the transfer, the Fund could provide training assistance to all workers – salaried, employed, self-employed or those seeking employment.

Like the NPB before it, the PSB functioned as a statutory board under the MTI. Nevertheless, the PSB operated the SDF with very tight linkages to the Ministry of Education, the Ministry of Manpower, the National Trades Union Congress, other MIT statutory boards (especially the NSTB and the EDB), and private industry.[32] Private industry participates directly on the board of directors for the SDF. As of the 1999 *Annual Report*, the chairman of the SDF technical committee was the CEO of a private Singaporean technology firm. In addition, both the EDB and NSTB function as a conduit for information from firms on their scientific and technical skills needs, as well as an indirect connection to the universities and public research institutes; the Ministry of Manpower (MoM) coordinates initiatives and funding to develop corporate training centers to provide SDF sponsored training; the Ministry of Education (MoE) provides training facilities; and the National Trades Union Congress (NTUC) provides information and coordinates participation from organized labor. This dense interconnected network of participants creates a mechanism of checks and balances that makes it difficult to use the Fund inappropriately.[33]

As the focus of the Fund shifted toward both productivity and higher-level technical knowledge and skills, labor's participation in education and training became even more important. In 1996 the NTUC concluded that MNCs were still not providing sufficient training to lower-paid employees. Furthermore, many of these workers were over the age of 40 and, if retrenched, would find it difficult to secure new employment in a rapidly changing economy. Initially the NTUC presented a plan to the government to create a new, labor-led training initiative aimed at these lower-end workers. The government, however, responded that, while necessary, the program would have to be developed and implemented within the current training infrastructure.

On 20 December 1996, the NTUC launched the 'Skills Redevelopment Program' with support from the EDB, PSB, Singapore National Employers' Federation (SNEF), ITEs and the four polytechnics. To run the new program the NTUC brought in Lim Swee Say, a high-level official at the EDB with significant knowledge of the private sector. His aim, coming from the EDB, was to involve as many players as possible in the new venture. Also, since the government had mandated that the program be implemented using existing resources, only by cooperating and coordinating with other public and private actors could the program succeed. First the program would use the existing SDF to pay for upgrade training. Productivity-enhancing skills would be taught by the PSB in their Institute for Productivity Training while job skill training, on the other hand, was to be provided by the Ministry of Education's polytechnics and ITEs. Finally, to ensure the participation of private firms, additional funds were offered to firms to offset the costs of absentee workers.[34] Since funds are used to cover both the costs of training and the time the worker is absent from the job, firm investment appropriation dilemmas are minimized. The result has been extremely high private participation, especially among firms trying to transition from labor-intensive manufacturing to more knowledge-intensive industries.[35] Originally these funds came from the PSB. But in 1998 both the funds and the people responsible for administering them went to the MoM, which was created from the old Ministry of Labor as well as from parts of the NTUC, PSB, EDB and MTI. In 2002, all of the responsibilities of the PSB for the SDF were transferred to the MoM.

The leadership of the SDF reflects deep institutionalized public–private relationships. The SDF technical committee consists of 11 representatives from business, three from labor and one from government. The technical committee reports to the MoM, whose board of directors is chaired by the managing director of the NTUC. Including labor, government and industry in the formation of SDF policy ensures that the Fund will benefit all stakeholders, which in turn increases support, participation and credibility.

There are several metrics attesting to the success of the Fund. By fiscal 1986, employers were investing $2 in training for every dollar of SDF grant funds disbursed. By 1998 the ratio was 17:1, with private firms averaging 3.6 percent of payroll on training, up from 1 percent in 1986. Total number of hours of training has likewise risen dramatically, from 17.4 hours per employee in 1990 to 31.5 hours in 1998. In 1999, well over half a million occurrences of formal training were funded by the Skills Development Fund in a country with only slightly more than 3 million total population. In this same year, in what is nothing short of an amazing statistic, 100 percent of firms with more than ten employees and 33 percent of firms with fewer than ten employees participated in the SDF (Singapore SDF, 1999a and 1999b).[36] Finally, since the mid-1980s the SDF has run a deficit. In fiscal year 1998, the Fund accumulated just over S$20 million but paid out S$97 million, over four times as much. In other words, if firms are willing to invest in training beyond their contributions, the government is prepared also to extend its participation.[37]

Malaysia

It wasn't until much later that Malaysia created a similar program for training and skills development. In 1992 the government passed the Human Resources Development Act, primarily to increase technical training and education, but also to accelerate technology transfer on the shop floor and improve productivity. This Act provided for the creation of the Human Resource Development Fund (HRDF) and the Human Resource Development Council (HRDC) to supervise and administer it.[38] The HRDC, in turn, is part of the Manpower Development Department (Jabatan Tenaga Rakyat) in the Ministry of Human Resources (formally the Ministry of Labor).

Like the SDF in Singapore, the HRDF extracts a levy from companies that can then be used for education and training. But even though the HRDF looks similar to the SDF at first glance, subtle differences provide different incentives for participation. First, rather than base contributions on wage levels, as in Singapore, the HRDF bases contributions on firm size. Those firms that meet the qualifications must contribute 1 percent of the monthly wages of all their employees to the HRDF. Second, cut-off points for participation – 50 employees and/or RM2.5 million in paid-up capital – means that most SMEs are exempt from participating in the HRDF.[39] Third, the Fund is administered as individual firm-level accounts. Each participating firm contributes to an individual account, rather than to a general-purpose fund. The funds are then only made available to the contributing firm. Fourth, although there is board-level participation from private businesses, there is little connectivity between the HRDC and other government ministries. Even starker in comparison, however, is the fact that there is no participation in the HRDC by organized labor.

Differences in implementation have led to variation in outcomes. The overall participation rate among companies registered with the Fund is just over half the rate in Singapore. Since its inception in 1993, the HRDF has collected over RM562 million, but paid out just over RM345 million (61.4 percent).[40] Second, exempting smaller firms places the emphasis of private sector education and training on larger firms, which on average are already providing much more training and education than are SMEs. Among the SMEs not required to register with the Fund, only approximately 5001 of more than 100 000 participated. For companies with fewer than ten employees or RM2.5 million paid-up capital, only approximately 300 of the more than 16 000 participated.[41] Third, since the levy is based on the wages of all employees, there is a perverse incentive to employ the lowest-cost, and hence lowest-skilled, labor available. When development strategies stress competitive advantage based on low-wage labor, this approach makes sense. And yet, by 1995 Malaysia was experiencing full employment and chronic labor shortages. Fourth, individual firm accounting means that while it is true that contributions not used are forfeited, there exists no time-sensitive competitive insecurity that unused funds might go to more aggressive rivals. And finally, without active policy-making participation from labor, academia and other bureaucratic agencies, levels of training, especially for lower-paid workers, are not qualitatively or quantitatively sufficient.[42]

But even though early implementation of the HRDF was marked by low take-up, inefficient bureaucratic claims procedures and excessive rigidity (Edwards, 1999: 244), between 1993 and 1996, grants were allocated to train over 800 000 people. In 1997 alone, over RM99 million was dispersed for training – certainly significant by any metric of industrial education and training (Malaysia HRDF, 1998). But much more remains to be done if Malaysia is to reach Singapore's standards. Indicators show that Malaysia continues to be plagued by poaching and other forms of high labor mobility, especially for employees with middle- to high-level skills (Edwards, 1999; Kondo, 1999). This suggests that the investment appropriation dilemma has yet to be fully resolved. Second, incentives are needed to upgrade the level of training that employees receive. This is especially true of scientific and technical education and training. Not only are improvements needed in curriculum design, but also in teacher training, teacher salaries and access to foreign knowledge and skills. Third, the Fund must be implemented differently to improve the participation of SMEs as well as the overall participation of firms at every level. Fourth, incentives to use low-cost labor in labor-intensive industries must be removed. And finally, funds should be made available to any firm that will use them, rather than limit usage to contributions.

What is needed to effect these changes is an expansion of the working participants. In particular, the key to many of these changes is to include the perspective and resources of groups currently excluded, such as labor, research institutes, think tanks and academia, not simply as consultants, but as equal participants with a role in the bargaining process.

When education and training processes are marked by such broad-based participation, outcomes approach those in Singapore. As mentioned earlier, the experience of the PSDC has been different from that of any other state skills development center. Although the PSDC still lacks active participation of labor, it has successfully included local industry, foreign industry, academia (the Science University of Malaysia), the Penang State government and the HRDF to design curricula, loan equipment and trainers, supply technical and scientific consulting and direction, and provide financial resources.[43]

The success of the PSDC encouraged the national government to call for skill development centers modeled after the PSDC to be built in each state. One of these, the Selangor Human Resource Development Center (SHRDC), was established in 1995 near the industrial concentration in the Klang Valley. Nevertheless, because the Selangor State Economic Development Corporation has been unable to replicate the intermediary role of the PDC, participation of private firms has not approached the level experienced by the PSDC in either quantity or quality.[44] Thus, when the International Disk Drive Equipment and Materials Association (IDEMA) recently introduced its series of training courses into Malaysia, it chose to partner with the PSDC for all of Malaysia instead of partnering with each skill development center individually.[45]

Thailand
As in Malaysia, much of Thailand's training system has been modeled after that of Singapore.[46] Nevertheless, there is much that is different. In 1994 the government implemented the Vocational Training Promotion Act to engage and assist manufacturing companies in educating and training their employees. The Act had two components. First, firms that conducted approved training would be eligible to deduct up to 150 percent of the costs from income taxes. And second, the government created an SDF to help finance training.

The initial intention of the Skills Development Department in the Ministry of Labor was to establish a skills development fund modeled after the SDF in Singapore, the finer points of which the Thais had gleaned from multiple visits to Singapore.[47] Ultimately, however, the private sector effectively lobbied the government to take the teeth out of the initiative. What was finally signed into law bore little resemblance to the ambitious initial conception. Instead of a grant-levy scheme, the Thai SDF (TSDF) was simply a yearly lump sum allocated by the government to be disbursed as loans to individuals at favorable interest rates to fund training for un- or underemployed workers. Both programs were assigned to the Ministry of Labor and Social Welfare's Skills Development Department.[48] The TSDF at this point made no attempt to involve firms or other economic actors other than the individual in the training process.

Firms could also deduct training costs from their taxes. The process for claiming these funds, however, is daunting. Interested firms must first register with the Ministry of Labor and Social Welfare. Next, the ministry must pre-approve every training program. After the training program has been completed, the firm must apply to the ministry for reimbursement. If approved, the ministry grants the firm a voucher, which they must then take to the Ministry of Finance for approval. If it is approved, the firm may then attach the voucher to its tax return as proof of deductions made.

Table 7.1   Training in Thailand

Budget year	Number of companies	Number of training courses	Number of training incidents	Training expenditures (in baht)
1996	2	2	132	152 136
1997	69	639	51 702	116 964 216
1998	271	2 377	199 592	314 727 958
1999	207	2 154	191 592	214 894 369
2000	204	2 077	190 019	229 082 532

Source: Thai Department of Skill Development, Ministry of Labor and Social Welfare.

In the current program, collective dilemmas are not adequately addressed. Because firm participation in the scheme is not mandatory, free-rider dilemmas are not resolved. Also, because the process of claiming the rebate is costly and complicated, firms choose to forego subsidies that would alleviate investment appropriation dilemmas.

The initial intention of the government was to make participation mandatory. Powerful business interests, however, resisted the effort. In the end, participation was completely voluntary and, as a result, the number of firms claiming the tax deduction has been very small (see Table 7.1). Most firms using the deduction would have trained anyway. Of the 204 firms that registered and claimed training-related tax deductions in 2000, most are large multinational firms that conduct training with or without the incentives.[49]

Comparisons of all three countries can be seen in Table 7.2.

DEVELOPMENTAL LINKAGES AND DEMAND

Firm-level R&D, both formal and informal, is the primary source of demand for technical intellectual capital (Booth and Snower, 1999; World Bank, 1997).[50] As with supply, initiatives must foster coordination and cooperation through public–private linkages. Nevertheless, whereas labor plays a prominent role in public–private linkages for effective supply, labor's role in R&D is much less, although likely to increase in the future as technological and innovatory processes are pushed ever further toward the shop or production floor.

Two primary mechanisms countries use to encourage formal R&D are direct and indirect subsidies and efforts to develop agglomeration economies. Subsidies directly address the investment appropriation dilemma.

Table 7.2   Country training comparison

	Malaysia – HRDF	Singapore – SDF	Thailand – 150% tax refund
Training places			
1997	533 227	502 686	51 702
1998	409 242	530 755	199 592
Training expenditures[a]			
1997	$41.97 m	$50.89 m	$2.60 m
1998	$36.52 m	$52.01 m	$6.99 m
Courses/Applications			
1997	Not reported	52 990	639
1998	Not reported	53 368	2 377

Note:
[a]   Malaysian ringgit are easily converted to dollars at the fixed exchange rate of RM3.8 per $1. I used S$1.7 to $1 and B45 to $1. The figures for both Thailand and Singapore are therefore approximations.

Sources: Singapore SDF *Annual Report, 1998/99*; Malaysian HRDF *Annual Report, 1998*; Thai Skills Development Office data, 2001.

Agglomeration economies, in turn, create externalities and spillovers, thereby alleviating both free-rider and investment appropriation dilemmas. Moreover, agglomeration economies foster increasing returns which, as Kaldor concludes, foster 'the development of skill and know-how; the opportunities for easy communication of ideas and experience; [and] the opportunity of ever-increasing differentiation of processes and of specialization in human activities' (quoted in Waldner, 1999: 171).[51] In these ways agglomeration economies encourage innovation by lessening the costs of development and hastening the return on R&D investments.

Singapore
In the 1970s, the EDB balanced investment incentives against requirements for both employment and levels of industrial upgrading.[52] Increasing demands for technological development made close working relationships between the EDB and private firms vital to the success of the economy. As one high-ranking official in the MTI put it, 'It is not too clever to simply give cash to companies. We must develop incentives that encourage these firms to upgrade technologically.'[53] Thus R&D requirements are becoming increasingly evident in the incentive packages offered by the EDB to new and existing firms, both foreign and domestic.[54]

But as the demands for innovation and technological upgrading intensify, the government has expanded its technological development policy to both strengthen existing linkages and to create new ones. While it is true that all three countries provide tax incentives for firms to conduct formal R&D, Singapore has been able to combine requirements for R&D initiatives and industrial upgrading with tax and other direct incentives associated specifically with R&D. Interestingly, there are no hard-and-fast rules for when firms receive certain incentives and when they do not. Each is reviewed on a case-by-case basis.[55] Moreover, incentives other than tax breaks, e.g. grants and subsidies, are being used more often to supplement tax incentives when forming firm-specific incentive packages to improve R&D.

In one case a newly formed micro-sized hard disk company chose Singapore as its new manufacturing base. As part of the tax holiday incentive package, the firm had to commit to an extremely aggressive ramp-up schedule to create a corporate product design center in Singapore.[56] In another case, Seagate, the largest hard disk drive manufacturing company in the world, initiated a product design center in 1984. Much of the early effort was aimed at determining if the company could develop a sufficient base of engineering capacity in Singapore to create a regional R&D center. By the early 1990s some progress had been made, but no significant design work was being done. During this same period the firm's initial tax incentive package expired. When the firm went to the EDB to renew the tax incentives, the EDB made continuing incentives contingent upon advancing the firm's earlier plans to create the R&D center. But in addition to tax incentives, the EDB directly funded a large portion of the costs of finalizing the creation of the center. Without these funds a company official admits that the center would probably never have become what it is today: one of the firm's four main research centers with over 120 engineers (the other three being in the USA). But, most impressive, new technology in the center's first product, released in 1998, combined outstanding performance with low-cost production, resulting in the company's best-selling drive ever.[57]

The government is also concentrating heavily on creating indigenous technological capacity. The EDB formed the Local Industry Upgrading Program (LIUP) in 1986 to upgrade the technological capacities of Singaporean supplier firms. The EDB helps 'match' local suppliers with potential MNCs. The EDB then enters into a partnership with the MNC to mentor the local supplier(s) through a less formal letter of understanding. An experienced engineer from the MNC is seconded to the EDB to become the LIUP manager for a specified period of time, usually two to three years. The sole purpose of the LIUP manager is to translate sourcing requirements of the MNC into upgrading programs for the local supplier(s). In return, and again on a case-by-case basis, the EDB enters into remunerative terms with the MNC.[58]

The Singapore government is also working with a variety of economic actors to nurture new, mostly Singaporean, techno-entrepreneurial ventures. For example, the NSTB provides startup funds for new, private firms spun off from the public research institutes. Increasingly these are joint ventures between the government and local, private firms. Internal auditors for the Kent Ridge Digital Labs, a public research institute involved in high-resolution imaging technology, report that since 1998 13 new ventures have been spun off.[59] The NSTB is also providing zero- and first-stage funding to promising new technologies developed in the universities. As of 2008, the National University of Singapore's INTRO department, which is tasked with identifying commercially promising technologies within the university, had set up 20 private companies and spun out eight more in 2000.[60]

The NSTB works actively to connect university students with firms. Students are assigned a mentor from the faculty. As technologies take shape, engineers are brought in from private firms and the public research institutes to provide feedback and direction. But equally important, techno-preneurial managers, venture capitalists and other business experts are brought in to educate students on the business of technology. As with other ventures, initial-stage funding is provided by the NSTB to develop business plans and VC funding presentations for commercially promising technologies.[61] Although the NSTB has allocated over US \$1billion to fund new ventures, the NSTB recognizes that it has limited internal capacity to evaluate new technologies. Instead, the NSTB often invites foreign VC companies in to jointly evaluate new ventures. In some cases the NSTB partners with these firms to provide funding. In many cases, however, the international VCs reject the proposal after evaluating the technology. But rather than let an opportunity to learn pass by, the NSTB uses the criteria for rejection as a blueprint for improving the technology or the business. That is, the NSTB will provide early funding specifically to remedy the problems that prevented the technology from receiving international VC funding. When the problems are addressed, the venture will be presented to the international VCs again. As the number of new technologies has risen, so has the number of VC companies that have set up operations in Singapore.

These initiatives have paid off. From 1990 until 1999 gross expenditures on R&D (GERD) have increased from S\$571 million to S\$2.66 billion. In 1999, industry's portion of that spending increased 8.8 percent to S\$1.67 billion. The same year, GERD as a percentage of GDP rose to 1.84 percent, and in 2002 moved over the 2 percent threshold reached by most developed Organisation for Economic Co-operation and Development (OECD) countries. The private sector accounted for 62.9 percent of GERD, public research institutes and centers 14 percent, higher education 11.7 percent and the government 11.5 percent. Also, the number of research scientists and engineers holding advanced degrees increased from 4329 to 13 817.[62]

Malaysia

Malaysia's efforts to develop product and design R&D have been much more modest, albeit better than Thailand (Lall, 1999: 163). Partly due to colonial legacies and partly the result of early technology focus, primary sector R&D institutions, such as the Malaysian Agricultural R&D Institute, Palm Oil Research Institute of Malaysia (PORIM) and the Rubber Research Institute, are conducting R&D on the frontier of their respective industries (Rasiah, 1999b). Nevertheless, Lall (1999) notes that for the level of industrialization in Malaysia, R&D is conspicuously low. Within the disk drive industry, for example, no firms report doing product R&D. Outside the hard disk drive industry, Sapura, a local telephone manufacturer, has invested heavily in R&D, but has yet been unable to match foreign competitors on price or quality.[63]

In 1967 the government created the Malaysian Industrial Development Authority (MIDA) to foster industrial development. Between 1970 and the mid-1990s the agency focused primarily on promoting labor-intensive industry. Toward the mid- to late 1990s the government began to refocus developmental priorities away from labor-intensive to knowledge-intensive activities. First, the criteria by which new tax incentives were awarded were officially changed to reflect the new emphasis on knowledge-intensive industries. And second, the old Vendor Development program was upgraded to the Industrial Linkages Program (ILP), where MNCs are given incentives to help develop local suppliers and local suppliers are given incentives to work toward producing a list of promoted products.

Government also aggressively implemented a series of subsidies for formal R&D projects. The Ministry of Finance approved R&D expenses as eligible for a 200 percent tax deduction. The same deduction is available for monies donated to a public research institute or for services provided by a public research institute or research company. These subsidies are available to all firms, foreign and domestic.[64]

In addition, an impressive array of subsidies is available to majority-owned Malaysian firms. Under the Seventh Malaysia Plan, RM1 billion has been allocated to the Ministry of Science, Technology, and the Environment (MOSTE) to fund the IRPA R&D program. As part of this program, RM100 million has been allocated to the Industry

R&D grant scheme, RM100 million to the Multimedia Super Corridor R&D grant scheme and RM50 million to the Demonstrator or Application grant scheme.[65] In the fiscal 2000–01 budget, the government increased the Venture Capital Fund by RM500 million to RM1 billion, and made investments in high-tech startups tax deductible.[66] Finally, wholly owned government corporations are making R&D funds available to new startups. The Malaysian Technology Development Corporation (MTDC) assists in R&D commercialization, incubation and acquisition. The Multimedia Development Corporation has RM100 million set aside for VC investment in new technology ventures. Technology Park Malaysia also has an incubation VC fund.

Outcomes, however, have been mixed. On the positive side, although there is little evidence of formal product R&D outside of the primary sectors, there are clear cases of process innovation in many different industries (Bell et al., 1995; Arrifin and Bell, 1999). By the late 1990s, Malaysia had developed a core of firms that specialize in technologically advanced electronic processes and products (Bell et al., 1995; Hobday, 1999: 100). Moreover, a new group of fast-growing, large local firms, e.g. Sapura, Likom, HIL and UNISEM, were beginning to compete technologically in the world export markets by the mid-1990s (ibid.: 82). Companies outside the microelectronics industry have also flourished. Between 1987 and 1997, Proton, the national car company, doubled production to 170 000 cars and began exporting to the UK, all while developing a significant base of local Bumiputra (ethnic Malay) supply firms (Abdulsomad, 1999: 291).[67]

To support structural transformation, budget allocations for public investment in R&D, primarily in the public research institutes, rose dramatically, from RM540.5 million in 1986 to RM1160 million in 1991. By the end of 1996, the MTDC held equity positions in 15 ventures. Additional efforts to establish industrial linkages were also made by the University of Science Malaysia in Penang. During 1981–93, the University's Innovation and Consultancy Center worked with over 700 corporate clients (Felker 1999: 124). In 1995 alone, it concluded deals worth RM2.3 million from 600 companies. Finally, the MDC awarded MSC status to over 400 companies and successfully persuaded many of the world's top players in Internet and multimedia software technology to become members of the MSC. Between August 1998 and December 2000, the MDC invested over RM40 million in the R&D projects of 19 local companies.[68]

Although visually impressive, this industrial transformation has largely been a technological mirage. The lion's share of technological upgrading took place within foreign MNCs (Rasiah, 1996; Felker, 1999: 8). But even here, firms did not significantly alter the labor-intensive assembly operations they began with. Some argue that foreign-dominated industries were largely 'ersatz' industry, at least from the standpoint of long-term national development (Goh, 1999: 129). Although this characterization is probably overly harsh, it is true that foreign-dominated industry did not upgrade the level or quality of productive spillovers produced by similarly technical industries in developed countries.

Technological development and diffusion were also severely circumscribed by an acute scarcity of technical human resources. This shortage extended to teachers and trainers as well.[69] Scarce technical skills meant that MNC operations in Malaysia engaged primarily in the lower-skill, lower-technology processes of assembly and test (Lall, 1999: 157; Goh, 1999: 130). Fewer skills led to very few linkages by which technology could be transferred from MNCs to local companies (Rasiah, 1999a; Hobday, 1999). Finally, instead of encouraging linkages with the private sector, the new bureaucratic structure over-emphasized technology capacity in the public sector while ignoring the development of similar capacity in the private sector (Felker, 1999: 21).

At the root of these difficulties are years of ethnically divisive policies and initiatives designed to further Bumiputra economic interests at the expense of local Chinese and Indian entrepreneurs (Jesudason, 1989; Felker, 1999: 23). Not only have deep ethnic cleavages fostered inefficient economic outcomes, but they also continue to frustrate efforts to resolve them. Often, the growth of local, primarily Chinese-owned firms has been thwarted by ethnically sensitive, affirmative-action policies (Rasiah, 1999a; Goh, 1999: 129). In response, local firms tend to look unfavorably and suspiciously upon government initiatives, which are designed to develop linkages with them (Leutert and Sudhoff, 1999: 263). The tendency is to 'go it alone.'

In Penang the opposite is true. In Penang, 'a combination of a relatively autonomous Chinese-dominated state government, transnationals, and Chinese-owned SMEs . . . [led to] relatively strong government-business relationships . . . [and] competitive production linkages' (ibid.: 193). As Landa (1991) would predict, strong ethnic networks generated high levels of trust, which were used in place of more formal institutions to overcome market failures. Political leaders, top management of MNCs and directors of local industry used trust-based linkages to upgrade the technological capacity of both MNCs and local industry.[70]

Lower participation of private firms in other parts of the country makes it difficult for government to evaluate technology initiatives. In a glaring case, the budget for 2000 allocated RM500 million to a VC fund. RM200 million was channeled for distribution through Bank Industri and Teknologi Malaysia, while the remaining RM300 million was to be disbursed by Bank Negara, Maybank and Bumiputra-Commerce Bank.[71] One year later, not one ringgit had been disbursed. The bank's executive director Dtuk Ismail Shahudin said Maybank indicated that the bank would like to give their portion out as soon as possible, but has had trouble evaluating the risks involved with venture capital. Maybank MD, Amirsham A. Aziz, said that 'It is not easy to evaluate IT-related projects and the skills needed for such evaluation must be developed.' The bottom line is that Maybank, or any of the other banks, did not know how to function as a VC.[72]

As a result, the government revised downward its targets for total R&D spending in 2000 from 2 percent to 1.5 percent of GDP. By 2002 Malaysia had reached only 0.69 percent of GDP on R&D (MASTIC, 2006). Also troubling is the extremely low rate of R&D within the industrial sector, which remains at about 0.03 percent of GDP (Lall, 1999). Of this small amount spent on R&D within the private sector, virtually none of it came from SMEs. To counteract this trend, the government created the Industrial Technical Assistance Fund (ITAF), which funds up to 50 percent of R&D efforts in SMEs. Nevertheless, as in the case of the programs before it, only RM12 million was used out of the RM50 million allocated.[73] Government-supplied incentives and support without the participation of private firms has not been sufficient to stimulate innovatory activities.

Malaysia has been equally unsuccessful in linking R&D at institutions of higher learning with the private sector. Funding for university R&D has been small and inconsistent, equaling just over RM133 million in 1998. In the aggregate it accounted for roughly 13.2 percent of R&D expenditures between 1992 and 1998. The little R&D activity carried out in institutes of higher learning is not connected to the private sector. Nor are there significant initiatives to commercialize university R&D.[74] Without the institutional capacity to foster cooperative linkages among government, business and academia at the micro level, monitor and measure the R&D activity of firms, and flexibly tailor policies and initiatives to market exigencies, R&D capacity in Malaysia is likely to remain static.[75]

Thailand
In Thailand the state has taken a much more *laissez-faire* approach to technology development. Instead of pursuing industry-specific upgrading initiatives, the Thai government relies largely on a history of macroeconomic and political stability, a large pool of low-cost but experienced labor, and export-oriented financial incentives to encourage both foreign and local investment.

Thailand established the Board of Investments (BoI) in 1954 to encourage industrial development, but it was not until 1960 that the BoI was given charge of soliciting FDI. As in both Singapore and Malaysia, the impetus behind the initial push to solicit foreign investment was employment driven. In 1977 the government passed the Investment Promotion Act. But rather than redirect the focus away from generating employment and more toward technological development, the new Act continued to use FDI in the absence of a coherent industrial plan, only now it was focusing on developing 'zones' outside Bangkok while keeping a focus on jobs creation (Duenden, 2004). Whereas the EDB uses both tax incentives and grants to encourage foreign investment, the BoI relies only on tax incentives. Instead of nurturing the growth of specific industries or specific types of industry, the BoI establishes published criteria by which any firm can receive tax incentives. Approval is granted on a project basis, with the overarching consideration being the number of jobs generated.

Focusing only on employment handcuffed broader efforts to upgrade industries technologically. But employment was politically important. One official at the BoI insightfully pointed out that bureaucratic capacity was only one of the problems keeping the BoI from providing EDB-like incentives for industrial upgrading. The other, and perhaps bigger problem politically, was that graduates from vocational training programs, colleges and universities did not have the skill sets needed by high-tech firms. The result is that jobs must be found for over 100 000 new graduates every year. The political pressure on the BoI, then, is not for industrial upgrading but for additional employment opportunities for undertrained graduates. A vicious cycle ensues where undertrained graduates are funneled into low-skill, labor-intensive jobs, which drive down demand and capacity for higher-skilled graduates. This turns on its head the argument that low-skilled jobs lead to demand for low-skilled employees and argues instead that the causation begins in the education and training system. The reality is that the two are endogenous.

Finally, even if the BoI were focusing on industrial upgrading, demand, especially from the local sector, is extremely weak. One problem is that BoI efforts to upgrade certain industries often conflict with the Ministry of Industry's efforts to protect them.[76] 'Export-oriented protectionism' has resulted in a combination of policies that provide perverse incentives away from technology development and inter-firm linkages necessary for upgrading. To illustrate, discrepancies between import and raw material taxes encourage firms to import components rather than develop their own. As I argued in the last chapter, extensive and prolonged tariff protection has drained the innovative capacity of local firms and aggravated cost differentials for key product inputs, making it difficult for local firms to compete on cost or quality.[77]

But despite the challenges the BoI faces, it has been able to implement indirect tax incentives for R&D activity by allowing firms to claim 150 percent of the costs of R&D against income taxes. The procedures for claiming the refund, however, are even more cumbersome than for training. Firms must register with the Ministry of Finance. They must then submit a separate tax return for the R&D expenses. To make this accounting nightmare less difficult, most firms create R&D subsidiaries. Creating subsidiary R&D companies, however, effectively removes the innovatory activity out of the parent company, lessening potential spillover effects and making transmission and absorption of new technologies throughout the company difficult. And finally, it hinders attempts to claim expenses associated with process-oriented R&D undertaken in the parent company. Finally, the Ministry of Finance evaluates the claims and approves or disallows them. Post-expense evaluation lessens the firm's incentives to invest in R&D in the first place by making investment appropriation uncertain, but this tendency is exacerbated since the Ministry of Finance has little experience or capacity to assess the intricacies of R&D.

Again, as with training, only the large firms participate. One official at the NSTDA estimated that only about 26 firms in all of Thailand used the program.[78] In one case, Siam Cement, a well-respected and extremely successful company that is part of the Crown Property Bureau, submitted a claim for R&D expenses, which the Ministry of Finance disallowed. Siam Cement took the case to court, where deliberations lasted for over six years. In the end, Siam Cement lost. But officials at the Ministry of Finance admitted that their capacity to evaluate private R&D initiatives was limited. While erring on the side of conservatism certainly helps limit corruption, with R&D expenditures in Thailand being so low, erring on the liberal side may have been more beneficial to the country.[79]

In addition, a lack of technological sophistication among SMEs continues to be a problem. Using disk drive firms as an example, few local firms are able to meet the technology and quality requirements of the MNCs. Disk drive companies found that even simple metal and plastic injection-molded components could not be sourced locally (McKendrick et al., 2000). To encourage SMEs to upgrade technologically, the BoI created the Unit for Industrial Linkages (BUILD). The program is designed to match potential local suppliers with foreign MNC firms. Despite initial excitement from the private sector, the program eventually faded, for several reasons. First and most important, the BoI lacked the incentive tools to broker individually tailored agreements between MNCs and local firms that adequately compensated the MNCs for their mentoring assistance. Indeed, the process of selectively matching local and foreign firms cut against the very philosophy of equal and transparent access. Yet tax incentives alone are not sufficient motivators for the in-depth linkages required to build technological capacity in the indigenous firms. Thus BUILD has become little more than a roadshow, advertising the products and services of local Thai firms to the large MNCs without doing much or anything in the way of developing linkages for upgrading.[80]

Looking to provide new incentives to encourage foreign MNCs to partner with local firms, the new government announced a 100 billion baht matchmaker fund. But the ultimate purpose behind these linkages was not to increase technological development, but to increase employment, even though at the time the unemployment rate was only 3.6 percent.[81]

As in Singapore and Malaysia, the Thai government allocated significant funds to directly subsidize R&D in Thai-owned companies. But, more like Malaysia, these funds were not being used. For example, R&D grant programs administered by the NSTDA were disappointing: between 1992 and 1997 only eight grants were approved (World Bank, 2000) and subsequently the program was dropped (Arnold et al., 2000). In addition, the 100 million baht Innovation Development Fund had funded only three projects from over 62 applications, spending a total of between 15 and 24 million baht. Unlike Maybank in Malaysia, however, the NSTDA is capable of evaluating these projects, suggesting that the quality of the applications is the biggest hurdle. Besides the NSTDA, the Thailand Research Foundation set up in 1992 also technically has the ability to fund research activities in firms, universities and public research institutes. By 1997, though, it had disbursed only 0.8 percent of its funds on private sector R&D (ibid.).

Other R&D funding projects include the MOSTE's Research and Technology Development Revolving Fund, which, between 1987 and 1997, spent 324 million baht ($7.6 million) to support 40 projects. The NSTDA soft loan facility in the same ten-year period loaned 148 million baht ($3.28 million) for 30 projects. Finally, the Bank of Thailand soft loan facility for R&D projects, operated through the Industrial Finance Corporation of Thailand, funded two projects directly and two others in conjunction with the NSTDA with a total loan value of around 30 million baht ($0.66 million) (TDRI, 1998).

Lastly, although improving slightly, the Thai university system has traditionally not conducted R&D. As in Malaysia, little pressure is applied to professors to conduct research, nor are professional requirements of university faculty conducive to it. Most junior faculty are completely swamped by teaching responsibilities and, since most are already permanently employed in the civil service, they have little incentive, financial or otherwise, to conduct research. Senior faculty are also not required to do research or much of anything else. Most spend much of their time consulting for private firms. What little R&D activity does exist is largely disconnected from private firms.[82] The Thai government identified the problem in the Sixth Development Plan (1986–91) and detailed ways to help universities become more oriented toward industrial and commercial development (Duggan, 1991). Between then and 1999, however, little has been done. Educational reform undertaken with the passing of the Education Act of 1999 again specified steps to be taken to connect academia with the private sector. There is evidence that some firms began to establish productive educational linkages with local universities. In one case, Toyota Motors Thailand helped create the auto-engineering degree at Chulalongkorn University and supplied 34 engineers to help teach the courses. The bulk of the evidence, however, continues to suggest that the current education system is outdated, lacks sufficient technical capacity, and is often unresponsive to overtures from private firms for collaboration (Brimble and Doner, 2007).

Outcomes continue to reflect institutional weakness. GERD as a percentage of GDP has fallen from 0.14 percent in 1993, 0.13 percent in 1995, 0.12 percent in 1996, to 0.10 percent in 1997.[83] Expenditures rose to 0.25 percent in 2000 and 0.26 percent by 2003. The Brooker Group estimates that in 1996 only around 187 manufacturing companies were performing R&D. For Thailand in 1996 to *catch up* with where Korea was in 1980 would require a five-fold increase in R&D expenditures as a percentage of GDP (up from 0.12 percent to 0.6 percent) and more than a 20-fold increase in business-funded R&D (11 percent to 45 percent) (Arnold et al., 2000). In spite of these gloomy figures, small improvements were made, especially in the private sector: by 1999 the number of manufacturing companies performing R&D had increased to over 300.[84]

In addition to scarce linkages within the government, within the private sector (between local and foreign firms), and among the government, academia and the private sector, the government also does not prioritize scientific and technological progress. As a point of comparison, the Korean government committed US$100 million to developing the local software industry. Of all emerging, high-tech fields, software offers the most compelling opportunities for developing countries, especially where language and cultural differences open myriad possibilities for both program and content development. The Thai Software Park, which was created to nurture a local Thai software industry, was formed on less than US$750 000.[85] The executive director of the park points to the quickly receding potential when he notes, 'Every country in Asia is investing in manpower development, including Vietnam. The Vietnamese are now doing back-office projects for the Indian Software companies that we in Thailand should be getting.'[86]

Even though the initiative is underfunded, however, it is making significant strides in developing indigenous technological capacity. First, the Thai software companies housed in the Software Park are in the aggregate quite good. Second, with respect to R&D and training, the Software Park is pursuing innovative relationships with training institutes to provide English-based technical training and education and with MNCs to increase jointly funded and jointly developed software projects.

COORDINATING SUPPLY AND DEMAND: THE CENTRAL ROLE OF PUBLIC RESEARCH INSTITUTES

Clearly, supply and demand for technical intellectual capital are not independent of one another. A large pool of technically and scientifically trained human resources provides incentives for firms to increase R&D. Likewise, as firms develop R&D capacity, pressure mounts for increased numbers of scientists and engineers. But it takes institutions to link them. The core policy challenge is one of matching skills and knowledge formation to the present and future needs of the economy.

Business associations are one institutional option that can effectively link the supply of technical intellectual capital with the R&D initiatives driving demand for those skills. When business associations confer valuable selective benefits, have high member density, provide effective internal intermediation among members, and foster balanced relations between an association's members and its staff, they are often able to reduce transaction costs, lessen principal – agent problems, and resolve collective dilemmas (Doner and Schneider, 2000: 13–14). Taking an example from the hard disk industry, the International Disk Drive Equipment and Materials Association (IDEMA) has created a training program leading to a certificate of competence in storage technology for disk drive manufacturers in Singapore, Malaysia and Thailand. Not only has the association created a needed training program where none existed before, it has also effectively linked the hard disk drive firms with local education and training institutions, including the Singapore Polytechnic in Singapore, the PSDC in Malaysia and the Asian Institute of Technology in Thailand.

As development processes in both Singapore and Penang show, government bodies can also play a coordinating role. Much like Japan and Korea before them, the EDB in Singapore and PDC in Penang effectively coordinated supply with demand for knowledge and skills. Both worked by assessing the needs of MNCs, linking MNCs to local firms through purchasing and engineering, and then creating mechanisms for supply to meet determined demand.

Another potentially effective institutional linkage between supply and demand is centers of technological excellence that perform education and training as well as R&D. The most effective linkages between supply and demand occur when the center is capable of conducting education and training and R&D that are relevant to multiple actors simultaneously. Research institutes can be especially effective in performing these tasks, especially when they follow Singapore's model of being non-profit, government founded and initially funded, but subsequently corporatized and supported, at least partially, by private membership.

The central role that government research institutes have played in the technological development of both Taiwan and Korea has been well documented.[87] Thousands of high-level scientists and engineers first worked in these institutes before transferring to the private sector. In addition to this massive transfer of technology from the public to private sectors, the institutes developed intimate bonds with fast-growing high-tech corporations in electronics, chemicals and automobiles, as well as the downstream industries they spawned. For the techno-nationalist development strategies of these two countries, government-owned research institutes worked well to transfer technology to indigenous, often highly protected, local firms.

In a more technoglobal environment, however, the Taiwanese and Korean model for research institutes lacks two important features: first, an ability to effectively draw in MNCs; and second, the ability to link basic and blue-sky academic research to the demands for functional and applied R&D in the private sector. Singapore has been able to modify the framework for research institutes to retain all of the earlier benefits while meeting these new demands. Since 1992 the Singapore government has created 13 research institutes and centers[88] to meet the challenges of R&D and education and training in the 'critical' technology areas identified by the EDB.[89] But the aim of the government in creating these institutions was not to pursue these technologies in isolation from business or academia. Nor was it their intention to pursue only a narrow, commercializable band of R&D in each area. Instead, they aimed for technological breadth as well as depth through a unique three-way partnership.[90] First, the institutes and centers were created as private, non-profit firms with government holding the majority ownership and the NSTB having oversight responsibility. Although the institutes were created with the assumption of significant private funding in the future, yearly funding from the national budget is ongoing and necessary. Second, the government built the institutes on the campuses of the country's colleges, universities and research parks.[91] Significantly, the vast majority of the researchers not from the private sector are faculty from the tertiary education sector. Lastly, once established, the institutes offered corporate memberships, much as business associations would do. As members, corporations contribute not only physical resources – i.e. money and equipment – but also intellectual resources. Moreover, a combination of business executives and academic faculty fill top management positions.

Broad connections between these three groups allow the institutes to conduct R&D and education and training needed by all three. The Data Storage Institute (DSI) provides a representative example.[92] The chairman of a diverse board of directors is the chief executive officer of Hewlett Packard in Singapore. Virtually every firm of any significance in the data storage industry is a member of the DSI. Member firms assign engineers to work at the DSI and receive DSI engineers to work in the company. Often these engineers collaborate on firm-specific technologies. The rights to new intellectual property (IP) are then jointly owned, at which point the IP can either be purchased outright from DSI (recognizing the input from the firm), or licensed.[93]

In addition to firm-specific research projects, the DSI conducts basic and foundation research in areas critical to the whole industry, such as tribology, magnetics, advanced materials and microelectronics. Here the R&D more closely matches the initiatives of academia and the government. But again, the research effort is not disconnected from the private sector. Although usually not immediately commercially applicable, the research effort is informed by the potential future needs of the industry. In one case, officials at the DSI explained how hard disk firms had rapidly increased the capacity of magnetic media by bringing the read/write heads ever closer to the media. The closer the head gets to the media, the more data can be read or written in the same space. But now with new technologies bringing the heads into pseudo-contact with the media, there are diminishing returns from continued efforts to lessen the distance between heads and media. Instead, new advances must be now be made with the media itself. Recognizing this, the DSI is shaping a portion of its longer-term research to this endeavor, knowing that some of it at some point will be commercially viable and therefore of interest to the private sector. And yet the short-term success of the project is not driven by quarterly returns or stock prices.

Cooperative linkages also bind R&D with skills development. First, the DSI creates broad-based, general training in new and existing technologies. The idea is to offer a sequence of courses firms can use to quickly ramp up new engineers and technicians to speed in the data storage industry. Interestingly, these courses not only offer general information on well-worn knowledge, but also include information on the cutting-edge frontier of this industry, most of which is gleaned from the active, academically driven side of the research at the center. Second, the DSI cooperates with member firms to develop company-specific training programs.

Firm-specific training may be general training geared to a broad cross-cutting group of employees, or it can be training on a jointly developed and firm-specific technology for a select group of engineers. And third, the institute links students and their research directly to private industry. Every year the DSI awards 50 undergraduate and 50 graduate scholarships to university students. Most bachelor and masters students are assigned as interns and complete senior projects and master's research within member companies. PhD students are not formally attached to companies, but are encouraged to solicit input from private sector scientists and engineers into their research. One company reported that, upon completion, research interns in their firm make presentations to upper management, after which the firm makes employment offers to the best and brightest.[94]

Neither Malaysia nor Thailand has created similarly linking institutions. Research institutes in both countries are primarily government owned and have little if any connection to the private sector. In Malaysia, for example, MIMOS was created as the country's flagship microelectronics research center. But instead of forging links with the private sector and academia, its primary activity has been to develop commercial products and services, including personal computers, Internet service, consulting services and so forth. Very little of the R&D goes beyond short-term commercial applications, making linkages with academia difficult. On the other hand, tie-ins with the MNCs or local Malaysian technology firms are difficult since MIMOS is a head-to-head competitor.[95] Weak and competitive links between MIMOS and other electronics firms mean that MIMOS's training efforts are technologically basic and often do not meet firm needs.

In Thailand, research institutes are also government owned, but do not compete with the private sector. The three research institutes in the NSTDA – NECTEC, MTEC and BIOTECH – are all involved in substantive R&D. Even so, there are virtually no linkages to private industry. There are, however, better linkages between these institutes and academia than there are in Malaysia. For example, several of the institutes have laboratories in the local universities. The number, size and significance of these laboratories are, in the aggregate, however, quite small.[96]

These linkages between government research institutes and academia exist due to similarities of research design and objectives: long term and more foundational in nature. The number of research institutes doing commercially viable research is even smaller, and then primarily for primary commodity industries. The Thailand Institute of Scientific and Technical Research (TISTR) provides a stark example of the mismatch: TISTR is conducting *no* research in any industry commonly thought of as 'high-tech,' even though these industries provide the lion's share of export earnings.

CONCLUSION

Societies develop technical intellectual capital to the extent that their innovation system can foster both adequate supply through education and training, and demand through innovation (especially when that innovation follows from formal R&D). Sufficient supply that meets industry needs is possible only when broad yet deep connective linkages exist between government, business, academia and labor. In contrast, demand is driven primarily by linkages between business, government and academia. The coordinating role between the two is played most effectively in a liberal global economy by research institutes, which, if structured properly, can meld the interests of all of the actors and bridge supply and demand.

The important conclusion is that it is necessary to view the development of technical intellectual capital systemically. As stressed earlier, it is not simply the numbers of technically trained people that matter for economic development. Instead, a sufficient supply of technical skills and knowledge must match industrial demand, and institutions must exist to manipulate and allocate these skills appropriately such that innovation and technological development are sustainable for the long term.

NOTES

1. Lester Thurow estimated that private R&D spending returned 24 percent to the firms making the investment, but 66 percent to the broader public. If true, this is one area where public spending would be very beneficial indeed. Lester Thurow, 'Building Wealth,' *The Atlantic*, June 1999.
2. I draw the bulk of my industry-specific empirical examples from the IT industry, particularly companies in the data storage and software industries.
3. The People Developer Standard Program was developed by the PSB to recognize firms that have implemented systematic education and training programs. The program provides up to S$50 000 to help fund the planning and implementation of a company-wide training program. Not only did the PSB cooperate to coordinate the program with existing efforts by the MoM to encourage firms to develop internal training facilities, but the People Developer Standard Program also uses the funds allocated to the MoM for that purpose.
4. Author interviews, PSB, MoM, EDB, IDA, July–October 2000.
5. Author interview, NSTB, PSB, MoM, EDB, IDA, NUS and DSI, July–October 2000.
6. Author interview, PSB, MoM, July–October 2000.
7. The World Bank reported in December 2000 that levels of duplication and overlapping functions have diminished the effectiveness of the various training and research institutes within the Ministry of Industry.
8. One ex-minister of MOSTE lamented that the government gives no priority to the management of science and technology initiatives within the ministry, nor does it provide incentives for other ministries and agencies to work with MOSTE on science and technology policy impacting other agencies. Author interview, Rangsit University, April 2001.

9. Author interviews with NSTDA and the former minister of MOSTE, April–May 2001.
10. Author interview, ONEC, March 2001.
11. 'IT bureau planned.' *Bangkok Post*, 16 May 2001.
12. Author interview, MOSTE and MITI, November 2000–February 2001.
13. Some of those I spoke to suggest that fragmentation within the education and training system is to ensure that both ethnic groups control portions of this vital enterprise.
14. The government continues to encourage the formation of new, corporate-centered training facilities through the Ministry of Manpower's total corporate training programs. The PSB's People Developer Standard Program also encourages corporate-centered training.
15. Author interview, ITE (MoE) and EDB, July–October 2000.
16. Singapore Manpower 21 Report, Ministry of Manpower, 4 August 1999.
17. Author interviews.
18. See Chapter 5, especially the case of the Ministry of Labor and the $153 million training upgrade.
19. MIGHT *Annual Report*, 1999. Malaysian Industry–Government Group for High Technology, No. 320059-P.
20. Malaysia, HRDF (1997, 1998). Many of the 'private sector' representatives are in fact from state-owned corporations.
21. See Malaysia's new Knowledge Economy Masterplan. Much of the same analysis, vision and objectives can also be found in the 3rd Outline Perspective Plan.
22. See www.mdc.com.my.
23. Author interviews at Multimedia University, MDC and MOSTE, October 2000–January 2001.
24. If a firm must choose between paying the money and getting nothing as opposed to paying the money, conducting the training and appropriating whatever portion of expertise possible before the employee leaves the firm, then clearly the second option makes more economic sense.
25. In fact, labor-intensive strategies require that education and training be kept to minimal levels since increasing the skill levels of the workforce eventually drives wages up.
26. This tax has variously been as high as 4 percent. Currently it is back to its original 1 percent level. The wage ceiling was subsequently raised from S$750 to S$1000 in 1995, to S$1500 on 1 July 2000. Future plans are to continue raising the levels to S$1800 in 2002 and S$2000 by 2004.
27. Author interview, PSB, July 2000, Singapore Skills Development Fund (2000).
28. The history and most of the figures in this section on the SDF come from Singapore Skills Development Fund (1999a, 1999b).
29. Author interview, PSB, July 2000.
30. See Singapore SDF (1999a).
31. Author interview, SDF, July 2000.
32. See Singapore SDF (1999a).
33. Author interview, Singapore SDF July 2000.
34. Ironically, it was not the cost of the training that most hindered the training of lower-paid employees. Instead, these employees were often employed in repetitive positions that were highly dependent on the output of other employees on the production line. To release any of these employees for training was to effectively shut down the line. The absentee funds allowed the firm to hire temporary, often foreign, workers to keep the lines open while permanent employees went for training.
35. Author interview, PSB, SDF, July 2000.
36. As measured by requests for reimbursement.
37. Author interview, PSB, SDF, July 2000.
38. Majlis Pembangunan Sumber Manusia, 1998. Most of the history and data from this section come from this report unless otherwise specified.
39. The qualifications include the following: manufacturing firms with more than 50

employees; manufacturing firms with 10–49 employees but with paid-up capital of RM 2.5 million or higher; and firms with ten employees and above in nine selected industries in the services sector. Manufacturing firms that employ more than ten but fewer than 50 employees and have paid-up capital of less than RM2.5 million have the option of participating in the Fund at a rate of 0.5 percent of wages. Since these firms are considered SMEs and have been specially targeted by the government, the government will match any contributions 2:1. For all participants, the rate of assistance from the fund is between 75 percent and 95 percent of allowable costs for local training and up to 50 percent for costs incurred in overseas training, subject to the maximum amount contributed. See www.hrdnet.gov.my.

40. In 1998 the HRDF took in RM61 000 356 and paid out RM88 166 080, suggesting that the trend of underutilization is reversing. Nevertheless, it is difficult to assess if this is really the case since over 38 industries at one point or another were granted a reprieve on their contributions due to the Asian financial crisis. Moreover, the RM88 million in funds dispersed represents a drop in usage of over 12.5 percent from 1997's total of over RM99 million.

41. Author interview. HRDC, 31 October 2000. See also 'SMIs and the k-economy,' *The Sun*, 4 December 2000.

42. Author interviews at Exxon, Multimedia University, AMCHAM, MIMOS, SIRIM, PSDC, PDC and IKMAS from July 1998 to January 2001.

43. Author interview, PSDC, 2 July 1998.

44. In spite of differences in performance between the SHRDC and the PSDC, the SHRDC has made significant progress since its inception in establishing linkages with private firms. It may be that the SHRDC establishes that the model of state-run training facilities is much more effective at developing public–private linkages than are the various training institutes of the federal government.

45. Author interview, IDEMA Singapore, 13 July 2000.

46. When I was in Singapore conducting interviews at the SDF, I was told that on a number of occasions Thailand had sent delegations to the PSB to learn about the SDF. At one point Thailand was planning on employing the PSB as a consultant to help implement its own skills development fund.

47. Author interview, Skills Development Department, Ministry of Labor and Social Welfare, 27 February 2001 and 23 March 2001.

48. Author interview, Department of Skills Development, April 2001.

49. For example, Seagate and IBM – large hard disk manufacturers with operations in all three countries – both report using the tax deduction scheme extensively. Author interviews at Seagate Thailand and IBM Thailand, July 1998–April 2001.

50. While it is relatively straightforward to measure formal product R&D and design, it is much more difficult to capture the variety of incremental, often informal process, product and management innovation that can take place within firms (Freeman and Soete, 1997). Even so, innovation arising from formal R&D demands higher levels of technically trained human resources than process or management innovation. Where firms are capable of product and design engineering, I assume that process and management innovation is also occurring. It cannot be assumed, however, that where process and management innovation exist, product and design capabilities also exist.

51. See also Kaldor (1972).

52. Even though technological capacity, R&D, and industrial upgrading are the priorities, the EDB still requires significant employment potential before granting incentives. Nevertheless, the threshold for 'significant' is now in the hundreds as opposed to the thousands (author interview).

53. Author interview.

54. Author interview. One new firm in the data storage industry indicated that while export volumes and employment numbers were important, tax and investment incentives hinged first on the firm's willingness to develop R&D capacity in Singapore.

55. Author interview, EDB, August 2000. Officials at the EDB stress that while certain

concessions may be extracted from one company in return for incentives, a different package may be applied to another. In the end, very subjective criteria, such as future potential for technological upgrading, establishing regional or international headquarters, and potential for technological externalities and spillovers are all considered.

56.   Author interview, private firm, 3 August 2000.
57.   Author interview, private firm, 31 July 2000 and 21 August 2000. See also McKendrick et al. (2000).
58.   Local Industry Upgrading Program document, EDB Singapore, LIUP Center, 2000.
59.   Author interview.
60.   Author interview.
61.   The dean of the College of Engineering told me that these incubators are set up as closely as possible after the model of Silicon Valley: Nintendo and Coke machines in the corner, beanbags all around, and the newest and most powerful computing equipment (but no showers).
62.   NSTB, *National Survey of R&D in Singapore*, 1999.
63.   Interviews indicate that Sapura has abandoned the international communication market and has reverted to supplying components to Proton, where it is protected from direct international competition (personal communication with Rajah Rasiah).
64.   See www.mida.gov.my/mida policies.htm.
65.   See www.mastic.gov.my/kstas/.
66.   See 'Nurturing k-economy, but more expected,' *SunBiz*, 28 October 2000.
67.   Many debate the level of technological development in these companies. Fearing that even Proton would not survive in a deregulated economy, Malaysia has indicated that it will not adhere to the Asean Free Trade Agreement to open its auto market by 2003, instead insisting on continued protection until at least 2005.
68.   Author interview, MDC, December 2000 and April 2001. See also www.mdc.my.
69.   See 'Technical Teachers,' *The Sun*, 21 November 2000.
70.   Rajah Rasiah details the role of ethnic networks in the development of Eng Technology, a local supplier to the semiconductor and hard disk drive industries. See Rasiah (1999a).
71.   See 'Govt initiatives to promote k-economy,' *SunBiz*, 28 October 2000.
72.   See 'Maybank yet to give out VC funds,' *SunBiz*, 30 October 2000. It is also interesting that the banks chosen to distribute the funds are either the national bank or Bumiputra-owned banks. And what about the bank's own money? If they cannot distribute the government's funds, surely they are not distributing their own either – money everywhere and not a note to use.
73.   Author interview, MOSTE, December 2000.
74.   Author interviews, MMU, UKM, UM, MFI, GMI, UTiM, UPM, Universiti Tenaga, October 2000–January 2001. Figures from 1998 *National Survey of Research and Development*, MASTIC.
75.   McKinsey concluded a government-sponsored evaluation of the MSC where they determined that the MSC failed to accomplish its initial objectives. The report prompted Mahathir himself to admit that the MSC has not reached expectations. While the infrastructure development has been impressive, the R&D activities have not. Buildings, roads and wires are enough to create export-processing zones, but something more, specifically plenty of highly trained people, is needed to create a research, design and product development hub. See 'Malaysia's "Super Corridor" Fails To Attract Financial Attention,' *The Asian Wall Street Journal*, 26 March 2001.
76.   Author interview, BoI, March 2001.
77   .See 'Out of the Driver's Seat,' *Far Eastern Economic Review*, 17 August 2000, p. 46.
78.   Author interview, NSTDA (NECTEC), April 2001.
79.   Officials at NSTDA indicate that the Ministry of Finance will transfer review authority to NSTDA to evaluate R&D projects instead of Ministry of Finance officials. While such a move would certainly improve the evaluation process, many others see the NSTDA as being involved in too many such oversight and policy-oriented activities and not spending enough time doing the R&D the center was created to do.

80. Author interview, BoI, March 2001. There seem to be changes afoot in the BoI, however. Recently, the government announced sweeping changes for the BoI, which will change the focus from promoting FDI more toward local industry upgrading. Even so, the announced focus of the new development policy will be on agriculture, Thai crafts and other small traditional industries.

81. 'B100bn matchmaker fund to attract foreign investors,' *Bangkok Post*, 15 May 2001. Nowhere in this article is there any mention of linkages to further technological or innovatory gains.

82. There is evidence that the linkage between the universities and the public research institutes is improving as the research institutes establish research labs on the campuses of several universities. For example, the NSTDA has departments with research labs at Chulalongkorn and Mahidol Universities.

83. Thailand Ministry of Science, Technology, and the Environment (1998).

84. Personal conversation with Peter Brimball, President of the Brooker Group, Bangkok Thailand, 25 May 2001.

85. Author interview, Thai Software Park, March 2001.

86. 'Building a higher-tech future,' *Bangkok Post*, 21 May 2001.

87. See Lau (1990), Lee and Yamazawa (1990) and Jang-Sup (1996).

88. The institutes consist of the Environmental Technology Institute; Institute of Materials Research and Engineering; Center for Signal Processing; Data Storage Institute; Institute of High Performance Computing; Institute of Microelectronics; Center for Remote Imaging, Sensing and Processing; Center for Wireless Communications; Kent Ridge Digital Labs; Bioprocessing Technology Center; Institute of Molecular Agrobiology; Institute of Molecular and Cell Biology; and the GINTIC Institute of Manufacturing Technology.

89. These areas include electronics, chemicals, life sciences, engineering, education and healthcare, logistics, communications and media headquarters, world-class companies/promising local enterprises, innovation, international business, resource development and co-investment (EDB).

90. Author interviews, July–October 2000, particularly with the NSTB and the EDB.

91. The research parks were also built close to the universities. Hence the institutes are also close to one another.

92. The rapid pace of technological development has led to technological convergence across many industries and products. Increasingly the disk storage companies report that in addition to the DSI, they are finding that membership in the advanced materials and microelectronics institutes to be equally beneficial.

93. Author interviews, Seagate, IBM, Halo Data, IDEMA, July–October 2000.

94. Author interview, DSI, July 2000 and Seagate, 31 July 2000.

95. Author interview, MIMOS, 30 October 2000.

96. Author interview, NSTDA, April 2001.

8. The Asian financial crisis and technical intellectual capital formation

Up until the early part of 1996, the countries of Southeast Asia had experienced some of the fastest economic growth ever recorded. But just as rapidly as this happened, it all came to an abrupt end in 1997. Beginning with Thailand, the region plunged into the greatest economic decline since the great depression (Krugman, 1999). This chapter looks at the effects of this crisis and its aftermath on the formation of technical intellectual capital in the three countries, with particular attention paid to Thailand. Thailand was the country hardest hit and hence, we would assume, based on the theory, most likely to change.

Did the Asian financial crisis represent a new critical juncture during which institutions could be formed or reformed to shape the creation of technical intellectual capital? Clearly the crisis exerted hard budget constraints on all three countries, the same influence as would be experienced through a scarce resource endowment. But how did constrained resources influence institutional change within the context of existing institutional systems? And perhaps most intriguing, could we expect more ordinal relationships between resources, vulnerability and institutional outcomes?

To give an overview of the chapter's findings, in Malaysia and Thailand the initial severity of the crisis created pressures to reorient coalitional structures. But the relatively short duration of the crisis meant that these reorderings were not permanent and coalitional politics quickly returned to previous configurations and operations. Thus, although policy change was widespread, implementation was difficult, or policies proceeded along predictable time-tested routes. In the end, existing institutional systems influenced the range of choices available to policy-makers while simultaneously providing incentives for maintaining the *status quo*.

By comparison, Singapore's institutional system allowed it to respond flexibly to the crisis by generating new policy initiatives that included a broad cross-section of society in further upgrading. Malaysia's and Thailand's systems encouraged ruling elites to respond with 'more of the same.' In Malaysia this was increased investment in the 'bricks and mortar' of the education and training system. In Thailand, it was a dis-combobulated hodgepodge of initiatives at the national level, although at the sectoral level several industries responded with coherent and effective upgrading policies. Sectoral variation suggests that collective dilemmas can be overcome, at least at the more micro level. Firms operating in extreme uncertainty as to the technological future realize that cooperation may be the only way for survival.[1]

The remainder of this chapter evaluates the impact of the crisis and post-crisis periods on institutional formation and implementation to improve the formation of technical intellectual capital in each of the three countries. As Thailand was hardest hit, one would expect that, if the crisis were severe enough, the most change would happen here.

ASIAN FINANCIAL CRISIS: A NEW CRITICAL JUNCTURE OR STATUS QUO REFORM?

Were the constraints imposed by the Asian financial crisis severe enough to lead to institutional upheaval and change involving upgrading? And even if it was enough for policy change, was it enough for policy implementation? Policies that are created but not implemented or implemented to continue existing trajectories of institutional capacity can be termed '*status quo* reform.' The big question, then, is whether the crisis was strong enough to alter the political incentives behind coalitional configurations and, if so, was it sufficient to create the participation and linkages among business, government, academia and labor necessary for credible policy implementation?

Malaysia

Malaysia responded to slowing export sales in 1997 by implementing capital controls rather than accept a US-led International Monetary Fund (IMF) bailout. Although this response was initially castigated by the world financial experts, the evidence suggests that the strategy was at least as successful as any of the other responses in the region: from negative growth in 1998 the economy rebounded with 5.6 percent growth in 1999 and 7.5 percent growth in 2000. It has dropped somewhat since, but remained above 5 percent for most years.[2]

A return to growth has UMNO trumpeting the success of its heterodox economic strategy. From the government's perspective, Malaysia is still on track to reach Vision 2020.[3] As has been the case historically, the government continues to call on businesses to 'forgo some short-term profits in exchange for longer-term ethical [read ethnic] goals.'[4] The conclusion is that the government's focus remains on 'trying to balance the development of the indigenous people with the non-indigenous Chinese and Indians.'[5]

In spite of government optimism over a return to growth, government is emphasizing the need for the Malaysian economy to transition to a more knowledge-intensive economy. Put simply, Malaysians recognize that they must upgrade from labor-intensive to more capital- and knowledge-intensive industries to remain competitive. But despite government rhetoric for economic transition, real reform in Malaysia has been scarce, especially in the education and training system.

For example, one year after announcing that the education and training system must be overhauled to meet the requirements of a new, 'knowledge-based' economy (Felker, 1999: 24), little action has been taken to determine the substance of these reforms, let alone any implementation. The difficulty of turning rhetoric into implementable policy reflects continuing problems of bureaucratic politicization and fragmentation as well as continuing priorities for ethnic distribution.

The result is continuing low output of the education and training system. For example, by 1992 Malaysia had enrolled 60 percent of its secondary-age population, and the comparable figure for tertiary education was 6 percent for vocational and 7 percent for university. And yet by 1998 the number for secondary education had still not broken the 70 percent figure while tertiary education had risen to only 13 percent.[6]

Of the small numbers in Malaysia that do enroll in both secondary- and tertiary-level education, only 28 percent of secondary and 25.7 percent of tertiary students are studying technical subjects.[7] Potential deficiencies in technical human resources could measure in the hundreds of thousands by 2010 (Felker, 1999: 132). Equally alarming are actual trends. Recent government reports show that the numbers of research personnel are growing, but much more slowly than desired: still fewer than 300 per million capita as of 2002 (MASTIC, 2006).

Many of these initiatives continue to be hampered by ethnic quotas (Kondo, 1999: 207). In what is clearly a microcosm of Malaysian society, former Prime Minister Mahathir responded to the university student quota crisis in vintage style by saying 'I am leaving the decision to the people, whether they want it or not . . . If they feel that the government is implementing a bad policy imposing the quota, and they don't want the quota, then the government can abolish it.'[8] Such a statement is purely political and designed to address two crowds at once. On the one hand the statement gives hope to the Chinese that affirmative action policies might be changed in the future and reason to support the current government – support that has recently been waning. On the other, it reminds Malays of what the government has done for them. But it also exposes the disingenuous nature of the statement itself: surely the Malays will not allow a system to be reformed that they increasingly see as a birthright.

Most of the reform in Malaysia has come in the form of bricks and mortar, with little change in curricula, expertise or private sector involvement (Ritchie, 2005b). In Malaysia's case the policies that are being created are also being implemented. But there is little new policy or direction that promises substantial improvement in Malaysia's upgrading capacities. Levels of attainment for technical intellectual capital, R&D funding, patents and so forth reflect this lack of change.

Singapore

As early as 1990, the Singapore government began working on a strategy to transition from a capital-intensive to a more knowledge-intensive industrial structure. By the mid-1990s it was clear that two problems existed with Singapore's current MNC-led technology strategy. First, most of the country's SMEs were rooted in low- to mid-level technologies.[9] Where R&D did exist in SMEs it was primarily a process development rather than a product design variety. And second, although it was clear that the MNCs were upgrading the level of technology within their organizations, even to the point of high-level product R&D, the number of spin-offs was low. Thus the economy was technologically top-heavy: many MNCs and few small, 'technopreneurial' firms. To respond to this gap, the government has expanded its strategy to include the creation of new, and in many cases publicly funded, technology ventures.

To reach this objective, Singapore would have to create a world-class science and technology base (National Science Technology Plan, 1996: 6). The original NSTP envisioned that it would take until at least 2011 and more like 2015 to reach these objectives. The crisis, however, has accelerated these processes: an official at the Ministry of Trade and Industry told me that the crisis had compacted the original 10–15 year estimates into 5–7 years.[10] As an indicator of this acceleration, since 1997 there has been an explosion of government initiatives designed to foster the development of science and technology, with regard to both training and R&D.[11]

Perhaps it is more accurate, then, to characterize the crisis not as having spawned a change in direction, but as accelerating that change. Even though the crisis was relatively less severe in Singapore, it played upon the awareness of the people of their perpetual vulnerability. The crisis was able, therefore, to alter the strategy to develop indigenous technology from primarily one of leveraging the technology in MNCs to a more balanced strategy of levering foreign technology and creating a national base of technology independent of foreign firms.

Thailand

As brought out in Chapter 5, from the mid-1980s until 1996 Thailand was awash with FDI. Most of this investment was solicited and directed toward job creation, much of it lower wage and skilled, to accommodate the large numbers of high-school and post-secondary graduates in the kingdom. In the early 1990s bureaucrats in the Ministry of Labor and Social Welfare began to recognize that Thailand's boom would not be sustainable if skill levels did not rise. Other economies in the region, particularly Malaysia and Singapore, had embarked on the skills upgrading path much earlier, due to higher levels of exposure to the global market and tightening availability of labor.[12]

The initial push for technical education reform began in the early 1990s under Prime Minister Anand Panyarachun as part of a slate of technocratic reforms. Two factors help to explain Anand's reform efforts. One was his concern with external threats to Thai economic growth, including rising oil prices following the 1990–91 Gulf conflict and the need to prepare Thai firms for potential losses of FDI to NAFTA and the liberalization required by looming WTO membership (Doner, 2009). The second factor was political consolidation. Anand was selected to head two caretaker governments – the first after a military *coup* in 1991 and the second after civil unrest forced the (military-backed) elected government from power in 1992. As an unelected prime minister with no legislature, Anand did not have to negotiate the multi-party institutional environment that is the norm in Thailand. Veto authority over most policy domains was concentrated in the Prime Minister's Office.[13] While he was necessarily careful to respect the interests of the military, he was largely free to launch an extensive reform program (Hicken, 2001).

The result was decisive efforts to create world-class training policy. From 1990 through 1993, Thailand sent a delegation to multiple countries to study how to effectively implement a skills upgrading strategy. One of the key conclusions was that Thailand needed a skills development fund like that of Singapore, Malaysia and Korea. Skills development funds allow governments to tax firms a percentage of the incomes of their workers and then make those funds, usually in their entirety, available to be used by firms to train their employees. The program improves payoffs to firms for training while reducing payoffs for poaching. Anand also took steps to tie the hands of the elite to make sure that the policies were implemented successfully. He had been a respected businessman and his ties to the business community were evident in his efforts to seek its input and participation in the policy process. Business responded by supporting the reform program, including the initial plans for vocational reform.

Nevertheless, by 1992 FDI returned to pre-Anand growth trajectories and government returned to fragmented, multi-party democracy. As the number of veto players expanded and interests diverged, agreement on the basic tenets of the policy proved elusive. By the time the policy was completed and ready for implementation in 1994, it bore no resemblance to the recommendations of the delegation that was tasked to understand world-class policy responses to upgrading.

But even had policy formation remained decisive, evidence suggests that credibility for implementation would have been hard to come by.[14] The efforts of the newly elected government to draft a vocational education bill ignored the advice and participation of the business community. Worse yet, the increasingly fragmented political elites became sources to which the business community could go to pit policy-makers against each other to scuttle the policy. As a fall-back position, the Department of Skills Development (DSD) in the Ministry of Labor and Social Welfare (MLSW), who wrote the initial bill, created a one-time government appropriation to establish a fund from which potential students could borrow money for education at favorable rates. Even this watered-down version of the bill took nearly two years to pass and was not signed into law until 1994. The final bill set aside less than US$1 000 000 for these educational loans.

Even the implementation of the watered-down version of the SDF policy suffered from credibility problems. The very design of the fund as a revolving source of student loans meant that business would have little interest in participating in the program. Other groups more likely to participate in the program, such as academia and labor, were neither consulted nor included. Without broad participation from multiple actors, the funds could easily be allocated based on personal relationships and other non-economic criteria. Thus, instead of a healthy revolving fund, the initial capital endowment was quickly exhausted through mismanagement and non-repayment.

In sum, pre-crisis policies for upgrading training were hampered by problems of both decisiveness and credibility. The change in both policy form and the credibility of implementation was due largely to a change in veto players. As the crisis that brought Anand to power abated, changing political institutions dramatically expanded the effective number of veto players. Nor was there sufficient impetus for the ruling elite to tie their hands through broadened participation in the private sector to ensure policy credibility.

The failure of Anand's upgrading initiatives was thus a reflection of the country's overall strong economic performance. Over the course of more than a decade Thailand was one of the fastest-growing economies in the world. Between 1986 and 1996 Thailand's economy grew at an average annual rate of 9.2 percent as foreign investment poured attracted largely

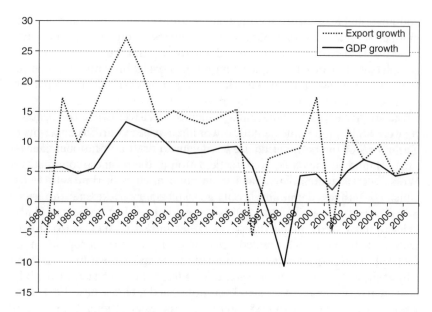

Source: World Bank Development Indicators, 2006.

Figure 8.1   Annual export and GDP growth, Thailand

by the country's reputation for sound macroeconomic management and its export-oriented development strategy (see Figure 8.1). Despite this impressive performance, by the mid-1990s the Thai economy was increasingly vulnerable. The tidal wave of foreign capital inflows, combined with weak financial sector regulation, produced speculative booms in the real-estate and stock markets. Simultaneously, capital inflows undermined Thailand's competitiveness by pushing up inflation and the value of the baht, eventually producing a decline in investment and a dramatic fall in export growth over the course of 1996 (see Figure 8.1). Large, higher-technology companies, such as Seagate, IBM and others, were laying off thousands of workers and moving their labor-intensive operations to China and their skill-intensive operations to Singapore, the USA and Japan (Ritchie, 2005a).

This vulnerability triggered attacks on the baht by currency speculators during the first half of 1997. By the time the Bank of Thailand was finally forced to let the baht float, investor confidence had been deeply shaken. The capital that had flowed so freely into Thailand during the boom quickly flooded out of the country, leading to a collapse of asset prices and of the rate of return on new capital investments. The collapse of these asset bubbles shook not only the financial sector, but the real sector as well. Gross domestic investment fell precipitously, per capita incomes declined, and the Thai economy contracted by nearly 14 percent.

There is not sufficient space here to go into detail about the multiple causes and consequences of the crisis, but for my purposes it is important to note that the crisis represented a substantial (though, as we shall argue, temporary) change in Thailand's vulnerability. Specifically, the contraction of the economy, the collapse of the financial sector, the near cessation of foreign investment and the downturn in corporate profits combined to significantly increase the resource constraints on both economic actors and political actors. Thailand's initial agreement with the IMF, which mistakenly directed the government to slash budgets and spending, further undermined the availability of resources. The crisis also increased the vulnerability of Thailand's domestic business class, many of whom had borrowed heavily in foreign currencies or were heavily exposed in the asset markets. Not only were these firms unable to repay their existing loans: the misallocation of investment resources during the economic boom meant that many of these firms were not internationally competitive, even with the steeply depreciated baht.

This decline in Thailand's competitiveness had been a long time coming. Long before the crisis there were signs that Thailand's ability to realize high rates of growth through accumulation and the export of labor-intensive goods was coming to an end (Richter, 2006; Bosworth, 2005; Jonsson, 2001). Competition for investment dollars meant that Thailand's access to foreign investment capital was probably going to decline relative to past levels. In addition, Thailand's export-led growth strategy was becoming less sustainable, given increased competition from other low-wage countries (Doner, 2009). Thailand was largely ill prepared to compete in this new environment. During the boom years it had 'failed to develop the design and innovation capabilities necessary to move toward [a] more sophisticated production [profile]' (Felker, 2001: 3).

In the end, the crisis deprived Thailand of both foreign and domestic capital resources while its diminished competitiveness meant that it could not rely on foreign investment and exports as it had in the past. In effect, the crisis (temporarily) increased the degree of Thailand's systemic vulnerability. The crisis did not change the fundamental nature of support coalitions or the degree of security threat, but it did significantly increase the resource constraint on the ruling elite, with predictable effects on incentives and behavior.

In the first place, as the financial crisis increased vulnerability, preferences for decisiveness also rose. As a result, we see more policies passed to improve skill levels and educational quality.[15] Central to these initiatives was a bottom-up exchange between officials in the Ministry of Industry and representatives from almost every major sector of the economy to devise a plan to move out of low-wage, mass-production activities through measures such as skills upgrading and SME support (Doner and Ritchie, 2003). Importantly, Thailand's industrial restructuring plan explicitly proposed to induce FDI to upgrade industries seen as strategically central for future industrial development, and to achieve this objective through more systematic public–private consultation through Thailand's Industrial Restructuring Plan.

To bring the education and training system in line with these industrial initiatives, the government implemented sweeping institutional reforms of the education and training bureaucracy. [16] In 1999 a new Education Act was signed into law and an overhaul of the Vocational Training Act of 1994 was promised to follow shortly thereafter. The reform was designed to centralize the education bureaucracy by combining the Ministry of Education with the Ministry of University Affairs and transferring all education responsibilities from under the Ministry of Interior. In addition, the 1999 law stipulates that universities must become autonomous from the civil service. The crisis has also had an immediate impact on the training activities of private firms. As an example, at the onset of the crisis fewer than 20 Thai companies claimed the 150 percent tax deduction for education and training. However, in the first quarter of 1998, the nadir of the crisis, over 140 firms applied (Asian Development Bank, 1999).

As the crisis deepened, pressures mounted on the ruling elite to reverse the downward trend in exports. Elite preferences converged on reform aimed at improving education and training. But even in the reform initiatives, innovation, technological development and scientific capacity as explicit objectives remain at the margins.[17] Quoting from the Education Act of 1999 in sections 6 and 7: 'Education shall aim at the full development of the Thai people in all aspects: physical and mental health; intellect; knowledge; morality; integrity; and desirable way of life so as to be able to live happily with other people [sic].' And,

> The learning process shall aim at inculcating sound awareness of politics; democratic system of government under a constitutional monarchy; ability to protect and promote human rights, freedom, equality and dignity; pride in Thai identity; promotion of religion; art; Thai culture; sports; local wisdom; Thai wisdom and universal knowledge; inculcating ability to preserve natural resources and the environment; acquiring thirst for knowledge and capability of self-learning and self-reliance [sic].

Noticeably absent is any concrete recognition of the place of technological knowledge and skills. Even section 23, which enumerates areas of emphasis, places community and political education above scientific and technological knowledge and skills.

There is little evidence that bureaucratic consolidation mandated by the Act will in fact translate into bureaucratic rationalization and cohesiveness: the current fragmented ministries, agencies and departments may get different names and report to different people, but many feel they will continue to operate largely as before. Even if there are significant changes for the Ministry of Education and Ministry of University Affairs, there is still the issue of the other powerful ministries – such as interior, labor and social welfare, and industry – and their roles in education and training.

In the end, the increase in vulnerability that resulted from the crisis was sufficient to induce preference convergence on the relatively uncontroversial tasks of immediate stabilization and financial system triage. But beyond these tasks Thailand's political elite remained divided. As the government pushed beyond simple stabilization, it encountered strong opposition from both business and political circles. In addition, by 1999 Thailand's economy had begun growing again, which dampened the initial enthusiasm for reform. While the government was able to act decisively to stabilize the economy, it made only limited progress on other fronts. Even in the area of financial sector restructuring, government efforts to reduce non-performing loans, encourage corporate restructuring, and induce banks to restructure and resume lending, stalled as a result of disagreements between veto player about how to proceed. On the upgrading front, although policies had been passed, efforts to implement them received some lip service but little else.

This might have been the end of the story were it not for two other by-products of the crisis – constitutional reform and the reconfiguration of Thailand's political economy. First, the crisis shone a spotlight not only on Thailand's economic vulnerabilities but also on the weaknesses and failures of Thailand's political system. The result was a significant convergence of preferences around the issue of constitutional reform – culminating in a new constitution debated and adopted in the midst of the crisis.[18] Second, the crisis and its fallout changed the face of Thailand's political economy. To begin with, Thailand's business elite, weakened by the crisis and facing threats of greater decimation under IMF-backed reforms, abandoned their traditional behind-the-scenes involvement in politics and instead moved to secure protection of their interests by playing a more direct role in politics and policy-making – coalescing within the newly formed Thai Rak Thai Party (Hewison, 2005). In addition, Thailand's largest existing political parties were greatly weakened as the result of the crisis, leaving something of a political vacuum. And finally, the crisis and the austere IMF recovery plan heightened the antipathy among the Thai public toward globalization and foreign economic interests.

Thaksin Shinawatra and his Thai Rak Thai Party seized on the prevailing nationalist sentiment, the fears of domestic business interests, and new opportunities and incentives under the 1997 constitution, and harnessed these to benefit of Thai Rak Thai's electoral fortunes. In the 2001 elections, Thai Rak Thai was able to secure a majority of the legislative seats – a drastic departure from the norms of past democratic governments. In effect, the crisis set in motion changes that not only reduced the effective number of veto players through preference convergence, but also dramatically reduced the formal number of veto players in the Thai system by converting the formally multi-party coalitional system into one controlled by a single majority party.

With a secure majority in control of government, the Thai model of political economy was drastically revised. Gone were the short-lived, indecisive multi-party governments that had been the distinguishing feature of Thailand's political economy since the 1970s. In its place was a majority party government that immediately demonstrated its ability to take decisive action on its policy priorities. Thaksin committed his government to address competitiveness problems in the real economy, promising to address the dual challenges of rural poverty and inequality on the one hand and industrial competitiveness on the other.[19] The prime minister's focus on industrial upgrading was striking for its departure from past governments' lukewarm attention to real sector problems. Thaksin and his advisors spoke of the 'nutcracker effect' created by the combination of cost pressure from low-cost rivals and technology pressure from more advanced rivals. They were explicit in their desire to move the country 'further up the value chain' and away from excessive dependence on exports that used cheap labor to produce goods relying on foreign technology and investment. They adopted a systematic, market-based approach, categorizing industries and focusing on adding value in sectors – autos, tourism, food and textiles – where Thailand had already succeeded. This strategy involved linkages through support for basic and support industries, related infrastructure and technical personnel, and it involved combining local knowledge and dedication . . . with world-class technology.

However, as the economy recovered, upgrading efforts faded as the government focused on addressing domestic business concerns, rewarding voters with promised populist programs, and further centralizing political authority within the Prime Minister's Office (Hicken, 2005). The government continued to employ the rhetoric of upgrading, but little else was accomplished. The concentration of political authority in the hands of the single veto player also raised new concerns about policy credibility – private and public actors had serious doubt about the credibility of the government's upgrading rhetoric given its ability (and incentives) to switch course if upgrading began to impose costs on Thai Rak Thai's business constituency. The institutional solution to the credibility concern is for the decision-maker to tie his/her hands. But absent the incentives that flow from sustained high levels of vulnerability, the government did not reach out to private sector actors. This truncated upgrading was reflected in the area of education and skills development following the 1997 crisis.

The early effects of the crisis created convergence of policy preferences around resurrecting the skills development fund initiative. With almost unanimous support among policy-makers, the Department of Skills Development submitted a policy that would levy a 1 percent tax (equal to what was being levied in both Singapore and Malaysia), to which business agreed, on the condition that the levy would not be adjusted upwards at any time in the future. The draft bill was sent to the Cabinet in 1998.

This alignment proved to be temporary. By 1999 the intensity of the crisis had begun to abate. Although Thailand was still feeling the effects of the crisis, by early 1999 exports and FDI were both recovering. As they did, policy fragmentation began to re-emerge. Despite earlier congruence on policy preferences, fragmenting preferences stalled the skills development bill's passage in the parliament, where it languished and was never passed in its proposed form.

The evidence again suggests that even had the bill passed, it would have lacked the credibility to be implemented effectively without the active participation of labor and business. Although the DSD convened a consultative group of business owners and government officials for input on how to reform education and training, no labor or academic representatives attended the meetings, and no one other than the DSD had any hand in actually creating the policy. But more problematic, there was little if any negotiation over how the program would be implemented. Firms were worried that the DSD lacked the capacity and the probity to manage the program well.

If other education and training policies were any indication of probable outcomes, businesses' fears were well founded. As discussed earlier, university restructuring reforms were passed, but only partially implemented, and then only with one or two universities already on the path of reform before the crisis. Vested interests were able to derail implementation efforts. Although the new Education Act was passed, very few of the key elements meant to improve skills upgrading were ever implemented.

Even the 'most ambitious effort to improve manufacturing performance,' the Industrial Restructuring Program, suffered from problems of credibility (Doner, 2009). Launched in late 1997 and led by a respected technocrat, Sompop Amatayakul, the 'IRP aimed to upgrade 13 sectors through 8 sets of measures ranging from equipment modernization to labor skills to product design.'

The overall policy for the program was developed through intensive consultation led by the Ministry of Industry. Industry and government collaboration led to 400 program proposals, from which 24 were chosen as part of the IRP's first 'action plan.' But despite the auspicious start, by the year 2000, a senior MoI official labeled the IRP a failure,' as weak business associations and fragmented and turf-conscious ministries led to confusion, discouragement and misinformation (Doner, 2009: ch. 4).

Thaksin's rise to power in 2001 and his explicit commitment to developing local skills for global competitiveness indicated real political support for improvements in education and technical training. Indeed, the DSD pushed again to get the skills development fund initiative through parliament. But skills upgrading through a skills development fund did not fit within the narrow preferences of local capital, which made up a significant portion of Thaksin's political coalition. Thaksin's stated reason for opposing the policy was his concern that Thailand's weak recovery would be dealt a significant blow if businesses were required to pay the levy. However, one MLSW official surmised that the true reason for his opposition was Thaksin's unwillingness to have his own companies participate in the program, especially since the fund would be used to provide training for potential competitors. He suggested instead that money for training be diverted from the funds that businesses were already paying into the Workers' Compensation Fund. The DSD pointed out that if this were done, then only those who were unemployed could access funds for training. In addition, there would be no incentive for firms to participate directly in such training.

Thaksin ignored the DSD concerns and within a short period of time returned the bill to the DSD for further revisions.[20] Without consulting business interests further, the DSD revised the bill, especially the provisions relating to the SDF. Instead of collecting 1 percent from every firm, the revised bill proposed to collect some percentage of wages (undefined) from only those firms that were found not to be doing any training. The revised bill was sent back to the Cabinet, which approved it. Parliament then passed this watered-down version of the bill.

As the crisis continued to abate, FDI began to return to pre-crisis levels, which reduced pressures on firms to upgrade the skills of their workers. Lessening pressures for upgrading allowed interests of the ruling elite to again proliferate, even within the Thai Rak Thai Party. Different faction heads within the Party each control different ministries. Thaksin's expansion of the ministerial structure from 14 to 22 ministries led to a further fragmentation.[21]

But even if policies were passed efficiently, it seems clear the Thai government was still not able and/or willing to broaden participation sufficient for credible and effective implementation. As a comparison, in Singapore, business has been a consistent, if sometimes reluctant, supporter of skills development programs. Although ambivalent about the policy, firms rightly expected that the government would pass an SDF initiative, with or without their participation and support. Since the government was offering the opportunity for firms to actively participate in forming and implementing policy, better to try to shape the policy while also enjoying the incentives offered by the government in exchange for cooperation. In Thailand, business interests opposed to reform had no reason to be confident that the government would have the stomach to implement the watered-down policy even when it was passed. As a result, it has been extraordinarily easy for firms to 'cheat' on training.

Second, the government's failure to solicit the active participation of business undermined business confidence in the proposed reforms. Given the limited capacity of the bureaucracy, in this case the DSD, business had very real fears about how the SDF would be implemented. Where would the bureaucratic resources and expertise come from to run the program? How could business be sure that the proposed levy would actually be put to productive use by the government? How could individual companies be certain that the levy funds would not be used to favor politically well-connected competitors? Allowing participation by companies, as one way to tie the hands of the ruling elite, especially in the implementation and monitoring phases, may have helped allay these concerns. Without it, the credibility of the SDF was jeopardized from the start.

The revised bill likewise lacks credibility in the eyes of the business community. The DSD does not have the capacity to carry out the firm evaluations necessary to implement the new program and a variety of key issues have yet to be addressed.[22] In addition, given the ability of one minister, acting as a veto player, to block the reallocation of resources among ministries, the necessary resources to implement the new program were not likely to be forthcoming.

CONCLUSION

In this chapter I have argued that the crisis was a sufficient critical juncture to encourage policy change in all three of the countries in our study. In Singapore these new policies were implemented with a high degree of credibility, due largely to the level of private sector participation in business, academia and labor. In Malaysia, policies were created and implemented with a high degree of credibility, but the policies did not attack the core of the problems of lack of technical capacity. In other words, the policies that were passed and implemented were the easy ones, primarily constructing new bricks-and-mortar outlets for education and training. But the more difficult issues of technological capacity that would have required significant participation to change were largely ignored.

Thailand has never experienced a sustained level of vulnerability sufficient to cause a nominal change from diversification to upgrading, either during or after periods of state-building (see Table 8.1).

Without sufficient hard budget constraints, Thailand has been unable and unwilling to expand its narrow coalitional structure to create the institutional capacity to implement upgrading policies. That it has been able to consolidate preferences within the ruling elite to develop good policy is not debated here. But credible implementation has been a severe and ongoing problem. Ultimately, Thailand's crisis conditions were severe enough to stimulate a clear reduction in the number of effective veto players leading to corresponding policy changes devoted to economic upgrading. This can be seen in the number of policies directed to change the education and training system. But the crisis was not sufficiently acute, in part owing to the very diversification of the country's economy, to prompt the kinds of institutional linkages that would have generated the credibility required to implement these technologically demanding policy changes.

Ironically, reform has been most dramatic in the country that has needed it the least. In Singapore, where the effects of the crisis were least severe, the policy and institutional change has been the greatest. Future studies will likely judge this period to be a critical juncture in Singapore, where priorities were focused on increased development of indigenous technological capacity.

NOTES

1. Seagate in Thailand is willing to cooperate despite the costs of informing the competition precisely because future growth and survival *might* depend on it (personal conversation with Peter Brimble, Bangkok, 15 May 2005).
2. World Development Indicators, 2006.
3. Mahatir Mohammad, 'Malaysia on track for 2020 Vision,' 10 January 1999.
4. Speech given by Mahatir on 29 August 2000 at the 21st Century Conference to Commemorate the Establishment of the Tun Ismail Ali Chair in Monetary and Financial Economics.
5. Mahatir Mohammad, 'Many Challenges Lie Ahead,' 5 June 2000.
6. These figures, although official, reflect only those for public education. Private higher

Table 8.1 Vulnerability and economic outcomes in Thailand

Vulnerability	Mitigating circumstances	Ruling elites
	1958–73	
Rural unrest Vietnam (cold war conflict) Falling aggregate rice productivity	Land frontier US support	Aligned. Power concentrated in Sarit. Exiled competing factions, unified military. Unified behind macro policy, fragmented behind sectoral policy
	1973–79	
Popular uprising (students and middle class) Falling agricultural productivity Vietnam conflict Domestic unrest in northeast	Multiple contending parties in democratic environment Ministries became cash cows funded by rice US and Chinese rapprochement Still land frontier Borrowing funds	Unaligned. Intensified party competition. Fragmented bureaucratic agencies and trade associations. High clientelism.
	1979–88	
Military oversight Rising debt and lack of financing Falling investment Rising oil prices Frontier effectively begins to close down	Semi-democratic system reduced internal conflict. Needed some sense of fiscal control to stave off *coups*. Trade off between macro agencies and line ministries 1985 inflow of capital from Japan and around the world Regional security relaxed China and Vietnam preoccupied with each other	Rapid consolidation in wake of military takeover. Technocratic macro and clientelistic sectoral. Transitioned to Prem and democratic institutions balanced business interests with the military. Still had political competition. Prem's royal backing helped him consolidate power. As a retired general, the military supported him.

Table 8.1 (continued)

Vulnerability	Mitigating circumstances	Ruling elites
	1988–92	
Coup by military (excesses controlled)	Boom-induced surpluses	Unaligned. Intensified party competition, high clientelism
Broad domestic discontent with corruption	Democratically elected leader	Consolidation of preferences around Anand and Military
NAFTA	Quick return to growing investments	
Rising oil prices		
	1992–97	
Few if any of the three	Lots of investments	Unaligned (rural vs. urban). Expanding number of veto players in the form of fractionalizing parties. Growing influence of rural business people. Factional conflict in ministries Expansion of veto players. Unstable coalition governments
	1997–2001	
Economy in tailspin	17 billion bailout	Aligned right after crisis. Bureaucratic reform to centralize power. But then bureaucratic fragmentation and coalitional rivalries
Full-blown crisis	Short in duration	
Non-performing loans, liquidity crisis, bankruptcies	Miyazawa fund 1.5 billion	
	Return of investment	
	2001–present	
Tight financial market	Return of investment	Aligned. Defragmenting the bureaucracy. Continued sectoral fragmentation and aborted policy reform
Rural unrest	Thaksin's populist policies, funded by agricultural and commodity exports	

education, which was approved by the Malaysian government in the mid-1990s, is also producing a significant number of graduates, although of very uneven quality. If the numbers for private education are also included, the percentage for tertiary education is often estimated to be between 15 percent and 20 percent.

7. The Ministry of Education Department of Higher Education puts the figure at 28 percent.

8. 'Quota System doesn't add up,' S.H. Chong, Kuala Lumpur. *Bangkok Post*, 15 May 2001. The analysis that follows the quote comes largely from this article.

9. Clearly this was not the case for all firms. Firms such as Creative Technologies led their respective industries in technological development.

10. Author interview, Ministry of Trade and Industry, July 2000.

11. As a director at the NSTB put it, 'we need to support the MNCs with a vibrant source of new, niche technologies that can enhance the capacities and technologies of foreign MNCs. In this way, new MNCs will be attracted to Singapore and existing MNCs will be encouraged to upgrade their facilities.' If spin-offs from the MNCs had been filling this gap, there would have been little reason for the government to get involved. But the crisis placed in stark relief the vulnerability of Singapore having all its proverbial eggs in one basket.

12. Singapore reached full employment in the late 1970s early 1980s. Malaysia reached full employment in the early 1990s.

13. The Anand case underscores an important point: changes in systemic vulnerability are a sufficient but not necessary condition of changes in the effective number of veto players. If we are correct, greater systemic vulnerability will induce a reduction in the effective number of veto players. But changes in the configuration can also occur independent of any change in vulnerability – in this case as a result of a *coup*.

14. Unless otherwise indicated, the evidence from this case study comes from a series of interviews conducted by Bryan Ritchie from 1997 to 2004.

15. But part of this initial Thai response to the crisis was to cut public expenditures. Interestingly, the ministry with the largest budget cut was the Ministry of Science, Technology and the Environment, whose budget was cut 13.5 percent (Thai Budget Bureau).

16. Before the crisis, levels of education and training in Thailand were troublingly low: only 37 percent enrolment in secondary education and between 16 percent and 19 percent in tertiary education.

17. In the government's nine stated 'urgent' policy initiatives, innovation, technological development, education, or skills and knowledge development do not appear once. On the other hand, the first three, debt relief for farmers, the million baht village fund, and a people's bank, focus economic development primarily on agriculture and the rural poor.

18. See Hicken (2005) for more on the constitutional reforms.

19. This discussion of Thaksin's upgrading commitments is drawn from Doner (2009, ch. 4).

20. His stated reason for doing so was that the Privy Council had rejected it. The Privy Council is appointed by the king and advises him on various matters, including draft legislation. While the Privy Council has no formal veto power, its opinions are not dismissed lightly.

21. Nor are these tendencies confined to skills development, but also apply to labor reform more broadly. Brown (2004) argues that despite commitments to the contrary, Thaksin's administration has failed to implement meaningful labor reform. Perhaps even more troubling, the implementation of previous reform laws and regulations continues to be weak.

22. These include the criteria for what constitutes sufficient training, who collects and disburses the training funds, how firms will access those funds, and whether funds will be held in individual firm accounts (as in Malaysia) or in a common pool (as in Singapore).

References

Abdulsomad, Kamaruding (1999), 'Promoting industrial and technological development under contrasting industrial policies: the automobile industries in Malaysia and Thailand,' in K.S. Jomo et al. (eds),
*Industrial Technology Development in Malaysia: Industry and Firm
Studies*, London: Routledge, pp. 274–300.

Ahrens, Joachim (2002), *Governance and Economic Development: A
Comparative Institutional Approach*, Northampton, MA: Edward Elgar.

Ake, Claude (1996), *Democracy and Development in Africa*, Washington,
DC: The Brookings Institution.

Alesina, Alberto and Enrico Spolaore (1997), 'On the number and size of
nations,' *Quarterly Journal of Economics*, **112** (4): 1027–56.

Alchian, Arman A. (1987), 'Rent control', in John Eatwell, et al. (eds), *The
New Palgrave: A Dictionary,* New York: The Macmillan Press.

Amsden, Alice (1989), *Asia's Next Giant: South Korea and Late
Industrialization*, New York: Oxford University Press.

Anderson, Benedict (1998), *The Spectre of Comparison: Nationalism,
Southeast Asia, and the World*, London: Verso.

Ariffin, Norlela and Martin Bell (1999), 'Firms, politics, and political
economy: patterns of subsidiary–parent linkages and technological
capability-building in electronics TNC subsidiaries in Malaysia,' in
K.S. Jomo et al. (eds), *Industrial Technology Development in Malaysia:
Industry and Firm Studies*, London: Routledge, pp. 150–90.

Arnold, Erik et al. (2000), *Enhancing Policy and Institutional Support for
Industrial Technology Development in Thailand*, Bangkok: The World
Bank.

Ashton, David et al. (1999), *Education and Training for Development in
East Asia: The Political Economy of Skill Formation in East Asian Newly
Industrialized Economies*, London: Routledge.

Asian Development Bank (1999), background papers on higher education, prepared by The Brooker Group, September.

Auty, Richard M. (1994), 'Industrial policy reform in six large newly
industrializing countries: the resource curse thesis,' *World Development*,
1: 11–26.

Auty, Richard M. (1998), 'Resource abundance and economic development: improving the performance of resource-rich countries,' *World

Institute for Development Economics Research. Research for Action 44. Helsinki: United Nations University.

Aziz, Arfah A. and Chew Tow Yow (1980), 'Malaysia,' in T. Neville Postlethwaite and R. Murray Thomas (eds), *Schooling in the ASEAN Region*, Oxford: Pergamon Press, pp. 98–145.

Balzat, Markus and Horst Hanusch (n.d.), 'Recent trends in the research on national innovation systems', *Journal of Evolutionary Economics,* **14**: 197–210.

Barnett, Michael N. (1992), *Confronting the Costs of War: Military Power, State and Society in Egypt and Israel*, Princeton, NJ: Princeton University Press.

Bates, Robert H. (1990), 'Macropolitical economy in the field of development', in *Perspectives on Positive Political Economy,* James E. Alt and Kenneth A. Shepsle (eds), New York: Cambridge University Press.

Bates, Robert et al. (1999), *Analytic Narratives*, Princeton, NJ: Princeton University Press.

Baum, Matthew, A. and David A. Lake (2003), 'The political economy of growth: democracy and human capital,' *American Journal of Political Science*, **47** (2): 333–47.

Becker, Gary (1983), *Human Capital*, 2nd edn. Chicago, IL: University of Chicago Press.

Bedlington, Stanley S. (1978), *Malaysia and Singapore: The Building of New States.* Ithaca, NY: Cornell University Press.

Bell, Martin et al. (1995), 'Aiming for 2020: a demand driven perspective on industrial technology policy in Malaysia.' final report for the World Bank and the Ministry of Science, Technology and the Environment, Malaysia, SPRU, October.

Bernard, Mitchell and John Ravenhill (1995), 'Beyond product cycles and flying geese: regionalization, hierarchy, and the industrialization of East Asia,' *World Politics*, **47** (2): 171–209.

Bhagwati, Jagdish (1982), 'Directly unproductive, profit-seeking (DUP) activities', *Journal of Political Economy,* **90** (5): 988–1002.

Biddle, Jesse and Vidat Milor (1999), 'Consultative mechanisms and economic governance in Malaysia,' World Bank Private Sector occasional paper no. 39 (March), Washington, DC.

Birdsall, N., D. Ross and R. Sabot (1997), 'Education, growth and inequality,' in N. Birdsall and F. Jasperson (eds), *Pathways to Growth: Comparing East Asia and Latin America*, Washington, DC: Inter-American Development Bank, ch. 4.

Booth, Alison L. and Dennis J. Snower (1999), *Acquiring Skills: Market Failures, their Symptoms and Policy Responses*, New York: Cambridge University Press.

Booth, Anne (1999), 'Initial conditions and miraculous growth: why is South East Asia different from Taiwan and South Korea?' *World Development*, **27** (2): 301–21.

Bosworth, Barry (2005), 'Economic growth in Thailand', transcript, World Bank and Brookings Institution.

Brimble, Peter et al. (1999), *The Broader Impacts of Foreign Direct Investment on Economic Development in Thailand: Corporate Responses*, Bangkok: The Brooker Group.

Brimble, Peter and Richard F. Doner (2007), 'University–industry linkages and economic development: the case of Thailand,' *World Development*, **35** (6): 1021–36.

Brown, Andrew (2004), *Labour, Politics, and the State in Industrializing Thailand*, London: Routledge/Curzon.

Brown, Ian (1988), *The Elite and the Economy in Siam c. 1890–1920*, Singapore: Oxford University Press.

Buchanen, James M. (1994), 'Introduction,' in James Buchanen and Yong J. Yoon (eds), *The Return to Increasing Returns*. Ann Arbor, MI: University of Michigan Press, pp. 3–16.

Bueno de Mesquita, Bruce et al. (1999), 'An institutional explanation of the democratic peace,' *American Political Science Review*, **93** (4): 791–807.

Bueno de Mesquita, Bruce, Alastair Smith, Randolph M. Siverson and James D. Morrow (2003), *The Logic of Political Survival*, Cambridge, MA: MIT Press.

Buripakdi, Chalio and Pratern Mahakhan (1980), 'Thailand,' in T. Neville Postlethwaite and R. Murray Thomas (eds), *Schooling in the ASEAN Region*, Oxford: Pergamon Press.

Cai, Kevin G. (1999), 'The political economy of economic regionalism in Northeast Asia: a unique and dynamic pattern,' *East Asia: An International Quarterly*, **17** (2): 6–46.

Campos, Jose Edgaurdo and Hilton Root (1996), *The Key to the Asian Miracle: Making Shared Growth Credible*, Washington, DC: The Brookings Institution.

Case, William (2002), *Politics in Southeast Asia: Democracy or Less?* London: Curzon Press.

Centeno, Miguel Angel (1997), 'Blood and debt: war and taxation in nineteenth-century Latin America,' *American Journal of Sociology*, **102** (6): 1565–605.

Christensen, Scott Robert (1993), 'Coalitions and collective choice: the politics of institutional change in Thai agriculture,' unpublished doctoral dissertation, University of Wisconsin.

Cleesuntorn, Athipat (1987), 'The development of vocational education policy in Thailand: twenty-five years of national planning,' unpublished PhD dissertation, Florida State University.

Coase, Ronald H. (1937 [1991]), 'The nature of the firm', in Oliver E. Williamson and Sidney G. Winter (eds), *The Nature of the Firm: Origins, Evolution, and Development,* New York: Oxford University Press.

Collier, Ruth Berins and David Collier (1991), *Shaping the Political Arena: Critical Junctures, the Labor Movement, and Regime Dynamics in Latin America*, Princeton, NJ: Princeton University Press.

Cox, Gary and Matthew McCubbins (2001), 'The institutional determinants of economic policy outcomes,' in Stephan Haggard and Matthew McCubbins (eds), *Structure and Policy in Presidential Democracies*, New York: Cambridge University Press, pp. 28–88.

Crone, Donald K. (1988), 'State, social elites, and government capacity in Southeast Asia,' *World Politics*, **40** (2): 252–68.

Crouch, Harold (1984), *Domestic Political Structures and Regional Economic Cooperation*, Singapore: Institute of Southeast Asian Studies.

Crouch, Harold (1996), *Government and Society in Malaysia*, Ithaca, NY: Cornell University Press.

Culpepper, Pepper D. (2003), *Creating Cooperation: How States Develop Human Capital in Europe*, Ithaca, NY: Cornell University Press.

Cumings, Bruce (1984), *The Two Koreas*, New York: Foreign Policy Association.

Dahlman, C.J. (1994), 'Technology strategy in East Asian developing economies', *Journal of Asian Economics,* **5**(4): 541–72.

Deininger, Klaus and Lyn Squire (1996), 'A new data set measuring income inequality,' *The World Bank Economic Review*, **10** (3): 565–91.

Deunden Nikomborirak (2004), 'An assessment of the investment regime: THAILAND Country Report,' March. The International Institute for Sustainable Development (IISD): Thailand Development Research Institute.

Deyo, Frederic C. (1989), *Beneath the Miracle: Labor Subordination in the New Asian Industrialism*, Berkeley, CA: University of California Press.

Deyo, Frederic C. and Richard F. Doner (2001), 'Dynamic flexibility and sectoral governance in the Thai auto industry,' in Frederic Deyo et al. (eds), *Economic Governance and the Challenge of Flexibility in East Asia*, Lanham, MD: Rowman and Littlefield.

Diesing, P. (1971), *Patterns of Discovery in the Social Sciences*, Chicago, IL: Aldine-Atherton.

Dittmer, Lowell (1992), 'Mainland China's position in the Pacific strategic balance: looking toward the year 2000,' *Issues and Studies*, **28** (1): 1–17.

Doner, Richard F. (1992), 'Limits of state strength: toward an institu-tionalist view of economic development,' *World Politics*, **44** (3): 398–431.

Doner, Richard and Anek Lathamatas (1994), 'Thailand: economic and political gradualism', in Stephan Haggard and Steven B. Webb (eds), *Voting for Reform: Democracy, Political Liberalization and Economic Adjustment*, Washington, DC: Oxford University Press for the World Bank, pp. 411–52.

Doner, Richard F. and Gary Hawes (1995), 'The political economy of growth in Southeast and Northeast Asia,' in Manocheher Dorraj (ed.), *The Changing Political Economy of the Third World*, Boulder, CO: Lynne Rienner Publishers, pp. 145–86.

Doner, Richard F. and Ansil Ramsay (1997), 'Competitive clientelism and economic governance: the case of Thailand,' in Sylvia Maxfield and Ben Ross Schneider (eds), *Business and the State in Developing Countries*, Ithaca, NY: Cornell University Press, pp. 237–76.

Doner, Richard F. with Peter Brimble (1999), 'Thailand's hard disk drive industry', report 99, The Data Storage Industry Globalization Project, University of California, San Diego.

Doner, Richard F. and Ben Schneider (2000), 'The new institutional eco-nomics, business associations and development,' Business and Society Programme discussion paper series, Geneva: International Institute for Labour Studies.

Doner, Richard F. and Bryan K. Ritchie (2003), 'Economic crisis and technological trajectories: hard disk drive production in Southeast Asia,' in Richard Samuels and William Keller (eds), *Crisis and Innovation in Asian Technology*, New York: Cambridge University Press, pp. 187–225.

Doner, Richard, with Ansil Ramsay (2009), *The Politics of Uneven Development: Thai Economic Growth in Comparative Perspective*, Boston, MA: Cambridge University Press.

Doner, Richard F., Bryan K. Ritchie and Dan Slater (2005), 'Systemic vulnerability and the origins of developmental states: Northeast and Southeast Asia in comparative perspective,' *International Organization*, **59** (2): 327–61.

Doner, Richard F., Allen Hicken and Bryan K. Ritchie (2009), 'Political challenges of innovation in the developing world,' *Review of Policy Research*, **26** (1–2): 151–71.

Doraisamy, T.R. et al (1969), *150 Years of Education in Singapore*, Singapore: TTC Publications Board, Teachers' Training College.

Dosi, G., C. Freeman, R. Nelson, G. Silverberg and L. Seote (eds) (1988), *Technical Change and Economic Theory*, London: Pinter.

Duggan, Stephen J. (1991), 'Education and economic development in Thailand,' *Journal of Contemporary Asia*, **21** (2): 141–51.

Dunning, John H. (1998), 'Location and the multinational enterprise: a neglected factor?', *Journal of International Business Studies*, **29** (1): 45–66.

Easterly, William R. (2001), *The Elusive Quest for Growth: Economists' Adventures and Misadventures in the Tropics*, Cambridge, MA: MIT Press.

Easterly, William and Ross Levine (1997), 'Africa's growth tragedy: policies and ethnic divisions,' *Quarterly Journal of Economics*, **112** (4): 1203–50.

Eckstein, Harry (1975), 'Case study and theory in political science', in *The Handbook of Political Science*, Boston, MA: Addison-Wesley Publishers.

Economic Development Board (2005), *Heart Work*, Singapore: EDB.

Edwards, Chris (1999), 'Skilled and unskilled foreign labour in Malaysian development – a strategic shift?', in K.S. Jomo and Greg Felker (eds), *Technology, Competitiveness and the State*. London: Routledge, pp. 235–66.

Engerman, Stanley L. and Kenneth L. Sokoloff (1994), 'Factor endowments, institutions, and differential paths of growth among new world economies: a view from economic historians of the United States,' National Bureau of Economic Research historical working paper no. 66.

Engerman, Stanley L. and Kenneth L. Sokoloff (2002), 'Factor endowments, inequality, and paths of development among New World economies,' *Economia*, **3** (1): 41–88.

Evans, Peter (1995), *Embedded Autonomy: States and Industrial Transformation*, Princeton, NJ: Princeton University Press.

Fearon, James D. (1991), 'Counterfactuals and hypothesis testing in political science', *World Politics*, **43** (2) (January), 169–95.

Fearon, James D. and David D. Laitin (1996), 'Explaining interethnic cooperation', *The American Political Science Review*, **90** (4): 715–35.

Feeny, David (1982), *The Political Economy of Productivity: Thai Agricultural Development 1880–1975*, Vancouver, BC: University of British Columbia Press.

Felker, Greg B. (1998), 'Upwardly global? The state, business and MNCs in Malaysia and Thailand's technological transformation,' PhD dissertation, Princeton University.

Felker, Greg (1999), 'Malaysia's innovation system: actors, interests, and governance,' in K.S. Jomo and Greg Felker (eds), *Technology, Competitiveness and the State*, London: Routledge, pp. 98–147.

Felker, Greg (2001), 'Southeast Asian industrialisation and the changing global production system,' *Third World Quarterly*, **24** (2): 255–82.

Felker, Greg, with K.S. Jomo (1999), 'Introduction', in K.S. Jomo and Greg Felker (eds), *Technology, Competitiveness and the State'*, London: Routledge.

Finegold, David (1991), 'Institutional incentives and skill creation: preconditions for a high-skill equilibrium,' in Paul Ryan (ed.), *International Comparisons of Vocational Education and Training for Intermediate Skills*, London: The Falmer Press, pp. 93–118.

Francis, Wong Hoy Kee and Ee Tiang Hong (1971), *Education in Malaysia*, Kuala Lumpur: Heinemann Educational Books.

Freeman, Chris and Luc Soefe (1997), *The Economics of Industrial Innovation*, Cambridge, MA: MIT Press.

Friedrich, Robert J. (1982), 'In defense of multiplicative terms in multiple regression equations,' *American Journal of Political Science*, **26** (November): 797–833.

Gaventa, John (1980), *Power and Powerlessness: Quiescence and Rebellion in an Appalachian Valley*, Urbana, IL: University of Illinois Press.

George, Alexander L. and Timothy J. McKeown (1978), 'Case studies and theories of organizational decision making,' *Advances in Information Processing in Organizations*, **2**: 21–58.

Geddes, Barbara (1990), 'How the cases you choose affect the answers you get: selection bias in comparative politics', in James A. Stimson (ed.), *Political Analysis,* Ann Arbor, MI: University of Michigan Press.

Gereffi, Gary, John Humphrey and Timothy Sturgeon (2005), 'The governance of global value chains', *Review of International Political Economy*, **12** (1): 78–104.

Gerschenkron, Alexander (1962), *Economic Backwardness in Historical Perspective: A Book of Essays*, Cambridge, MA: Belknap Press of Harvard University Press.

Goh, P.C. (1999), 'The semiconductor industry in Malaysia,' in K.S. Jomo, G. Felker and R. Rasiah (eds), *Industrial Technology Development in Malaysia Industry and Firm Studies*, London: Routledge, pp. 125–49.

Gomez, Edmund Terrence and K.S. Jomo (1997), *Malaysia's Political Economy: Politics, Patronage, and Profits*, New York: Cambridge University Press.

Gourevitch, Peter A. (1986), *Politics in Hard Times: Comparative Responses to International Economic Crises*, Ithaca, NY: Cornell University Press.

Grindle, Merilee S. (2004), *Despite the Odds: The Contentious Politics of Education Reform*, Princeton, NJ: Princeton University Press.

Grossman, Gene M. and Elhanan Helpman (1990), 'Comparative

advantage and long-run growth', *The American Economic Review,* **80** (4) (September): 796–800.

Grossman, Gene M. and Elhanan Helpman (1991), *Innovation and Growth in the Global Economy*, Cambridge, MA: MIT Press.

Gullick, John (1981), *Malaysia: Economic Expansion and National Unity*, London: Westview Press.

Hewison, Kevin (2007), 'Constitutions, regimes and power in Thailand,' *Democratization*, **14** (5): 928–45.

Hicken, Allen (2001), 'Parties, policy and patronage: governance and growth in Thailand,' in J.E.L. Campos (ed.), *Corruption: The Boom and Bust of East Asia*, Ateneo de Manila Press, pp. 163–82.

Hicken, Allen (2005), 'Thailand: combating corruption through electoral reform,' in *Electoral System Design: The New International IDEA Handbook*, Stockholm: International IDEA (Institute for Democracy and Electoral Assistance), pp. 120–22.

Hicken, Allen and Bryan Ritchie (2002), 'The origin of credibility enhancing institutions in Southeast Asia,' paper delivered at the annual meeting of the American Political Science Association, Boston Copley Place Marriott, 28 August–1 September.

Hirschman, A.O. (1958), *The Strategy of Economic Development*, New Haven, CT: Yale University Press.

Hobday, Michael (1995), *Innovation in East Asia: The Challenge to Japan.* Aldershot: Edward Elgar.

Hobday, Michael (1999), 'Understanding innovation in electronics in Malaysia,' in K.S. Jomo et al. (eds), *Industrial Technology Development in Malaysia: Industry and Firm Studies*, London: Routledge, pp. 76–106.

Hoff, Karla and Joseph E. Stiglitz (2001), 'Modern economic theory and development', in Gerald M. Meier (ed.), *Frontiers of Development Economics: The Future in Perspective,* New York: World Bank and Oxford University Press.

Horowitz, Donald L. (1985), *Ethnic Groups in Conflict*, Berkeley, CA: University of California Press.

Huxley, Tim (2000), *Defending the Lion City: The Armed Forces of Singapore*, St Leonards, NSW: Allen & Unwin.

Ingram, James C. (1955), *Economic Change in Thailand Since 1850*, Stanford, CA: Stanford University Press.

Jang-Sup, Shin (1996), *The Economics of the Latecomers: Catching-up, Technology Transfer and Institution in Germany, Japan, and South Korea*, London: Routledge.

Jesudason, James V. (1989), *Ethnicity and the Economy: The State, Chinese Business, and Multinationals in Malaysia*, Oxford: Oxford University Press.

Johnson, Chalmers (1982), *MITI and the Japanese Miracle: The Growth of Industrial Policy, 1925–1975*, Stanford, CA: Stanford University Press.

Johnson, Chalmers (1986), 'The institutional foundation of Japanese industrial policy,' in C.E. Barfield and W.A. Schambra (eds), *The Politics of Industrial Policy*, Oxford: Oxford University Press, pp. 187–205.

Jomo, K.S. (1986), *A Question of Class: Capital, the State, and Uneven Development in Malaya*, Singapore: Oxford University Press.

Jomo, K.S. (1993), 'Prospects for Malaysian industrialization in light of East Asian NIC experiences,' in K.S. Jomo (ed.), *Industrialising Malaysia*, London: Routledge, pp. 286–301.

Jomo, K.S. (1997), *Southeast Asia's Misunderstood Miracle*, London: Routledge.

Jomo, K.S. and Patricia Todd (1994), *Trade Unions and the State in Peninsular Malaysia*, Oxford: Oxford University Press.

Jonsson, Gunnar (2001), 'Growth accounting and the medium term outlook in Thailand,' in *Thailand: Selected Issues*, IMF Staff country Report No. 01/147.

Kaldor, Nicholas (1972), 'The irrelevance of equilibrium economics,' *The Economic Journal*, **82** (328): 1237–55.

Kassim, Hamzah (1995), 'Building a workable S&T infrastructure in Malaysia,' in Denis Fred Simon (ed.), *The Emerging Technological Trajectory of the Pacific Rim*, Armonk, NY: East Gate Press, pp. 171–85.

Karl, Terry Lynn (1997), *The Paradox of Plenty: Oil Booms and Petro-states*. Berkeley, CA: University of California Press.

Keefer, Philip (2004), 'What does political economy tell us about economic development – and vice versa', *Annual Review of Political Science*, **7**: 247–72.

Keller, William and Richard Samuels (2003), *Crisis and Innovation in Asian Technology*, Cambridge: Cambridge University Press.

Kennedy, Peter (1998), *A Guide to Econometrics*, 4th edn, Cambridge, MA: MIT Press.

King, Gary, Robert O. Keohane and Sidney Verba (1994), *Designing Social Inquiry*, Princeton, NJ: Princeton University Press.

Knight, Jack (1992), *Institutions and Social Conflict*, Cambridge: Cambridge University Press.

Kondo, Masayuki (1999), 'Improving Malaysian industrial technology policies and institutions,' in K.S. Jomo and Greg Felker (eds), *Technology, Competitiveness and the State*, London: Routledge, pp. 199–217.

Krasner, Stephen D. (1984), 'Approaches to the state: alternative conceptions and historical dynamics,' *Comparative Politics*, **16** (2): 223–46.

Krugman, Paul (1999), *The Return of Depression Economics*, New York: W.W. Norton.

Kuhn, Thomas S. (1962), *The Structure of Scientific Revolutions*, Chicago, IL: University of Chicago Press.

Kwong, John Yip Soon and Sim Wong Kooi (eds) (1990), *Evolution of Educational Excellence: 25 Years of Education in the Republic of Singapore*, London: Longman Press.

Lake, David and Matthew Baum (2001), 'Invisible hand of democracy: political control and public service provision', *Comparative Political Studies*, **34**: 587–621.

Lakatos, Imre (1970), 'Falsification and the methodology of scientific research programmes', in Imre Lakatos and Alan Musgrove (eds), *Criticism and the Growth of Knowledge*, Cambridge: Cambridge University Press.

Lall, Sanjaya (1999), 'Technology policy and competitiveness in Malaysia,' in K.S. Jomo and Greg Felker (eds), *Technology, Competitiveness and the State*, London: Routledge, pp. 148–79.

Landa, Janet (1991), 'Culture and entrepreneurship in LDCs: ethnic trading networks as economic organization,' in Brigitte Berger (ed.), *The Culture of Entrepreneurship*, San Francisco, CA: ICS Press, pp. 53–72.

Landes, David (1999), *The Wealth and Poverty of Nations: Why Some Are So Rich and Some So Poor*, London: W.W. Norton.

Lane, Philip and Aaron Tornell (1998), 'Voracity and Growth', National Bureau of Economic Research working paper no. 6498.

Lau, L.J. (1990), *Models of Development: A Comparative Study of Economic Growth in South Korea and Taiwan*, San Francisco, CA: ICS Press.

Lauridsen, Laurids (2008), 'The policies and politics of industrial upgrading in Thailand during the Thaksin era', paper presented at the 10th International Conference on Thai Studies, Thammasat University, 9–11 January, Bangkok.

Lee, Chung H. and Ippei Yamazawa (eds) (1990), *The Economic Development of Japan and Korea: A Parallel with Lessons*, New York: Praeger.

Leete, Richard (1996), *Malaysia's Demographic Transition: Rapid Development, Culture, and Politics*, Kuala Lumpur: Oxford University Press.

Leifer, Michael (1988), 'Israelís president in Singapore: political catalysis and transnational politicsm,' *Pacific Review*, **1** (4): 342–7.

Leutert, Hans-Georg and Ralf Sudhoff (1999), 'Technology capacity building in the Malaysian automotive industry,' in K.S. Jomo et al. (eds), *Industrial Technology Development in Malaysia: Industry and Firm Studies*, London: Routledge, pp. 247–73.

Lewis, W. Arthur (1955), *The Theory of Economic Growth*, Homewood, IL: R.D. Irwin.

Lijphart, Arend (1969), 'Consociational democracy,' *World Politics*, **21** (2): 207–25.

Lijphart, Arend (1971), 'Comparative politics and the comparative method,' *American Political Science Review*, **65** (3): 682–93.

Lijphart, Arend (1975), *The Politics of Accommodation: Pluralism and Democracy in the Netherlands*, Berkeley, CA: University of California Press.

Loh, Philip Fook Seng (1975), *Seeds of Separatism: Educational Policy in Malaysia 1874–1940*, Kuala Lumpur: Oxford University Press.

Luciani, Giacomo (1995), 'Resource, revenues, and authoritarianism in the Arab world: beyond the rentier state?,' in Rex Brynen, Bahgat Korany and Paul Noble (eds), *Political Liberalization and Democratization in the Arab World*, Boulder, CO: Lynne Reinner, pp. 211–28.

Lucus, Robert E. Jr (1988), 'On the mechanics of economic development,' *Journal of Monetary Economics*, **22** (1): 3–42.

MacIntyre, Andrew J. (2002), *The Power of Institutions: Political Architecture and Governance*, Ithaca, NY: Cornell University Press.

Majlis Pembangunan Sumber Manusia (1998), *Laporan Tahunan*, Malaysia.

Mahon, James E. Jr (1992), 'Was Latin America too rich to prosper? Structural and political obstacles to export-led industrial growth,' *The Journal of Development Studies*, **28** (2): 241–63.

Malaysian Economic Planning Unit (1999), *Mid-term Review of the Seventh Malaysia Plan: 1996–200,*. Kuala Lumpur: Percetakan Nasional Malaysia Berhad.

Malaysia Human Resource Development Fund (1997), *Annual Report*, Ministry of Human Resources.

Malaysia Human Resource Development Fund (1998), *Annual Report*, Ministry of Human Resources.

Malaysia Human Resource Development Fund (2004), *Annual Report*, Ministry of Human Resources.

Malaysian Industry Government Group for High Technology (n.d.), *1999 Annual Report: Shaping Hi-tech Agenda Through Consensus Building and Networking*, MIGHT.

Malaysian Ministry of Education (2000), *Annual Report*, Kuala Lumpur.

Malaysian Science and Technology Information Centre (1997), *1996*

National Survey of Research and Development, Ministry of Science, Technology, and the Environment, December.

Malaysian Science and Technology Information Centre (1998), *1996 Malaysian Science and Technology Indicators Report*, Ministry of Science, Technology, and the Environment, October.

Malaysian Science and Technology Information Centre (1999), *1998 National Survey of Research and Development*, Ministry of Science, Technology, and the Environment, December.

Malaysian Science and Technology Information Centre (2000a), *1998 Malaysian Science and Technology Indicators Report*, Ministry of Science, Technology, and the Environment, May.

Malaysian Science and Technology Information Centre (2000b), *1998 National Science and Technology Databook*, Ministry of Science, Technology, and the Environment.

Malaysian Science and Technology Information Centre (2006), *Science and Technology Indicators Report*, Ministry of Science, Technology, and the Environment.

Marshall, Monty G. and Keith Jaggars (2000), The Polity IV Project Integrated Network for Societal Conflict Research Program, Center for International Development and Conflict Management, University of Maryland, College Park, MD, accessed at www.bsos.umd.edu/cidcm/polity/.

Mauro, Paolo (1995), 'Corruption and growth,' *The Quarterly Journal of Economics*, **110** (3): 681–712.

McKeown, Timothy (1999), 'Case studies and the statistical world-view: review of K2V's *Designing Social Inquiry: Scientific Inference in Qualitative Research', International Organization*, **53**(1) (Winter): 161–90.

McKendrick, David, Richard F. Doner and Stephen Haggard (2000), *From Silicon Valley to Singapore: The Competitive Advantage of Location in the Hard Disk Drive Industry*, Stanford, CA: Stanford University Press.

Mendoza, Enrique G. (1997), 'Terms-of-trade uncertainty and economic growth', *Journal of Development Economics,* **54** (2): 323–56.

Metcalfe, J.S. (1995), 'Technology systems and technology policy in an evolutionary framework,' *Cambridge Journal of Economics*, **19**: 25–46.

Milanovic, Branko (2005), *Worlds Apart: Measuring International and Global Inequality'*, Princeton, NJ: Princeton University Press.

Mill, John Stuart (1884), *A System of Logic,* New York: Harper & Brothers.

Mowery, David C. and Joanne E. Oxley (1995), 'Inward technology transfer and competitiveness: the role of national innovation systems,' *Cambridge Journal of Economics*, **19**: 67–93.

Muscat, Robert J. (1994), *The Fifth Tiger: A Study of Thai Development Policy*, Helsinki: United Nations University Press.

Nankani, Gobind T. (1980), 'Development problems of nonfuel mineral exporting countries,' *Finance and Development*, **17** (1): 6–11.

Nelson, Richard R. (1993), 'Technical innovation and national systems,' in Richard Nelson (ed.), *National Innovation Systems: A Comparative Analysis*, Oxford: Oxford University Press, pp. 3–22.

Nelson, Richard R. and Nathan Rosenberg (1993), 'Technical innovation and national systems', in Richard R. Nelson (ed.), *National Innovation Systems: A Comparative Analysis,* Oxford: Oxford University Press.

Nipon Paopongsakorn and Belinda Fuller (1997), 'Thailand's development experience from the economic system perspective: open politics and industrial activism,' in Toru Yanagihara and Susumu Sombommatsu (eds), *East Asian Development Experience: Economic System Approach and its Applicability*, Tokyo: I.D.E., pp. 466–80.

North, Douglass C. (1990), *Institutions, Institutional Change and Economic Performance*, London: Cambridge University Press.

OECD (1998), 'Technology, Productivity, and Job Creation: Best Policy Practices.'

Olson, Mancur (1971), *The Logic of Collective Action: Public Goods and the Theory of Groups*, Cambridge, MA: Harvard University Press.

Olson, Mancur (1982), *The Rise and Decline of Nations*, New Haven, CT: Yale University Press.

Osborn, Martin J. and Ariel Rubinstein (1994), *A Course in Game Theory*, Cambridge, MA: MIT Press.

Parayil, Govindan (1999), *Conceptualizing Technological Change: Theoretical and Empirical Explorations*, Oxford: Rowman and Littlefield.

Pasuk Phongpaichit and Sungsidh Piriyarangsan (1994), *Corruption and Democracy in Thailand*, Bangkok: Silkworm Press.

Pempel, T.J. (2004), *Beyond Bilateralism: U.S.–Japan Relations in the New Asia Pacific*, Stanford, CA: Stanford University Press.

Perrson, Torsten and Guido Tabellini (2003) *The Economic Effect of Constitutions: What Do They Say?*, Cambridge, MA: MIT Press.

Pierson, Paul (2000), 'Increasing returns, path dependence and the study of politics,' *American Political Science Review*, **94** (2): 251–68.

Pigou, A.C. (1912), *Wealth and Welfare*, London: Macmillan.

Pontusson, Jonas (1995), 'From comparative public policy to political economy: putting institutions in their place and taking interests seriously', *Comparative Political Studies,* **28** (1) (April): 117–47.

Przeworski, Adam and Henry Teune (1970), *The Logic of Comparative Social Inquiry*, New York: Wiley-Interscience.

Ragin, Charles C. (1987), *The Comparative Method: Moving Beyond Qualitative and Quantitative Strategies*, Berkeley, CA: University of California Press.

Rasiah, Rajah (1996), 'Innovation and institutions: moving towards the technological frontier in the electronics industry in Malaysia,' *Journal of Industry Studies*, **3** (2): 79–102.

Rasiah, Rajah (1999a), 'Government–business co-ordination and the development of Eng Hardware,' in K.S. Jomo et al. (eds), *Industrial Development in Malaysia: Industry and Firm Studies*, London: Routledge, pp. 231–46.

Rasiah, Rajah (1999b), 'Malaysia's national innovation system,' in K.S. Jomo and Greg Felker (eds), *Technology, Competitiveness and the State*, London: Routledge, pp. 180–98.

Rasiah, Rajah (forthcoming), 'Politics, institutions, and flexibility: microelectronics transnationals, and machine tool linkages in Malaysia.'

Rauch, James E. and Peter B. Evans (2000), 'Bureaucratic structure and bureaucratic performance in less developed countries,' *Journal of Public Economics*, **75** (1): 49–71.

Richer, Kaspar (2006), 'East Asia poverty reduction and economic management,' World Bank policy research working paper no. 3912, May.

Riker, William (1980), 'Implications from the disequilibrium of majority rule for the study of institutions,' *American Political Science Review*, **74**: 432–6.

Ritchie, Bryan K. (1999), 'The resource curse, ethnicity, and the origins of technical education and training', paper delivered at the annual meeting of the American Political Science Association, Atlanta, GA.

Ritchie, Bryan K. (2000), 'Innovation systems, collective dilemmas, and the formation of technical intellectual capital in Malaysia, Singapore, and Thailand', National University of Singapore Center for Management of Innovation and Technopreneurship working paper.

Ritchie, Bryan K. (2005a), 'Progress through setback or mired in mediocrity? Crisis and institutional change in Southeast Asia,' *Journal of East Asian Studies*, **5** (2): 273–314.

Ritchie, Bryan K. (2005b), 'Coalitional politics, economic reform, and technological upgrading in Malaysia,' *World Development*, **33** (5): 745–62.

Robinson, Lindon J. and Bryan K. Ritchie (2010), *Relationship Economics: The Social Capital Paradigm and its Application to Business, Politics, and other Transactions*. Aldershot: Gower (Ashgate).

Rodan, Gary (1989), *The Political Economy of Singapore's Industrialization: National State and International Capital*, London: Macmillan Press.

Rodrik, Dani (1995), 'Getting intervention right: how South Korea and Taiwan grew rich.' *Economic Policy*, **20**: 55–107.

Rodrik, Dani (1999), 'Where did all the growth go? External shocks, social conflict, and growth collapses,' *Journal of Economic Growth*, **4** (4): 385–412.

Romer, Paul M. (1986), 'Increasing returns and long-run growth,' *Journal of Political Economy*, **94** (October): 1002–37.

Romer, Paul (1994), 'The origins of endogenous growth,' *Journal of Economic Perspectives*, **8** (1): 3–22.

Root, Hilton (1996), 'The right kind of corruption,' in *Small Countries/ Big Lessons: Governance and the Rise of East Asia*, Hong Kong and New York: Oxford University Press, pp. 145–78.

Ross, Michael L. (1999), 'The political economy of the resource curse,' *World Politics*, **51** (January): 297–322.

Ross, Michael L. (2001), 'Does oil hinder democracy?' *World Politics*, **53** (3): 325–61.

Sachs, Jeffrey D. and Andrew M. Warner (1995), 'Natural resource abundance and economic growth', Harvard Institute for International Development discussion paper no. 517a, October.

Sachs, Jeffrey D. and Andrew Warner (1997), 'Natural resource abundance and economic growth,' November, Cambridge: HIID.

Samuels, Richard J. (1994) *Rich Nation, Strong Army: National Security and the Technological Transformation of Japan*, Ithaca, NY: Cornell University Press.

Scharpf, Fritz W. (1997), *Games Real Actors Play: Actor-Centered Institutionalism in Policy Research*, Oxford: Westview Press.

Schein, Edgar H. (1996), *Strategic Pragmatism: The Culture of Singapore's Economic Development Board*, Cambridge, MA: MIT Press.

Scherer, F.M. and D. Ross (1990), *Industrial Market Structure and Economic Performance,* 3rd edn, Boston, MA:

Schoppa, Leonard J. (1999), 'The social context in coercive international bargaining,' *International Organization*, **53** (2): 307–42.

Schumpeter, Joseph A. (1975) *Capitalism, Socialism, and Democracy,* New York: Harper & Row.

Scott, James C. (1985), *Weapons of the Weak: Everyday Forms of Peasant Resistance*, New Haven, CT: Yale University Press.

Shafer, D. Michael (1994), *Winners and Losers: How Sectors Shape the Developmental Prospects of States*, Ithaca, NY: Cornell University Press.

Singapore Economic Development Board (EDB) (1999), *A Knowledge-based Economy: Industry 21,* EDB (January).

Singapore Ministry of Education (2000), *Education Statistics Digest*.

Singapore Ministry of Manpower (1999), *Manpower 21: Vision of a Talent Capital*, Ministry of Manpower (August).

Singapore National Science and Technology Board (1996), *National Science and Technology Plan*, NSTB.

Singapore National Science and Technology Board (n.d.), *National Survey of R&D in Singapore 1999*, NSTB.

Singapore Skills Development Fund (n.d.), *Annual Report 1999*, Singapore Productivity and Standards Board.

Singapore Skills Development Fund (1999a), *Reflections: Setting Directions for the New Millennium*, Singapore: Productivity and Standards Board, The Skills Development Fund.

Singapore Skills Development Fund (1999b), *Towards a Skilled and Competitive Workforce*, The Singapore Skills Development Fund annual report for 1998–1999. Productivity and Standards Board.

Skinner, William G. (1958), *Leadership and Power in the Chinese Community in Thailand*, Ithaca, NY: Cornell University Press.

Smith, Anthony (2004), 'Trouble in Thailand's Muslim south,' *Asia-Pacific Center for Security Studies*, **3** (10): 1–50.

Snidal, Duncan (1991), 'Relative gains and the pattern of international cooperation,' *American Political Science Review*, **85** (3): 701–26.

Solow, Robert (1957), 'Technological change and the aggregate production function,' *Review of Economics and Statistics*, **39**: 312–20.

Soskice, David (1991), 'The institutional infrastructure for international competitiveness: a comparative analysis of the U.K. and Germany,' in A.B. Atkinson and R. Brunetta (eds), *The Economics of the New Europe*, London: Macmillan, pp. 45–66.

Soskice, David (1993), 'Innovation strategies of companies: a comparative institutional explanation of cross-country differences', unpublished manuscript, Wissenschaftszentrum, Berlin.

Steinmo, Sven et al. (eds) (1992), *Structuring Politics: Historical Institutionalism in Comparative Analysis*, New York: Cambridge University Press.

Stevens, Margaret (1999), 'Transferable training and poaching externalities,' in Alison J. Booth, and Dennis Snower (eds), *Acquiring Skills: Market Failures, Their Symptoms and Policy Responses*, New York: Cambridge University Press, pp. 19–40.

Streeck, Wolfgang (1989), Skills and the limits of neo-liberalism: the enterprise of the future as a place of learning,' *Work, Employment and Society*, **3** (1): 89–104.

Swat Sukontarangsi (1967), *Development of Thai Educational Bureaucracy*, Bangkok: National Institute of Development Administration.

Tan, Andrew (2004), *Security Perspectives of the Malay Archipelago: Security Linkages in the Second Front in the War on Terrorism,* Cheltenham, UK and Northampton, MA, USA: Edward Elgar.

Tan, Andrew (2006), *Southeast Asia: Threats in the Security Environment,* Singapore: Marshall Cavendish Academic.

Taylor, Zachary Mark (2007), 'Political decentralization and technological innovation: testing the innovative advantages of decentralized states, *Review of Policy Research,* **24**(3): 231–57.

Thai Government (1999), National Education Bill, Office of the National Education Commission, Office of the Prime Minister, Thailand.

Thailand Board of Investments (1987), *Thailand: Investor's Guide,* Office of the Board of Investment, Office of the Prime Minister.

Thailand Development Research Institute (1998), *Effective Mechanisms for Supporting Private Sector Technology Development and Needs for Establishing Development Finance Corporation,* Bangkok: Science and Technology Development Program, Thailand Development Research Institute.

Thailand Ministry of Science, Technology, and the Environment (n.d.), *1997 National Survey on R&D Expenditure and Personnel of Thailand,* MOSTE.

Thailand Office of the National Education Commission (1999), *Thailand Education Statistics Report 1999,* ONEC (December).

Thak Chaloemtiarana (1978), *Thai Politics, 1932–1957,* vol. 1, Bangkok: Social Science Association of Thailand.

Thelen, Kathleen (2002), 'How institutions evolve: insights from comparative historical analysis', in *Comparative Historical Analysis in the Social Sciences,* James Mahoney and Dietrich Rueschemeyer (eds), New York: Cambridge University Press.

Thelen, Kathleen and Ikuo Kume (1999), 'The rise of nonmarket training regimes: Germany and Japan compared,' *Journal of Japanese Studies,* **25** (1): 33–64.

Thomas, R. Murray, Goh Kim Leong and R.W. Mosbergen (1980), 'Singapore,' in T. Neville Postlethwaite and R. Murray Thomas (eds), *Schooling in the ASEAN Region,* Oxford: Pergamon Press, pp. 185–223.

Tilly, Charles (1975), *The Formation of National States in Western Europe,* Princeton, NJ: Princeton University Press.

Tremewan, Christopher (1994), *The Political Economy of Social Control in Singapore,* New York: St Martin's Press.

Tsebelis, George (2002), *Veto Players: How Political Institutions Work,* Princeton, NJ: Princeton University Press.

Tullock, Gordon (1987), 'Rent seeking', in John Eatwell et al. (eds), *The*

New Palgrave: A Dictionary of Economics, New York: The Macmillan Press.

Unger, Danny (1998), *Building Social Capital in Thailand: Fibres, Finance and Infrastructure,* New York: Cambridge University Press.

Viner, Jacob (1952), *International Trade and Economic Development*, Glencoe, IL: Free Press.

Viscusi, W. Kip, et al. (2000), *Economics of Regulation and Antitrust*, Cambridge, MA: The MIT Press.

Wade, Robert (1990), *Governing the Market: Economic Theory and the Role of Government in East Asian Industrialization*, Princeton, NJ: Princeton University Press.

Waldner, David (1999), *State Building and Late Development*, Ithaca, NY: Cornell University Press.

Weingast, Barry R. (1997), 'The political foundations of democracy and the rule of law,' *The American Political Science Review*, **91** (2): 245–63.

Weiss, Linda (1994), 'Government–business relations in East Asia: the changing basis of state capacity,' Chung-Hua Institution for Economic Research occasional paper series no. 9407, October.

Weiss, Linda (1995), 'Governed interdependence: rethinking the government–business relationship in East Asia.' *Pacific Review*, **8** (4): 589–616.

Williamson, Oliver E. (1985), *The Economic Institutions of Capitalism: Firms, Markets, Relational Contracting*, New York: Free Press.

Wilson, David A. (1962), *Politics in Thailand*, Ithaca, NY: Cornell University Press.

Wong Poh Kam (n.d.), 'From leveraging multinational corporations to fostering technopreneurship: the changing role of S&T policy in Singapore,' unpublished ms.

Woo-Cumings, Merideth (1999), *The Developmental State*, Ithaca, NY: Cornell University Press.

Wood, Adrian and Kersti Berge (1997), 'Exporting manufactures: human resources, natural resources, and trade policy,' *Journal of Development Economics*, **34** (1): 35–59.

Woo-Jung-en (1991), *Race to the Swift: State and Finance in Korean Industrialization*, New York: Columbia University Press.

World Bank (1993), *The East Asian Miracle*, Washington, DC: World Bank.

World Bank (1997), *Development Indicators*, CD-ROM. Washington, DC: World Bank.

World Bank (1997), *Expanding the Measure of Wealth*, Environmentally Sustainable Development Studies and Monograph series 17, Washington, DC: World Bank.

World Bank (1999), *World Development Report*, Washington, DC: World Bank.
World Bank (2000a), *Thailand Economic Monitor*, February, Washington, DC: World Bank.
World Bank (2000), *Thailand: Economic Monitor,* June, accessed at www. worldbank.or.th/monitor.
World Bank (2002), *World Development Report: Building Institutions for Markets*, New York: Oxford University Press.
World Bank (2005), *World Bank Development Indicators*, Washington, DC: World Bank.
World Bank (2006), *World Bank Development Indicators*, Washington, DC: World Bank.
World Bank (2007), *World Bank Development Indicators*, Washington, DC: World Bank.
World Bank (2007), *Thailand Economic Monitor* (November), Washington, DC: World Bank.
World Bank (2008), *World Bank Development Indicators*, Washington, DC: World Bank.
Yusuf, Shahid and Kaoru Nabeshima (2007), *How Universities Promote Economic Growth*, Washington, DC: World Bank.
Zeufack, A. (1999), 'Employee-provided training under oligopolistic labor markets: evidence from Thai manufacturing firms,' mimeo, World Bank, Washington, DC.

Index

Action Plan for Industrial Technology Development (APITD) 155
adaptive expectations 116, 117, 128–29
ADB *see* Asian Development Bank (ADB)
affirmative action *see* Malaysia
African coalitions 23–5, 38
agglomeration economies 150, 151, 169–70
Ake, Claude, *Democracy and Development in Africa* 22
Alesina, Alberto, 'On the number and size of nations' 22
Anand Panyarachun 153, 194, 195, 206, 207
APITD Action Plan for Industrial Technology Development (APITD)
ASEAN 23, 38, 40–41, 58, 91, 188
Asia, economic growth in 1, 4, 8, 22, 28
 Northeast compared to Southeast 36–41, 58, 89, 97–8, 130
 see also coalitions; East Asia; Malaysia; Northeast Asia; Singapore; Southeast Asia; Thailand
Asian Development Bank (ADB) 133, 134
Asian Institute of Technology 181
Association of Muslim Professionals 163
Auty, Richard M., 'Resource abundance and economic development' 33, 115

Bangkok 30, 105, 115, 119, 177
 Chinese in 75, 87
 elites of 81, 88
banks 207
 ADP 133
 Bank of Thailand 179, 196

Bumiputra-Commerce Bank 175, 188
 in Singapore 81, 91
 in Malaysia 123, 175, 188
 Maybank 123, 175–6, 179
 in Thailand 75–6, 82, 179, 196, 199
 see also World Bank
Barisan Socialis (BS) 80
Bates, Robert, *Analytic Narratives* 35
Baum, Matthew A., 'political economy of growth, The' 14, 15
Becker, Gary, *Human Capital* 6, 14
Bedlington, Stanley S., *Malaysia and Singapore* 99
Bioprocessing Technology Center 182, 189
BIOTEC *see* National Center for Genetic Engineering and Biotechnology (BIOTEC)
Board of Investments (BoI) 176–8, 189
BOI *see* Board of Investments (BoI)
Borneo 34, 70, 90
Bowring, Robert 66
Bowring Treaty 67, 74
Brown, Andrew, *Labour, Politics, and the State in Industrializing Thailand* 207
Brown, Ian, *Elite and the Economy in Siam c. 1890–1920, The* 74, 76, 114
Brunei 80
BS *see* Barisan Socialis
Buchanen, James M., *Return to Increasing Returns, The* 147
Bueno de Mesquita, Bruce, 'Logic of Political Survival, The' 13, 42, 43, 65
BUILD *see* Unit for Industrial Linkages (BUILD)
Bumiputra-Commerce Bank 175, 188